D1265533

The Plays of David Storey

Carbondale and Edwardsville

A Thematic Study

WILLIAM HUTCHINGS

SOUTHERN ILLINOIS UNIVERSITY PRESS

Copyright © 1988 by the Board of Trustees,
   Southern Illinois University
All rights reserved
Printed in the United States of America
Edited by Teresa White
Designed by David Ford
Production supervised by Natalia Nadraga

The part of chapter 6 on *The Changing Room*
is reprinted with permission of *Proteus,*
Shippensburg, Pennsylvania; copyright 1986.

Library of Congress Cataloging-in-Publication Data

Hutchings, William.
        The plays of David Storey : a thematic study / William Hutchings.
            p.   cm.
        Bibliography: p.
        Includes index.
        1. Storey, David, 1933–   —Criticism and interpretation.
        I. Title.
        PR6069.T65Z69 1988
        822'.914—dc19   87-35985
        ISBN 0-8093-1461-4   CIP

Contents

Preface

On 4 August 1983, after correspondence of several months, I arrived at the home of David Storey in northern London for an interview on his career as a playwright. For the next one and one-half hours, our conversation covered a variety of topics ranging from alleged literary influences on his work to his opinions of the current state of English theatre, his reactions to critics' and reviewers' assessments of his plays, and details of various productions and particular performances in them. Throughout his literary career, which now spans over a quarter of a century, Storey has granted very few interviews—apart from those related to forthcoming productions of his plays. "I've been in a predicament where I've always felt obliged, particularly working in the theatre, to give interviews, not because I've wanted to but because I have a sense of loyalty to the production because it's so exposed—and you've got to make some sort of immediate impact or you're lost. Things just vanish." Under those circumstances, he says, with the urgency of the publicists' deadlines and the limited number of column inches for journalists to fill, the result is too often that an author "tend[s] to be drawn into making statements which . . . [at] best are half-truths, really," since they cannot be developed at ample length or in sufficient detail.

Even in the absence of such constraints, as in our own conversation, Storey feels that readers "ought to be chary of interviews of *all* sorts. . . . Interviews, at least in my experience, are of no more value than other commentators' comments on that particular work, and to a large extent I think they're much more suspect, as the author has a vested interest in his comment, whereas most commentators tend to be more objective. I mean, they *are* subjective, but they have a much more objective attitude, seeing it from the outside, whereas the author always has this vested interest in talking about his own work, in putting across what he consciously made or wrote or acted or what he hopes will be there, whereas the best things in writing or art are those which are placed there unconsciously by the artist. Very often to these he's completely oblivious to their relative merit or even to the presence of these elements. Dostoyevsky is a primary example. He saw his work in evangelical terms, not the really extraordinary psychology and the characterization, the relationship between those characters."

Despite Storey's innate reservations about interviews of all kinds, he was frank, cordial, and genuinely helpful throughout our conversation—and throughout our correspondence as well. He has been particularly forthright in discussing details of the plays' productions and other background information, including their chronology and the circumstances under which they were written, which he modestly described as "through default or through ignorance. I mean, I didn't know—I'd no theatrical background." Repeatedly, Storey has denied most suggestions of literary influences on his own works—especially those of Harold Pinter and Samuel Beckett, to whose writings his own have often been compared. "My experience of the theatre when I wrote most of the early plays was virtually nonexistent. I'd only been to the theatre a half-dozen times in my life, and most of those were with relatives to see a West End comedy, Wilfred Hyde-White, Rex Harrison, or something like that. I'd never seen a Shakespeare play except when I was very very young: there was *Hamlet* when I was going on ten or eleven and Donald Orfett's *Lear*, which again was not my choice. But apart from that, . . . my only real theatrical experience had been seeing the production of [his first play, *The Restoration of*] *Arnold Middleton* at the Royal Court, which is what inspired me."

Nevertheless, as our conversation turned to such matters as dramatic technique and the prevailing tone of his plays, Storey remarked that such comparative assessments in the general context of modern drama constitute "an outsider's view, which is quite legitimate," though his own "insider's view" is, he insists, that he "couldn't write a sort of [traditionally plotted] narrative play. I mean, I've certainly tried over the years; I've obviously no facility whatsoever." Further, he contends, "I never actually analyze any of the characters for what they represent . . . I think you'd have to tell me." Beyond suggesting rather general categories within which his writing falls (e.g., "I'm very much an urbanized writer," "I think in looking back at the work there's always an interest in writing about groups, but beyond that I haven't any conscious [consistent theme]"), Storey also prefers to leave consideration of his major themes to "outsiders," suggesting that "you'll have to work on that one," since it is "another thing I don't really consciously do." Clearly, the view expressed by the central character of his play *Life Class* is also its author's own—that the creation of a work of art, in the theatre no less than on canvas or in any other medium, is "an instinctive process ... the gift, as it were, of song. * * * A bird sings in its tree * * * but doesn't contemplate its song ... similarly the artist sings *his* song, but doesn't contemplate its beauty, doesn't analyze, doesn't lay it out in all its separate parts ... that is the task of the critic" (*LC*, 30). Accordingly, in the following chapters, the assessments of Storey's works, the interpretation of his themes, and the comparisons of his works with those of other modern authors (including those whose influence he continues to deny) remain solely my own—an "outsider's view" that I hope will be, in Storey's terms, "quite legitimate." Wherever possible, the factual details have been corroborated by the playwright himself, for whose "insider's view" I remain grateful.

As at the end of the passage from *Life Class* quoted above, all parenthetical citations of Storey's plays (identified by their acronyms) refer to their first English editions, published by Jonathan Cape—with the exceptions of *Mother's Day* and *Early Days*, which first appeared in separate three-play collections of his plays published by Penguin; all are cited in full in the Bibliography.

Because Storey's plays are often punctuated with ellipses, deletions within quotations from the plays are indicated by three spaced asterisks; those consisting of three periods occur within the texts themselves and do not indicate omissions. In quotations from prose works and interviews, however, the asterisks have been used *only* when "period-ellipses" occur within the original source; otherwise, the ellipses indicate deletions of my own.

In view of the fact that a number of Storey's lesser-known works have been neither produced nor published in the United States, where others are currently out of print or not widely available, I have found it necessary to include more detailed summaries and quotations than would otherwise be needed or even desirable. Since this is primarily a *thematic* study, the plays are not discussed in chronological order (though a chronology has been provided in the first chapter); instead, they have been grouped according to subject and dramatic strategy, theatrical technique, and literary theme—toward a fuller understanding of which a detailed familiarity with the less renowned works is in many ways crucial.

Acknowledgments

I am grateful to the Graduate School of the University of Alabama at Birmingham for the Faculty Research Grant that made it possible for me to conduct my interview with David Storey in London in 1983 and to undertake additional research at the British Theatre Association. For Mr. Storey's consent in granting the interview, for his helpfulness in answering questions about even the smallest details, and for his permission to quote from the plays, I extend heartfelt thanks; his cooperation with, and interest in, this project made it an especially enjoyable experience.

I particularly want to thank Mrs. Enid Foster and Miss Joan Tracey of the British Theatre Association's reference library. Their kind assistance, their promptness in responding to inquiries during our correspondence, and their meticulous attention to detail are all greatly appreciated.

I also wish to thank the Kentucky Branch of the English-Speaking Union for the fellowship that enabled me to study at the University of London's Summer School in "English Theatre, Literature, and Culture of the Twentieth Century" during the summer of 1975, when my scholarly interest in Storey's works was first stimulated and a preliminary version of the final chapter of this book was written. The suggestions and encouragement offered by Dr. Katherine Worth, Dr. Philip Roberts, and Mrs. Helen Carr were in many ways the impetus for the further study of Storey's plays.

To Professors Guy Davenport, Jerome Meckier, Joseph Bryant, William Campbell, and Michael Brooks—all at the University of Kentucky—I am grateful for suggestions in shaping the earlier version of this study. Dr. Davenport's insights and guidance have been especially valuable, as always.

I am also indebted to Alan Perlis for his helpful suggestions and his always-thoughtful critiques; to Martin Sinclair of Edinburgh for information on the finer points of professional rugby; and to John Yozzo and Marilyn Kurata for their sustaining interest and encouragement, for friendship expressed in countless ways.

Most of all, I am grateful to my parents for their never-failing patience, love, and understanding. This study, therefore, is dedicated to them.

The Plays of David Storey

David Storey:

An Introduction

Among the group of modern English playwrights known as the "Second Wave" of the Royal Court group, the second generation of "Angry Young Men" (following John Osborne, Arnold Wesker, John Arden, and others), David Storey is one of the most prolific—and one of the most widely acclaimed. The author of twelve plays produced since 1966 and eight novels published since 1960, Storey has not only achieved considerable popular success but received numerous favorable reviews as well. When, at the end of the 1970s, *Time* magazine selected the ten best plays of the decade, Storey was the only author to be cited more than once[1]—a distinction that was hardly surprising, since he had also been selected three times during the decade to receive the New York Drama Critics' Circle Award for Best Play (in 1971, 1972, and 1974), becoming the only playwright to have been so honored. In his own country, he received London's *Evening Standard* Drama Award twice (in 1967 and 1970) and the Variety Club Award in 1971, and his novels were recognized with an equally lengthy list of prizes (the Macmillan Fiction Award in 1960, the John Llewelyn Rhys Prize, the Somerset Maugham Award, the Faber Memorial Prize in 1972, and Britain's most prestigious literary award— the Booker Prize—in 1976). More than any other modern playwright, Storey has used a variety of traditional dramatic forms: his works include a history play, a farce, and several domestic comedy dramas that have the familiar structure of the "well-made play." But his best-known plays are less conventional, since they are almost entirely without "dramatic incidents" or contrivances of plot. Although they have been widely acclaimed as meticulously detailed "slices of life" in which traditional action and conflict have been muted in scenes from workaday life, revealing character and theme with subtle elaborations of tone and mood, *The Changing Room*, *The Contractor*, and *Home* are also surprisingly innovative works whose subtly contrapuntal dramaturgy achieves and sustains a

---

[1]"Theatre: The Best of the Seventies," *Time* 7 January 1980: 97.

unique and delicate balance between seen and unseen events, even as his (often minimal) dialogue blends naturalistic speech and poetic nuance.

Throughout Storey's career as a playwright, while exploring a range of dramatic forms, he has consistently been deeply concerned with the nature of the modern family, the types of rituals that families honor, and the importance of such rituals in a world that has, since the industrial revolution, undergone a process of radical desacralization that has greatly accelerated in the twentieth century. Among the families in his plays (the Ewbanks of *The Contractor*, the Shaws of *In Celebration*, the Slatterys of *The Farm*), the changing mores and values of twentieth-century Britain become readily apparent; the working-class parents of the now-adult "professional" offspring in Storey's plays find themselves unable to understand their grown children's anxieties, their discontentedness with life, their unstable marriages, and their inability to enjoy the benefits of the education and "advantages" that the parents labored so hard for so many years to provide. The younger generation, though acknowledging the loving sacrifices that made possible their social "advancements," often find themselves cut off from their class origins (having been "educated out of" the working class at universities) and equally ill at ease among the "professional" classes. The mutual incomprehension that divides the generations is at best only temporarily and strainedly overcome by the ties that bind their hearts through often-painful memory and less-than-blessed familial love. In a number of Storey's plays, the occasion of the family reunion is a traditional ritual: an anniversary dinner in *In Celebration*, a planned wedding announcement in *The Farm*, and a wedding and reception in *The Contractor*. Yet, for a variety of reasons, such traditional rituals fail to unite the family in any significant way; differences among the generations and among siblings are suppressed only temporarily and through an exertion of will. Still, in *The Changing Room* and *The Contractor*, an alternate means of overcoming such alienation through the shared endeavor and common goals of a nonfamily unit is revealed; the workmen constructing a tent and the players of a rugby team take part in activities that are, in effect, major but nontraditional rituals in their lives, affording them a temporary but significant unity that the more traditional counterparts fail to provide to the families involved.

Storey's plays are deliberately uneventful; that is, their major "events"— the wedding and reception in *The Contractor*, the rugby match in *The Changing Room*, the anniversary party in *In Celebration*, the military battles in *Cromwell*—occur offstage and between the acts. In several of the other plays, anticipated events—a parental visit in *The Restoration of Arnold Middleton*, an engagement announcement in *The Farm*—simply never come to pass. Storey's deliberate "dislocation" or "removal" of his plays' central "dramatic" events—and the resulting (often-alleged) "plotlessness" of his plays—is unique in contemporary theatre. By placing the ostensibly important and "dramatic" events offstage, the playwright effectively shifts the audience's attention to the *impact* or *consequences* of such events on the individual characters' lives. The resultant unobtrusive yet significant transformations constitute what Storey has termed the "invisible events" of his plays. Subtly, yet with poignancy and frequent humor, amid seemingly banal activities and mundane dialogue, with their "dramatic" actions occurring offstage or between the acts or not at all, the plays deftly and eloquently reveal insights into not only the lives of the characters but the life of their times as well.

In many ways, Storey's plays seem to form a synthesis of traditional realism and the antirealistic conventions associated with various modern European dramatists, though the playwright has consistently denied any such direct influences of their works on his own. During an interview in 1973, Storey identified the "three broad categories of plays which I write," noting that "one is what you might call poetic naturalism, along the lines of *The Contractor* and *The Changing Room*. Then there's the kind of very traditional literary [i.e., "well-made" three-act] play like *In Celebration* and *The Farm*. Thirdly, there's the more overtly stylistic play like *Home* and *Cromwell*."[2] European affinities are most evident in the "overtly stylistic" dramas: in *Home*, the minimalism of Samuel Beckett's universal tragicomedies is transferred to a specifically English setting; in *Cromwell*, the devices of Brecht's historical parables are applied to English history—as well as to the conventions of the English history play. Nevertheless, the most important literary precedent in terms of which Storey's achievement must be assessed is Anton Chekhov, in whose works the major events also occur off-stage (e.g., the duel at the end of *The Three Sisters*, the auction of the estate in *The Cherry Orchard*, the attempted liaison occurring between the last two acts of *The Sea Gull*), while dramatic interest is focused on the *effects* of actions rather than on the actions themselves. Storey's plays are, in effect if not by design, a late flowering of the Chekhovian tradition, a type of theatre in which the causes of events are less important than their consequences and their impact on the characters' lives. But such plays as *The Contractor, The Changing Room, Home, The Restoration of Arnold Middleton,* and *The Farm* are not mere reiterations of Chekhov's insights or imitations of his style. By examining the effects of commonplace events (a rugby match, a wedding reception, an anniversary reunion, a homecoming) rather than exceptional or sensational ones, Storey's plays portray truly *ordinary*—even mundane—life and find there a significance and expressiveness that is uniquely his own. In his most successful plays (unlike those of "the English Chekhovian

[2]Peter Ansorge, "The Theatre of Life: David Storey in Interview with Peter Ansorge," *Plays and Players* September 1973: 32.

movement" earlier in the century—J. B. Priestley, Rodney Ackland, Ronald Mackenzie, et al.), the dialogue is spare and functional, punctuated with meaningful silences, always appropriate for the character, and seldom deliberately "profound"; his workmen, athletes, and other "ordinary people" rarely explain their feelings at great length (a tendency to which his teachers, Allott in *Life Class* and Arnold Middleton, are somewhat more prone). A clear and poignant subtext recurs throughout the plays, subtly revealing the disintegration of the modern family, the devaluation of traditional rituals, and the effects of ever-increasing secularity and commercialism on mid-twentieth-century society. Yet while the effects of such trends are manifest in the characters' lives, few are consciously aware of their causes or could articulate their impact; a perennial theme in Storey's plays is the way in which men and women attempt to cope (not always successfully) with the complexity, the uncertainty, and the rapid—often bewildering—changes that characterize modern life.

Notwithstanding their subtlety, their precise detail, and their carefully wrought structure, Storey's plays were written with astonishing speed, often being completed in just several days. As the playwright acknowledged in an interview in 1976, he seldom alters plays during rehearsal and production, and he spends

> very little time writing them . . . they seem to write themselves . . . [in] about five days or so usually. The main thing is to establish an immediate rapport. There are plays that have taken me longer . . . *The Contractor*, for example, all that stuff about the marquee was technically complicated and it took me longer. *The Changing Room* had twenty-three characters and it took me some time to work out mechanically what to do with them. The only real exception I remember is *In Celebration*, which was cut quite a lot in production.[3]

In bringing his plays into production at London's Royal Court Theatre, Storey's relationship with his director, Lindsay Anderson, has been particularly important. Their association—and Storey's career as a dramatist—began when, in the early 1960s, Anderson directed the film version of Storey's first novel *This Sporting Life*, for which the author himself wrote the screenplay. "We spent about two and a half years, I think, making that," Storey remarked during an interview in 1970, adding that "it was the first time he'd directed a feature film, it was the first time I'd written one, the first time Karel Reisz had produced one, the first time Richard Harris had ever taken the lead in a film. So it was a very exploratory period for all of us really, and I think we reached an understanding through what might be called the nightmare of making that

---

[3]"David Storey in Conversation with Victor Sage" *New Review* October 1976: 65.

particular film."[4] Shifting with surprising ease and effectiveness from the book's first-person narrative to the "externalized" point of view required for film, Storey found it "technically very easy" to adapt his novel for the screen. The sole difficulty, as he remarked during my interview with him, was in "going over material that I'd written" nearly six years before which now felt "completely dead":

> I wrote *This Sporting Life* when I was about twenty-one. The film was produced when I was twenty-seven. . . . So by the time the film was made, it was really very old hat to me. I found it terrible to have to go back six or seven years, poke around in all that stuff; it was completely dead. . . . The only stimulation was the novelty of making a film, and . . . I think if the people making the film hadn't been such a curious combination of temperaments, I couldn't really have gotten through it. . . . It had that kind of experimental feel about it.

In practice, the "understanding" that Storey and Anderson achieved was a synthesis of seemingly antithetical—but actually complementary—perspectives, which Storey has described as follows:

> Lindsay starts off from a kind of Tolstoyan viewpoint which is a sort of total picture of what you're doing, an overall conception, whereas my temperament is inclined to start off from a molecular viewpoint, starting off from a detail and working up towards a complete picture, all being well. So in terms of actual work we arrive at a common ground from opposite points of departure, as it were. . . . We never actually discuss what it's all about. The whole thing works without that kind of self-conscious exposition beforehand. It's an intuitive response. . . . Lindsay's tendency with actors and with writers is to let them have their head and if what happens is real, then [he] accepts it and if it's not, will say so, rather than determine beforehand what's required—I mean for that objective. It's an empirical way of working.[5]

Empiricism is, in fact, a key term for David Storey, who disdains "intellectualism" as "the English disease"[6] and maintains that to "see concepts first and life secondly rather than the other way around" constitutes "the disability of being educated. . . . Plays which are mere illustrations of an idea never become real."[7]

Nevertheless, he maintains that his plays are not merely the theatrical counterpart of *cinéma-vérité*, and he declines to call them "realistic," insisting on the term "poetic naturalism" instead, for reasons that he explained in my interview with him:

> I don't think they're "realistic." I think the contents of them are . . . not "idealised" but to a degree abstracted from the literal or what you might call

---

[4]Ronald Hayman, "Conversation with David Storey," *Drama* 99 (Winter 1970): 50.
[5]Hayman, "Conversation" 47, 50.
[6]"Conversation with Victor Sage" 63.
[7]Ansorge 32.

"literalism." There is a *choice*: it's the selection, I think, where the poeticism comes in, the selection of the actual elements within the play, and the naturalism is the method by which the elements are portrayed. So, I wouldn't call them "realistic" in that sense.

Although they work (as Storey himself acknowledges) "on many levels"[8] and differ in their dramatic styles and theatrical techniques, Storey's plays share a central trait that establishes them within the Chekhovian tradition. As he explained in 1970, "they're all plays of understatement in a way and if you don't get what they're understating, then you've really had it, because there's nothing great going on on the surface. It's all got to be going on in the audience's mind really, particularly in *Home*."[9] The development of *Home* from an initial "molecular" detail best exemplifies Storey's creative process:

> When I'd finished *The Contractor* I was struck by the image of the white table at the end, the white metalwork table which is left on the stage. . . . Perhaps two or three weeks later [I] sat down one morning to write and thought of that white table sitting by itself and thought "Well that's the beginning of something" and just wrote this description of a white metalwork table sitting by itself on stage with two white metalwork chairs, then bringing this chap on—somebody has to come on—so he sits down and somebody else has to come on because he can't sit there too long. . . . I wrote two plays called *Home* and this is the better of the two, I think.[10]

Like Flaubert's *Bouvard et Pécuchet*, *Home* opens with a coincidental meeting and deliberately mundane dialogue; Harry and Jack, Storey's central characters, are basically similar to Flaubert's, since they are representative but wholly undistinguished men of their times, though they lack the grandiose plans of the Frenchmen to master all knowledge and have not enough self-confidence to initiate even the most modest undertakings.

The speed with which Storey completes his plays is, of course, the opposite of Flaubert's slow and painstaking labor of composition; yet whereas the plays were composed in a number of days, Storey's novels are usually the product of several years of careful work. As Mel Gussow observed in his profile of Storey in the *New York Times*,

> For [Storey], writing novels is guilt-ridden hard labor. "It's like working in a coal mine," he said. "I sit down to eight hours of slog a day and do a kind of shift of prose. If I don't, I begin to feel very uneasy, irritable and frustrated. Even if nothing comes out, I do a great block of work each day." But though

---

[8]Mel Gussow, "To David Storey, a Play is a 'Holiday,'" *New York Times* 20 April 1973: 14.

[9]Hayman, "Conversation" 49.

[10]Hayman, "Conversation" 50–51.

he spends years mining his novels, his plays flow quickly and spontaneously. "Plays are a holiday," he said.[11]

Accordingly, Storey feels that he is "more a novelist than a playwright," as he remarked in another interview, adding that "the sentimental attachment is always to the novel."[12] Nevertheless, he finds a number of advantages in writing for the stage, avoiding the expansiveness and diffusiveness that prose fiction allows: "Writing a novel is like launching an unmanned ship. You may direct it in a certain direction, but thereafter you have no further control over it, it's out of your hands. A play is like a properly crewed ship: you can modify from moment to moment, take account of the climate of feeling at any particular performance, test out ideas and if they don't work as you want them to, change them."[13] His dual career as a novelist and a playwright (unmatched by any other modern English author) has led to an anomalous division of opinion about his works, which was reflected in the title of one of the first critical articles about his works: "David Storey: Novelist or Playwright?"[14]

Even today, as Storey admits himself, there is no critical consensus on the answer to that question; in his own country, he is acclaimed primarily as a novelist, while in the United States he is much better known for his plays. Yet, as he remarked during our conversation, such success in two quite different genres has also had certain drawbacks in critical assessments of his work:

> In the theatre I'm dismissed as a novelist and in literary circles as a playwright, so there's no real credibility in either. I don't know what category that comes under. . . . There's a kind of theatre which is very fashionable over there [in the United States] which has a convention of poetic naturalism, whereas over here the fashion is very much a sort of neo- or pseudo-Brechtian tradition amongst intellectuals or people who write seriously about theatre, [to whom] poetic naturalism is not very interesting or not very relevant, so I think that may be the reason also why the plays aren't much appreciated in this country.

Scrupulously recorded naturalistic detail is a hallmark of Storey's fiction, and he consistently attempts to avoid making a work (whether prose or drama) the mere illustration of a thesis. "You can't write a novel by an act of will," Storey remarked in 1976, adding that "it's no use telling everybody 'Look, this is what I'm doing.' It's no use beating a fool about the head."[15]

[11]Gussow 14.

[12]Hayman, "Conversation" 47.

[13]John Russell Taylor, "British Dramatists: The New Arrivals, III—David Storey, Novelist into Dramatist," *Plays and Players* June 1970: 23.

[14]Mike Bygrave, "David Storey: Novelist or Playwright?" *Theatre Quarterly* 1.2 (April–June 1971): 31-36.

[15]"Conversation with Victor Sage" 63.

David Storey

Storey's first novel, *This Sporting Life*, is a first-person narrative about a professional rugby player and his complex relationship with the widow from whom he rents a room; it involves a sophisticated use of flashbacks and shows considerable narrative subtlety, closely observed psychological nuances, and surprisingly mature characterization for a first novel by a twenty-one-year-old writer. The sophistication of its narrative technique was perhaps due in part to the fact that he had written six or seven novels by the time *This Sporting Life* was accepted, winning the 1960 Macmillan Fiction Award after having been rejected by eight other British publishers. Encouraged and excited at having won such recognition (and having spent the award money on a white Jaguar), he wrote *Flight into Camden* in only eighteen days. Like its predecessor, it also appeared in 1960; it, too, is a skillful first-person narrative, though quite different from *This Sporting Life* in technique and subject matter. It does not use flashback techniques, it does not involve sports, and it is told from a woman's point of view. As the initial outburst of enthusiasm and creative energy waned (and as reviews came in), Storey began work on *Radcliffe* in what he has described as "a state of irritation. I was angry at the reception—or rather lack of reception—of my first two novels. *This Sporting Life* was just some bloody provincial thing about rugby players. I hadn't learnt then that there's nobody out there . . . nobody knows what the hell you're doing."[16] As a result, he discarded the nuance and subtlety (and critically unrecognized artistry) of the first two novels, producing instead a long, shrill, deliberately shocking (even lurid), and blatantly schematic novel whose stereotypical central characters lack the complexity of those in the previous books, epitomizing instead a simplistic dichotomy between body and soul. *Radcliffe*, he now insists, is a novel he dislikes, "a willful book . . . a young man's desire to make himself heard at all costs. There's a lot of theorising and self-consciousness to it . . . too pretentious."[17]

At the same time that he was writing *Radcliffe*, Storey was adapting *This Sporting Life* for the screen. Having earned enough money to devote himself full-time to writing, he then began a lengthy novel that he has since abandoned; it was to have been, he says, "a big thing, with four or five characters all inhabiting different worlds and I thought it would take me five years. . . . After four years, I knew it was beyond me. . . . I kept on with it for the final year, but I knew it was no good. . . . It was about a group of people finding out about a nineteenth-century evangelical preacher and seeing him as a revolutionary figure and deciding to make a film about him."[18] From this diffuse work, Storey shaped his

[16]"Conversation with Victor Sage" 63.
[17]"Conversation with Victor Sage" 63.
[18]"Conversation with Victor Sage" 63–64.

fourth novel, *Pasmore*, which was published in 1972; he now acknowledges it to have been "a transposition . . . the only way to recoup on five years' work."[19] The abandoned work also provided the raw material for his fifth novel, *A Temporary Life*, which was published in 1973 after substantial revisions, including changes in the setting (moving it from London to the provinces) and in point of view (from that of one of the characters to a more detached narrative perspective). About this work too, he has expressed distinct reservations, finding it "too vicarious . . . after about two-thirds of the way through it started to get too abstract. . . . The material wasn't organic to the work."[20]

Storey's sixth novel, *Saville*, for which he won the Booker Prize, is a lengthy *Künstlerroman*, reiterating themes and situations from a number of his earlier works; he has said that it "was written over a period of years as a kind of relaxation from writing plays"[21]—much as the plays had begun as a respite from writing novels. *A Prodigal Child*, his seventh novel, also traces the growth and development of a young artist in England's industrial northlands; it was published in 1982. The central character of *Present Times* (1984) is a sportswriter and former rugby player who, at the age of forty-seven, finds himself beseiged by domestic crises amid the chaos and radical ideologies of the modern world.

Clearly, Storey's plays were written and produced at two of the most crucial points in his career—when he was meeting the least success as a novelist. His first play, *The Restoration of Arnold Middleton*, had been written during the late 1950s, when *This Sporting Life* was being considered and rejected by the English publishers. "I got so cheesed off trying to get [novels] published that after *Sporting Life* had been turned down about eight times, I thought 'Well I've got nothing left here really so perhaps I'm a dramatist,' " Storey told Ronald Hayman, adding that "I was teaching in the East End and at half term I took off and wrote a play and didn't feel perhaps I'd got very far, then left it and went on with cooking away at *Sporting Life* and about two years later it was published. . . . *The Restoration of Arnold Middleton* . . . came to light of day about eight years after it was written."[22] The play was first performed at the Traverse Theatre Club in Edinburgh on 22 November 1966 (directed by Gordon McDougal) and opened at the Royal Court Theatre in London on 4 July 1967 (directed by Robert Kidd). Although he did not direct either version of the play, Lindsay Anderson was responsible for the beginning of Storey's career as a playwright when, after completing work on the film of *This Sporting Life*, he asked whether Storey had ever written a play.

[19]"Conversation with Victor Sage" 64.
[20]"Conversation with Victor Sage" 64.
[21]"Conversation with Victor Sage" 64.
[22]Hayman, "Conversation" 47.

David Storey

Originally titled *To Die with the Philistines*, the play underwent substantial revisions between 1964 and 1966, when Storey had completed *Radcliffe* and still believed that blatant symbols were needed to make himself understood. The central symbol of *Arnold Middleton*, a suit of armor that prompts much discord between the protagonist and his wife, was inserted at this time. "I don't know that that was an improvement," Storey remarked in an interview in 1970, adding that "I think it's just that bit too much pushing something right under people's noses."[23] The ending of the play was also changed (as the title suggests), since in the original version the central character committed suicide at the end of the play, although Storey remained ambivalent about this revision as well:

> I don't know if that was right: it might have been better to follow out the logic of the story, as I did at first. But it was honest in another way, because I was I suppose in a rather despairing state myself when I first wrote the play, and when I came to revise I said to myself, but I'm still alive, and working, so I must see some sort of possibility of going on and getting somewhere, so in a certain sense the original ending was not really "true" either.[24]

Notwithstanding the playwright's uncertainties, *The Restoration of Arnold Middleton* received generally favorable reviews and won the *Evening Standard*'s Drama Award as the Best Play of 1967. This success occurred four years after the publication of *Radcliffe*, just when the complex 350,000-word novel was foundering. Exactly as the acceptance of *This Sporting Life* at a time of much frustration had prompted him to write *Flight into Camden* in less than three weeks, the acclaim accorded Storey's first play brought about a period of creative exhilaration during which he wrote almost all of his subsequent major plays.

The order in which the plays were written, however, is not the order in which they were produced. After writing them out in longhand, Storey would typically leave them alone for a period of months or years before rereading them and typing them for production and eventual publication. The following chronology summarizes the order in which the plays were written and first produced:

	Written	*Produced*
1964–66	*The Restoration of Arnold-Middleton* (revised from previous version, *To Die with the Philistines*)	
1966		*The Restoration of Arnold Middleton*

[23]Taylor, "New Arrivals" 23.
[24]Taylor, "New Arrivals" 23.

10

Year		
1967	The Contractor	
	Home	
	In Celebration	
1969		In Celebration
	Cromwell	
		The Contractor
	The Changing Room	
1970		Home
1971		The Changing Room
1972		
1973	Life Class	Cromwell
	Mother's Day	The Farm*
1974	Early Days	Life Class
1976	[Sisters?]	Mother's Day
1978		Sisters*
1980	[Phoenix?]	Early Days
1985		Phoenix*

*The dates when *The Farm* and *Sisters* were written have not been definitely established, and Storey maintained during my interview with him that he does not now recall. *Sisters*, he says, would have been written at some time between 1974 and 1978. *Phoenix*, which has not been published and has received only limited exposure through regional and amateur productions in England, was said in one review to have been written five years earlier, though this information was not attributed directly to Storey and its accuracy has not been confirmed.

    Although their production history spans a twenty-year period, at least eight of the eleven plays were written between 1967 and 1974—a period of extraordinary creative output, made possible in part by Storey's remarkable facility in writing plays. During this time, when working on plays having a relatively small cast (e.g., *In Celebration, The Farm,* and *Home*), he typically wrote one entire act per day; those that involved larger casts (*The Changing Room* and *Cromwell*) or particularly intricate stage directions (*The Contractor*) took five days at the most; *Life Class* and *Mother's Day* were written during the same week. "I can't do it any more," he remarked during our conversation in 1983, adding that it was

> obviously a combination of circumstances. I'd been for many years working on a novel and got rather bogged down with it, and I think it was opening a fresh window and suddenly being able to look in a new direction as a writer. There must have been a lot of steam there that had accumulated from the frustration of not being able to come to terms with the novel. I imagine it was that kind of energy being released.

11

David Storey

Given his "molecular" method of composition, starting from a single detail or image and developing the entire work from it, the plays are interrelated in ways that their production order does not reveal. In much the same way that *Home* began with the image of the white table that had been used in *The Contractor*, the conception for *The Changing Room* came as he observed the rehearsals of *The Contractor* in 1969. *Cromwell*, written at the height of the Vietnam War and the troubles in Northern Ireland, was an attempt (as he explained in an interview with Peter Ansorge) "to get away from the idea of a static play . . . placed in one specific location" as the previous ones had been. With the resumption of his career as a novelist, when *Pasmore* was published in 1972, the phase of his career during which almost all of the major plays were written came to an end.

Numerous autobiographical motifs recur throughout Storey's novels and plays, although they more often provide contextual details and background information rather than specifics of plot or characterization. Born in 1933 in Yorkshire, where many of his works are set, Storey was the son of a collier who, like the fathers in *In Celebration* and *Saville*, insisted that his sons receive educations so that they would not follow him into the mines. Yet, like the sons in those works, Storey found himself unsatisfied with the life that his father envisioned for him; "after going through the grammar school I decided I'd rather be a collier than a teacher," he later explained,[25] though he also felt that he could paint and write. At age eighteen, he joined the professional rugby league team in Leeds, using his initial bonus of $1,700 to enroll in an art school in his hometown, Wakefield. The following year he received a scholarship to the prestigious Slade School of Art in London, though he continued to play rugby for Leeds, commuting by train for the matches and becoming increasingly resented by his teammates, who "were all young colliers or factory workers and I was a bloody student. . . . They thought it was absurd to be carrying on as a painter."[26] As he explained in an essay entitled "Journey through a Tunnel" and published in the *Listener* in 1963, Storey found that, because he came from "an intensely and even obsessively puritan region [which] carries with it that profound and ironical puritan distrust of the isolated and solitary man," his choice of a career as an artist and writer brought about an inevitable sundering from both his parents and his native region, about which he feels both guilt and compassionate understanding: "What else could my father think when, nearing sixty, he came home each day from the pit exhausted, shattered by fatigue, to find me—a young man ideally physically equipped to do the job which now left him totally prostrated—painting

[25]Martha Duffy, "An Ethic of Work and Play," *Sports Illustrated* 5 March 1973: 68.
[26]Duffy, "Work and Play" 68.

a picture of flowers, or writing a poem about a cloud? There was, and there is, no hope of reconciliation."[27]

Such generational conflict—stimulated in large part by the education that the father had himself desired for his children—forms a principal theme in *In Celebration*, *The Farm*, and *Saville*, and similar confrontations are depicted more briefly in *The Contractor*, *This Sporting Life*, and other works as well. Increasingly, during this period of his life, Storey found himself leading a dual existence, with art and sport, London and Leeds, the aesthetic and the physical as its polarities. Separating these distinct existences were "four dragging hours of darkness . . . [which] took on a metaphorical reality which I still feel I inhabit."[28] Furthermore, Storey contends that during these "unhappiest years of [his] life" he was

> trying to resolve two sides of my temperament which were irreconcilable— the courtship of a self-absorbed, intuitive kind of creature with a hard, physical, extroverted character: the one the very antithesis of the other. . . . This, then, was the situation to which, not undramatically, I felt I had been condemned: to be continually torn between the two extremes of my experience, the physical and the spiritual, with the demand to be effective in both. I went on painting pictures, I went on playing football, but with increasing despair, obsessed with guilt at the one thing and by the futility of the other.[29]

Each of Storey's first three novels embodied this conflict between the physical and the spiritual in a different way: *This Sporting Life* presents it from the point of view of the "hard, physical, extroverted character," a professional rugby player whose love for the widow from whom he rents a room is roughly but earnestly expressed, though he is never fully accepted or understood; *Flight into Camden* is in many ways the reverse of its predecessor, since it is the first-person account of "a self-absorbed, intuitive" woman who leaves her provincial home and settles in London with her lover. In *Radcliffe*, the embodiments of both the physical and the spiritual are male, and their attempt at achieving a union of their respective attributes (a union that is itself both physical and spiritual) leads to a lurid and brutal murder. The plays—and the later novels— tend not to display this dichotomy as prominently: *Life Class* and *A Temporary Life* return to it, in altered form, making art itself—rather than any single character—the representative of the "spiritual." Their protagonists, both of whom are artists and teachers, struggle to cope with physical (often sexual) realities that they believe art can and should transpose. These works, too, reflect autobiographical details: after his career as an athlete ended, Storey taught school (like Allott in *Life Class*

[27]David Storey, "Journey through a Tunnel," *Listener* 1 August 1963: 160.
[28]Storey, "Journey" 159.
[29]Storey, "Journey" 160.

13

and Arnold Middleton) and worked as a laborer for a tent-constructing firm, gaining experience that he later shaped into *The Contractor*.

In addition to their recurrent autobiographical motifs, a number of details—and several characters—appear in more than one of Storey's works: Ewbank, who employs the central characters in *Radcliffe*, is himself the major figure in *The Contractor*; Foley, the eccentric headmaster of the school where Allott teaches in *Life Class*, also appears in *A Temporary Life*, which is apparently set in the same unnamed school; the brothers in *In Celebration* and *Saville* have the same first names (though they are separate families), and in each of these works—as in *The Restoration of Arnold Middleton*—the trauma resulting from the death of an infant son has scarred the memories and the adult lives of all members of the family. But such reiterations are less important than the variety of literary forms into which Storey has shaped his subject matter, since—like the plays— the novels display his mastery of a variety of literary techniques: the first-person narrative (masculine) in *This Sporting Life* and (feminine) in *Flight into Camden*, the modern Gothic novel in *Radcliffe*, the ironic novel in *Pasmore* (third-person) and *A Temporary Life* (first-person), and the *Bildungsroman* in *Saville* and *A Prodigal Child*. During an interview in 1976, when asked about the recurrence of such motifs throughout his works, Storey replied that "to work the same thing over from different angles . . . it's a bit like Cézanne or someone painting the same thing over and over again in different versions. I like to work like that."[30] Nevertheless, he insists that he does not deliberately adopt a new technique for each work, as he explained during our conversation:

> It's not a deliberate choice of an artistic position in a conscious sense. It really is the material that determines the way it comes out. It's more an organic choice than an intellectual choice, and the way the material comes out is just a matter of starting with the first page and seeing what happens. The material really just shapes the form, dictates the form. And so, I don't see them as being a change; it just seems that each one is true to its own material.

Despite the frequent recurrence of a number of characters, motifs, settings, and themes, Storey's works—when considered as a whole—display not only an extraordinary mastery of two very different genres but also an impressive range of forms within each.

The most often alleged literary influence on Storey's work is that of D. H. Lawrence, who, like Storey, was the son of a coal miner, the recipient of scholarships for his education, and a schoolmaster before embarking on his career as both a novelist and playwright. *Radcliffe* is the most clearly Lawrencian of Storey's novels, with its resurgent passions, its schematic "polarities," and its prominent though seldom subtle or

---

[30]"Conversation with Victor Sage" 64.

14

ambiguous symbols. Yet, with unusual vehemence, Storey scorns almost all of Lawrence's work, preferring only the scenes that are least typical of it, as he remarked to Victor Sage:

> Lawrence was a prick actually, and the more he went on, the more of a prick he showed himself to be. He became self-conscious and started intellectualising and striking attitudes all over the bloody place. After *Sons and Lovers*, it's all rubbish ... *The Rainbow* and all that ... He just got taken over by these middle-class pricks all dancing round him. But there's some fine writing in *Sons and Lovers*. Rereading it, I've noticed the character of the father ... the father is fascinating. Lawrence obviously thought he was a cunt and didn't want to reveal any of his opinions ... so he doesn't tell you anything about him. There's a scene where he goes to the pit and tells him about someone's death. The father just puts his hands over his eyes ... doesn't say a thing ... just goes over and leans against the side of a truck. It's only about three sentences, but *so* moving ... that's fine writing to me ... I suppose it suits me temperamentally to describe things through gritted teeth.[31]

Significantly, Storey's rereading of *Sons and Lovers* apparently occurred as he was writing *Saville*, his own most autobiographical novel, which was published only shortly before the interview in which these remarks were made. Seven years later, during my conversation with him, he insisted that connections between his work and Lawrence's overlook vital differences in their subjects as well as their styles:

> The easiest way of reviewing or writing criticism is to find a bracket or some means of encapsulating what this particular artist stands for . . . and Lawrence, because we share an identical or very similar background, seems to be the one I've been stuck with from the very beginning. My work is, I'm quite sure, the kind of writing Lawrence would have loathed, because he was very much a writer of flux and movement, and light and illumination, and certainly a writer of movement and not a static writer. He came out of and remained in a very strongly marked rural tradition of writing. I'm very much an urbanized writer. I write basically about and organize with very static situations, and I would say the difference is it's a very urban way of writing in the context of the situation and identification of character. The works actually present themselves very much in urban or social terms, certainly not in the varying terms they are in Lawrence. So I think it's a sort of facile view of my work which enables a kind of identification to be made. It also helps it in being dismissed, I think. The moment you sort of encapsulate it in that way, the person either reviewing or reading it tends to not look at it except in terms of that particular "identity."

Having repudiated *Radcliffe*, his most Lawrencian novel, and having adopted the restraint and understatement of subtler art, Storey's lack of admiration for Lawrence is as understandable as his resentment at being frequently cited as writing in Lawrence's shadow.

[31]"Conversation with Victor Sage" 64.

David Storey

More surprising, however, is the literary figure with whom Storey feels more affinity—Wyndham Lewis, the novelist and Vorticist painter (educated, like Storey, at the Slade School of Art), whose works include the acerbically satirical *The Apes of God* as well as *Self-Condemned*, about which Storey spoke at length in 1976:

> Wyndham Lewis has affected me a lot, and he's the opposite of Lawrence. Lawrence was an emotional writer until he started thinking he was an intellectual, but Lewis had this intellectual approach ... he saw himself as an artist ... the perfect machine of art and all that. But very moving because, despite his determination not to allow his feelings about his awful life to show, they're coming out on every page. *Self-Condemned* I found very moving, all that stuff about the exile in Canada, the terrible life he led ... very moving, but in the opposite way, you see, to Lawrence.[32]

In fact, Wyndham Lewis was a constant influence throughout Storey's early career, as he acknowledged in the 1963 essay entitled "Journey through a Tunnel," noting that one of Lewis's works accompanied him on the weekly trips to and from Leeds to play rugby:

> The book I invariably took with me on this "black journey" was Wyndham Lewis's autobiography, *Rude Assignment*—one which I eventually read six times. ... Lewis's view of the artist as a man isolated in an alien society and therefore of necessity clothed in armour of the most rigid and impenetrable design, was an attitude to which I was instinctively drawn. How else could I survive, I would ask myself, if it were not as an armoured protagonist? ... I began to write about my situation, trying to understand some of those sensations that accompanied me on that dark journey. ... I started making notes which two years later, while I was still at the Slade, resulted in the writing of a novel which I called *This Sporting Life*.

Like Lewis's protagonist René Harding, Storey's Arthur Machin is unable to realize that the desires of the woman in his life are independent of his own, unable to reconcile two aspects of his personal life (the physical and spiritual in Storey's work, the intellectual and emotional in Lewis's); each recognizes the value of the woman's love and the depths of her sufferings only after her death.

The influence of Lewis's work is even more apparent in Storey's first play: like Harding, Arnold Middleton is a teacher of history who, when deprived of his (literal) armor, faces the most acute spiritual crisis of his life. Although neither Storey's fiction nor his views of art resemble Lewis's own, lacking the acerbity and wit of the novels and the avant-garde qualities of the paintings, Storey particularly admires Lewis's technique,

[32]"Conversation with Victor Sage" 64.

16

as he explained during our conversation: "[Whereas] Lawrence was a writer who wrote from the inside out, Lewis was very much a writer who wrote from the outside and endeavored to go in. He certainly dramatized everything he was writing from an external viewpoint, and I suppose as an artist that certainly appealed to me: to sort of solve things visually and then form the visual, to write clearly, then try to decide what was in or behind it." Furthermore, Storey remains particularly indebted to *Self-Condemned* not only for its demonstration of the means whereby autobiographical material can be transformed into art but also for its image of the isolated artist and/or teacher struggling in a harsh or alien landscape, cut off from his class, home, and love. He has explored this theme through a broad range of literary forms, shaping and reshaping aspects of his own experience as a teacher, construction worker, athlete, and artist, creating works in which the details of these autobiographical experiences remain relatively unimportant—works that address more serious themes of life and art, exactly as Lewis believed they should do.

Throughout all his works, however, there is a recurrent concern that Storey himself has acknowledged: "an interest in writing about groups"—whether a family or a rugby team or a construction crew—as the individuals within them overcome their isolation and integrate (even if only temporarily) into a significant unit that transcends the self. Traditionally, such integration has been accomplished through rituals of various kinds, though in Storey's works these traditional rituals seem ineffective or devalued in modern society; in their stead, new and heretofore unrecognized patterns of ritualistic behavior are found, even though the characters themselves seldom understand or could articulate their significance. The contrast between the devalued traditional rituals and the more significant non-traditional ones is a central thematic and structural principle underlying and uniting Storey's diverse works. In 1967, during a panel discussion published in *New Theatre* magazine three months after his first play had been produced in London, Storey remarked on a general tendency toward ritual in the development of English drama since 1956— a trend that his plays would culminate in a unique way:

If you trace back a pattern over the past ten years, you can see a kind of evolution from romance to ritual. In the middle-nineteen-fifties, when the theatre became a more fashionable medium, as a form of intellectual currency, the theatre was a sort of polemical instrument; one could cite the early plays of Osborne, for example, or Wesker, where the dramatist attempted to intervene actively in social life by making certain dramatic assertions about it. The currency of the drama at that time seemed to be to present ideas about the world we live in at a social level—the way it destroys or appeases us, or the way it makes us; and the evolution of the last ten years has been towards a sort of introversion, or if you like toward ritual. In other words it seems now that the problems are within us and not without.[33]

In their various ways, all of Storey's characters confront inner or "spiritual" crises, problems *within* themselves and, by extension, within us all; whether public or private, secular or sacred, collective or individual, traditional or idiosyncratic, the methods by which they cope with these crises constitute the significant rituals of their lives. In fact, their problems often arise from the modern devaluation of traditional rituals that (although many are still regularly reenacted) are apparently no longer wholly viable or satisfactory. His most significant plays suggest that these problems can be resolved only through types of behavior that, although hitherto unrecognized as ritualistic, are in fact more efficacious than their traditional counterparts.

Any collective ritual, whether public or private, reaffirms for its participants that the life of the community subsumes that of the individual and enables him to become an effective part of a group that transcends himself—a reassurance that may be, as Jane Harrison observed, "a perennial need."[34] Further, as Mircea Eliade contends, "even non-religious men sometimes, in the depths of their being, feel the need for this kind of spiritual transformation"[35] that is confirmed through ritual. Formerly, organized religion provided such reassurance; in an increasingly secular society, however, the "perennial need" for reassurance and transformation remains unabated but is often unfulfilled by the traditional religious forms. This predicament is the basis of what Storey termed "the problems . . . within us" that, in his most significant plays, are overcome— at least temporarily—through types of collective activity that apparently satisfy the "perennial need" but have heretofore remained unrecognized as inherently ritualistic.

Although Storey has never defined precisely what he means by ritual, his understanding of the term becomes clear in the context of his works. Whatever the disagreements among social scientists, theologians, and others, in Storey's works a ritual has three essential characteristics: it is a *patterned, purposeful,* and *significant* (i.e., *status-affirming*) event.

First, a ritual is a *patterned* activity in that it follows an exact sequence of performance that has been prescribed (whether by long tradition or by the participants themselves) and from which variation seldom if ever

[33]Quoted in John Willett et al., "Thoughts on Contemporary Theatre," *New Theatre Magazine* 7.2 (1967): 7.
[34]Jane Ellen Harrison, *Ancient Art and Ritual*, rev. ed. (1918; London: Oxford University Press, 1948) 206.
[35]Mircea Eliade, *Rites and Symbols of Initiation: The Mysteries of Birth and Rebirth* (1958; New York: Harper & Row, 1965) 135.

occurs. From the repetition of the procedure, a sense of rightness develops, as both the *matter* (content) and the *manner* (method) of the ritual are standardized by the individual, group, or community. Thus, as Susanne Langer pointed out in *Philosophy in a New Key,*

> Before a behavior-pattern can become imbued with secondary meanings, it must be definite, and to the smallest detail familiar. Such forms are naturally evolved only in activities that are *often repeated.* . . . [It] acquires an almost mechanical form, a sequence of motions that practice makes quite invariable. Besides the general repetition of *what* is done there is a repetition of the *way* it is done by a certain person.[36]

The pattern of the ritual is also reinforced by the regularity of the intervals that separate the performances of it, whether daily, weekly, or seasonally. Thus, in *Pasmore,* the title character finds that "he could measure out his sickness now in the regularity of those visits [from his friend Coles] . . . the gaoler who came with those meager rations: the whole ritual of outside sounds, of feet ascending, of handles turning, of doors being opened, the long derangement of waiting."[37] In such cases, the standard by which the pattern is enacted and imposed may be wholly subjective, even idiosyncratic, as Storey observed in *Radcliffe*: "His voice was suddenly indulgent, as though some familiar ritual were to be performed. . . . She had a strange restlessness, almost ritualistic, as though each movement were pre-determined and conformed to some eccentric pattern in her mind."[38] When the regularity of the occurrence is altered or the relationship among the participants changes, however, the ritual fails to reassure. Accordingly, in *Pasmore* the children find that their usual weekly outing has been disrupted because their father has abandoned his familiar role (during a separation from his wife and family) and may see them only during prearranged visitations:

> He drove them from park to park. At each deserted playground they got out, were encouraged to climb onto swings where, motionless, they were pushed to and fro, their faces white, their eyes red and swollen, gazing sightlessly around.
>
> From the wet swings he led them to the wet slides, to the wet roundabouts and rocking horses, then back to the van.
>
> At each park the same ritual began, pushing and coaxing, a kind of terror running through him at their incapacity to be reassured.[39]

[36]Susanne K. Langer, *Philosophy in a New Key: A Study in the Symbolism of Reason, Rite, and Art* (Cambridge, MA: Harvard University Press, 1942) 160.

[37]David Storey, *Pasmore* (New York: E. P. Dutton, 1972) 163-64.

[38]David Storey, *Radcliffe* (New York: Coward & McCann, 1963) 121.

[39]Storey, *Pasmore* 126.

David Storey

Such reassurance (a product of all successful rituals) is conveyed primarily through the regularity and continuity of the ritual pattern, which is here undermined by Pasmore's abandonment of the responsibilities of the familial role that he tries temporarily—with uneasiness, self-consciousness, and guilt—to reassume.

Such reassurance, in one form or another, is often the *purpose* of a ritual—the aspect that differentiates it from the merely repetitive behavior of *habits*, which serve either no distinct purpose (e.g., pacing the floor or compulsively drumming the fingers on a tabletop) or none beyond their immediate utilitarian ends (e.g., brushing teeth, dusting furniture, washing hair). This absence of a purpose in patterned activity produces monotony and routine (the hallmarks of *habit*), as the narrator of *Flight into Camden* remarks: "The routine [of office work] no longer had a purpose; before it had been a preoccupation, a relief; but now it was boredom itself, dolorous, ineffective, embalmed in its uselessness, cold with its uninvolvement of me. The letters, the contracts we had to type—everything we did was a yawning, shuffling silliness that was carried out with us as its apparently inanimate components."[40] Traditionally, the purpose of a ritual often involves the indirect achievement of an intercession (the aid of gods, nature, luck, or some other impersonal force), but the purpose of Storey's wholly secular rituals is not a consciously articulated or deliberately enacted part of the process.

Often, the purpose of a ritual in Storey's works is the tacit affirmation of the participant's *significance*, conferring or confirming the "place" or *status* of the individual within the group; as such, it is a primary means whereby personal identity is established and maintained. Typically, a ritual performs a dual function of confirming the role or status of the individual within a hierarchy (vertical orientation) and within a collective entity (horizontal orientation). Thus, for example, an athlete accepts the role or function assigned to his position and experience in relation to the coaches and "captains" as well as his identity as a part of a team; a soldier assumes the responsibilities and privileges of his rank, even as he learns to identify with his "unit"; a child is taught his "place" in relationships with his parents and siblings, which also confirms his identity as a member of the family; a worshiper acknowledges both his status in relation to the priests and gods and his identity within a congregation of peers. Although such orientation may be deliberately, consciously, and graphically demonstrated to the participant—particularly during processes of initiation—it is most often accepted implicitly in the interest of achieving a goal, which is typically both collective and individual (e.g., victory in a game or battle) and often coincides with the purpose of the ritual itself.

[40]David Storey, *Flight into Camden* (New York: Macmillan, 1961) 167.

The fact that a habit can become a ritual when infused with purpose and significance is made particularly clear in *This Sporting Life*. Mrs. Hammond's habit of polishing her husband's boots and placing them on the hearth becomes a ritual only after his death, as it gains both a memorial purpose and an added significance, visibly confirming her status as a loyal and bereaved widow. When that status is threatened as she finds herself reluctantly but strongly attracted to her lodger (the narrator, Arthur Machin), her idiosyncratic ritual gains an additional purpose: to help her withstand the temptations of her new situation by reminding herself of her status in relation to her former husband.

Whereas such personal rituals confirm individual status in particular roles (which sometimes conflict—as in Mrs. Hammond's situation of being a widow, landlady, mother, and lover), collective rituals typically develop *morale*, the source of any group's identity, unity, and security. Accordingly, they contribute to the individual's awareness of his membership in a community within a larger, more diverse society. In such a society, no prevalent system of belief or actions unites its diverse constituencies, and no fundamental ritual provides the individual with the horizontal and vertical orientations that foster a common morale; such is particularly the problem, as Mircea Eliade has shown, in the modern "desacralized" world, wherein the "sense of the sacred" and a consensus of values based on it can no longer be found. Within smaller groups, however, shared values *can* prevail as common experiences and goals are shared and the individual subordinates himself to the collective purpose that rituals help to confirm. The contrast between the "collective" morale of such groups and the disunity of the diffuse society at large is a frequent theme in Storey's plays; the most significant "change" in *The Changing Room*, for example, occurs as the rugby players abandon the divergent interests and occupations that they pursue in the society at large and assume their places within the community of the team—participating in its locker-room rituals and preparing themselves to work toward their common (though temporary) goal, victory over the opposing team in that day's match. In *The Contractor*, the goal is even more mundane—the construction of a tent in which a wedding reception is to be held—but it too provides a common purpose and demands a unified effort that unites them at least temporarily and subsumes their individual differences as they pursue a shared aim.

The desacralization of modern society—and the consequent loss of any significant experience of what Eliade terms "the sacred" and "the holy" within society—is the ultimate cause of what Storey termed "the problems within us," which traditional rituals do little or nothing to assuage; for this reason, the crisis is more appropriately described as *spiritual* rather than merely psychological. In *Radcliffe*, for example, Blakely

David Storey

expresses a longing for the authority, order, coherence, personal responsibility, and individual accountability that were confirmed through ritual in the traditional societies but are lacking in the relatively normless modern world:

> That's the trouble. . . . At one time you were responsible, but now no one demands it of you, no one bothers you with it, torments you with it. It isn't that God's no longer relevant, no longer real, it's simply that God's no longer interesting. . . . And the result is what? . . . Nothing! Nothing but this soot and rock and smoke, and the scuffling of workmen. And nothing, not one drop of these acres of blood can be shown to mean one mortal thing. . . . I want a king, I want dignity, and authority . . . and *certainty*. Because without it it's the death of all extremes, and it's only at the extremes that man is finest and noblest of all. . . . But no one cares. . . . It's no longer even a part of life. . . . The fact is, we're of no more importance than if we'd never existed.[41]

The absence of "meaning" and "certainty" is, as Eliade has shown, among the foremost consequences of life in a desacralized and normless world, while such protests against the modern plight are manifestations of the "perennial need" for transcendence and external (traditionally imposed) order. Susanne Langer described such feelings as "an imperious demand for security in the world's confusion: a demand for a world-picture that fills all experience and gives each individual a definite *orientation* amid the terrifying forces of nature and society."[42] When such a world-picture is unforthcoming—that is, when there is no consensus about it among the diverse factions of a normless society—it becomes necessary for each individual to define himself within a social order that he finds amenable, confirming his orientation through the rituals (however mundane, workaday, secular, or untraditional) that they entail. The need for such orientation is a recurrent theme in Storey's novels and many of his plays (particularly *Home*, *In Celebration*, and *The Restoration of Arnold Middleton*); the effects of such orientation through "ordinary" ritual are demonstrated in *The Changing Room* and *The Contractor*, his most innovative—and arguably most important—plays.

The implications of having lost the core of communal beliefs and values but having found no replacement for them was eloquently summarized by H. G. Wells in 1905:

> The ideal community of man's past was one with a common belief, with common customs and common ceremonies, common manners and common formulae; men of the same society dressed in the same fashion, loved, worshipped, and died in the same fashion. They did or felt little that did not find a sympathetic publicity. . . . But . . . the old order has been broken up or is now being broken up all over the earth, and everywhere societies deliquesce,

[41]Storey, *Radcliffe* 267–68.
[42]Langer 158.

everywhere men are afloat amidst the wreckage of their flooded conventions, and still tremendously unaware of the thing that has happened. The old orthodoxies of behavior, . . . the old accepted amusements and employments, the old ritual of conduct in the important small things of daily life and the old ritual of thought in things that make discussion, are smashed and scattered and mixed discordantly together, one use with another, . . . and no wider understanding has yet replaced them.[43]

More than eight decades later, amid a heterodoxy that would astonish if not dismay Wells himself, such a "wider understanding" seems more remote than ever, and the "old rituals" remain devalued, vestiges of a more conventional—and more decorous—time. Accordingly, as Storey has remarked, modern "organized religion" is for him "touching, but irrelevant, touching though."[44] Yet paradoxically, despite the desacralization of all aspects of modern life, many actions necessarily—and often unconsciously—recapitulate the manner and/or matter of their sanctified counterparts in much the same way that, according to the nineteenth-century biologist Ernst Haeckel, ontogeny (the individual) recapitulates its phylogeny (its group or tribe). Thus, as Eliade has shown in both *Rites and Symbols of Initiation* and *The Sacred and the Profane*,

> Whether he wants to or not, the nonreligious man of modern times continues the behavior patterns, the beliefs, and the language of *homo religiosus*—though at the same time he desacralizes them, empties them of their original meanings. . . . The festivals and celebrations of a nonreligious, or ostensibly nonreligious society, its public ceremonies, spectacles, sports competitions, youth organizations, propaganda by pictures and slogans, literature for mass popular consumption—all still preserve the structure of myths, of symbols, of rites, although they have been emptied of their religious content.[45]

Such are, in effect, the nontraditional rituals of Storey's plays, responses to the "perennial need" for patterned, purposeful, and significant behavior even in a desacralized world. In *The Sacred and the Profane*, Eliade suggests a particular transformation in the perception of sanctified space, which is particularly relevant to Storey's plays. Formerly the publicly and traditionally consecrated setting for religious rituals, the "sanctified space" assumes wholly private significance in a desacralized world:

> The experience of profane space still includes values that to some extent recall the nonhomogeneity peculiar to the religious experience of space. There are, for example, privileged places, qualitatively different from all others—a man's birthplace, or the scenes of his first love, . . . All of these places still retain an

---

[43]H. G. Wells, *A Modern Utopia* (1905; Lincoln: University of Nebraska Press, 1967) 39–40.
[44]"Conversation with Victor Sage" 65.
[45]Eliade, *Myths and Symbols* 127–28.

exceptional, a unique quality; they are the "holy places" of his private universe, as if it were in such spots that he had received the revelation of a reality *other than that in which he participates through his ordinary daily life.*[46]

The significance of such personally "sanctified" places is a frequent theme in Storey's works: the locker room in *The Changing Room* elicits such feelings from the players, while the lawn in *The Contractor* is transformed into such a place by the construction of the tent for the wedding festivities (and, in the third act, is restored to its original "ordinary" state after the ceremony). The family home is the center of the crises in *In Celebration* and *The Farm*, and the physical exclusion of the title character of *Pasmore* from his home and family contributes substantially to his mental break-down. Yet, even the modern sense of a sanctified physical place has been devalued and deprived of spiritual significance; in *Life Class*, the class-room—a space sanctified for the purposes of secular art, in the central character's view—is profaned by the violent intrusion of vulgar, normless "life." Unprotected by the traditional weight of religious "sanctity" in earlier societies, the modern "sanctified space" is at best only tenuously—and temporarily—held.

In their study entitled *Ritual in Family Living*, James H. S. Bossard and Eleanor S. Boll summarized a number of the key distinctions between "primitive" rituals and their modern counterparts, which "tend to be (a) more secular and simple; (b) more intimate and less public; (c) less traditional, i.e., of shorter duration in their original rigidity; (d) less repressively and autocratically prescribed; (e) more frequently of the consciously constructed and adjusted type; (f) more narrowly restricted in number and scope; and (g) more personalized to particular family groups."[47] Whereas *literally* "primitive" rituals are often reenacted in Harold Pinter's plays and can be found beneath the seemingly mundane surface level of their plots, as Katherine Burkman has shown,[48] Storey's plays depend on a less radical dichotomy; no rites of savagery or ritualistic sacrifices are there to be found. Instead, in the ordinary lives of his workmen and athletes and teachers and others, the drastic effects of the loss or devaluation of familiar traditional rituals in modern society can clearly be seen. It is, as one of his characters describes it in *Saville*, the "destitution . . . of belonging nowhere; of belonging to no one; of knowing that nowhere you stay is very real."[49] For many, the result is an acute spiritual crisis; for others, fulfillment and consolation are found through

[46]Mircea Eliade, *The Sacred and the Profane: The Nature of Religion*, trans. Willard R. Trask (New York: Harcourt, Brace & Co., 1959) 24.

[47]James H. S. Bossard and Eleanor H. Boll, *Ritual in Family Living: A Contemporary Study*, 2nd ed. (Philadelphia: University of Pennsylvania Press, 1956) 29.

[48]Katherine H. Burkman, *The Dramatic World of Harold Pinter: Its Basis in Ritual* (Columbus: Ohio State University Press, 1971) 10.

[49]David Storey, *Saville* (New York: Harper & Row, 1976) 503.

new, nontraditional rituals—activities that have been unrecognized as ritualistic heretofore.

Through the depiction of these "invisible events" onstage, with subtlety, insight, and humor but without the contrivances of traditional plot, David Storey has achieved a unique innovation in modern drama and an advancement in Chekhovian form. When thematically considered as an oeuvre, notwithstanding their remarkable diversity of forms, the plays constitute a significant and surprisingly consistent exploration of the effects of desacralization on life in the modern world. After demonstrating the consequences of modern existence without meaningful ritual in such works as *The Restoration of Arnold Middleton, In Celebration,* and *Home,* Storey presents the seemingly ordinary, wholly unselfconscious rituals of *The Changing Room* and *The Contractor.* Unadorned by contrivances of plot (and without the self-conscious artificiality of participatory "reenactments" and theatrical "happenings"), these plays suggest the hitherto unrecognized means through which, at least temporarily, individuals may find the vital orientation and security that are perennial human needs. Therein lies his major achievement as a playwright.

Cromwell:

Parable, Paradox, Paradigm

Theatregoers who purchased tickets for *Cromwell* when it opened in 1973 might well have expected an historical drama like John Osborne's *Luther*, Robert Bolt's *Man for All Seasons*, T. S. Eliot's *Murder in the Cathedral*, or Bertolt Brecht's *Galileo*, all of which are based on well-known facts and biographical details about their famous subjects. *Cromwell*, however, is quite different: the title character never appears in the play, nor is he directly involved in its action, nor is he ever named by any of the characters. Even critics who were familiar with Storey's earlier works found *Cromwell* disconcerting for a number of reasons: it is the author's only work that is not set in contemporary England; it is presented on a bare stage with minimal props, unlike the realistically detailed settings of most of his previous plays; its language is poetic and relatively formal, with the metrical regularity of blank verse sustained throughout—in marked contrast to the spare and prosaic dialogue of his other plays; its action is occasionally violent and intricately plotted (unlike the allegedly "plotless" subject matter of *The Changing Room*, *Home*, and *The Contractor*), and it resonates with an ambiguous symbolic significance that critics considered portentous if not pretentious. Perhaps because the play failed to fulfill the expectations of both ordinary theatregoers and critics who had praised Storey's previous works, *Cromwell* was unenthusiastically received and closed after only thirty-nine performances at the Royal Court. Clearly, the play is not a traditional "history play" as the genre has developed since the Renaissance, nor is it typical of Storey's works; nevertheless, its significance among his works should not be underestimated, and it exemplifies his use of ritual on the stage in a way that clarifies its presence in his other plays. The play about which Storey has been most explicit in discussing his use of ritual is also his least typical work, which is best understood in terms of Brecht's "dramatic parables"—though he denies any *direct* knowledge or influence of the German works at the time of the play's composition.

As *Cromwell* begins, two young Irish laborers await conscription into a battle that continues in a nearby wood; they are soon joined by a

Welshman, followed by Proctor (the protagonist of the play), and finally their recruiting sergeant arrives. Only women and children remain in their village, whose inhabitants have been deprived of their livestock as well as their crops and have reportedly been reduced to eating rats, grass, leaves, and even corpses. On their way to join the regiment, they come across an abandoned cart bearing a single coffin; their attempt to remove the casket and commandeer the cart is interrupted by the return of the bereaved family—the elderly brother and middle-aged daughter of the dead man, his granddaughter Joan (whose father also died in the war), and their servant, a mentally retarded mute named Mathew. The priest of the village having fled or hidden himself, the family is attempting to transport the corpse for burial in sanctified ground, at the insistence of his daughter. The granddaughter reveals that, on the day of the old man's death, a soldier had had his throat slit while resting near a hedge on their farm; after a raid in which other soldiers confiscated the family's cattle and crops, the body of the slain soldier was no longer to be found, and the mourners set out across a landscape of "burnt fields, houses, even churches left in ruins" (*C*, 25) in order to bury their dead. At the insistence of the soldiers who intercept them on their journey, the coffin is opened to reveal the body of the murdered trooper, and—along with the members of the family except Mathew, who runs away—Proctor and his companions are taken into custody and tied together with ropes after being forced to dig the soldier's grave. While the women are being questioned and beaten, the old man reveals that he secretly substituted the body of the trooper for that of his brother because he feared that his family would be held responsible for the soldier's death. Suddenly Mathew returns, bringing the concealed knife with which he had murdered the trooper; after persuading the mute to cut him free, Proctor disarms him, ties him among the hostages so that the escape will not be detected, and flees into the night. When the soldiers return to announce their plan to execute the old man for the murder of the soldier and to free the other members of the family, they discover that Proctor is missing and dispatch a search party to recapture him as the first act of *Cromwell* ends.

At the opening of the second act, the two Irishmen and the Welshman who were to be conscripted into the Catholic forces have instead enlisted in the Protestant army rather than face execution alongside their former recruiting sergeant. Proctor, however, has joined the opposing forces and, encountering his erstwhile colleagues, considers them traitors for having so readily changed their allegiance. The Irishmen decline the taunts and challenges of their former friend, who kills the Welshman during a sword fight and makes the others his captives. Attempting to rejoin Proctor's forces, the group comes across the ruined farmhouse of the family that they met on the road during the first act; Mathew and the girl (whose mother has since died) bring them bread and water, the only provisions that they have after the battle—although the question of which side won remains unclear. Having nowhere else to go and no further ties to their destroyed farm, Joan and Mathew join Proctor, who has resolved to "find a place where no one fights ... with words, with ideas, with philosophies ... but not with these. (*Kicks his sword aside.*) * * * a place where we can rest awhile * * * a place for moral argument" (*C*, 54). Their journey is interrupted by Cleet, a "long-haired, almost naked" zealot (*C*, 55) who brandishes a sword, claims the woods to be his own, and escorts them to an enclave of fellow insurrectionists against "the Big One * * * the one who took the land" (*C*, 57); they claim that, after ousting the occupying forces, they hope to establish "a place where everything is shared" and there is "no land, no property, not common to us all" (*C*, 57). While such a place seems quite similar to the one that Proctor seeks, he soon realizes that such an ideal is unattainable, and war-torn reality again intrudes:

> PROCTOR. I'm tired of war ... We travelled to a place, I thought, where men took sides with words, not swords.
>
> WALLACE. There is no such place.
>
> DRAKE. No words stake out their claims but swords are not drawn up behind.
>
> JOAN. Yet if we don't ... Or if we can't.
>
> WALLACE. No don't, or can't.
>
> JOAN. Yet take up neither side.
>
> PROCTOR. But stand aloof ...
>
> JOAN. Looking to our own and nothing else.
>
> CLEET. Your own is ours ... and ours is yours to share.
>
> DRAKE. Our side, or theirs. (*Draws out his sword too.*)
>
> PROCTOR. We fall between the two.
>
> (*Vast explosions on either side.*)
>
> CLEET. To arms! The troops have reached the woods!
>
> (*C*, 57-58)

Escaping the insurrectionists in the ensuing disarray, Proctor and Joan resolve to return (with Mathew) to the farm, rebuild it, and begin anew. In the final scene of the second act, the Irishmen (who also escaped from Cleet and his men) arrive at a river and encounter a boatman who has apparently transported them all on a prior occasion, since he inquires about Proctor, Joan, her mother, and the others; because the Irishmen have no money to pay the ferryman, they too decide to turn back and work until they can buy their passage across the stream.

An unspecified number of years pass during the interval between the second and third acts, for as the latter begins, Joan and Proctor have a child who is "running in the fields" (*C*, 62) of their now-successful farm, where they employ the Irishmen as laborers. That night, being pursued by soldiers, Cleet and his fellow insurrectionists hide in Proctor's barn; during the confrontation between the guerrilla and the landowner, the question of whether political reform must precede or develop from a spiritual reform is thoroughly discussed, although neither is persuaded of the other's point of view. Soon the troops arrive to search for Cleet, and finding evidence that a fugitive has been sheltered there, they burn Proctor's barn and house (from which the child does not escape) in addition to seizing all of his lands and property. Proctor and his wife, along with Mathew and the Irishmen, are taken prisoner but are freed during a raid by the rebels, with whom they now resolve to fight. In the next scene, after another unspecified amount of time, the soldiers of the state offer a coalition to the insurrectionists, but their proposal provokes a curious response:

> CLEET. I need no coalition ... coalesce with what? The people are disaffected ... Look through these woods ... an army made up from all your towns and forts ... The battle's lost. Take off your medals. Join with us. Generals and captains are not political men. We hold no grudge. Exchange your uniform for one of ours and we'll march together to the city wall and proclaim our confederacy with such a shout that tyranny itself will come running out. What say you then?
>
> BROOME (*looks to* KENNEDY. *Then:*) Aye ...
>
> CLEET. And you?
>
> KENNEDY. Aye ... Where the people lead ... The order follows.

(*C*, 72)

Such an assertion should not necessarily be construed as the theme of the play, however, since Proctor seems equally convincing in his claim that "Oppression makes reflections of itself—and calls it revolution ... change ... the end to discontent ... And change it is ... the beggar usurps the horseman and takes the whip himself" (*C*, 66). Despite the reservations of his wife, who advocates a Stoic endurance, Proctor resolves to "have no more of living as it comes ... I must have goals and ways and means ... if men are victims what value are the things they struggle to?" (*C*, 73). Alone, he prays for illumination that, he tells the Irishmen, he has received "in part" (*C*, 75); a new battle has begun, producing yet more refugees who report a massacre and further insurrections as they flee "To a lighter place than this" (*C*, 77). In the final scene of the play, Joan and Mathew join Proctor at the river, where the boatman transports them across the stream from the dark land to another that is "darker still" (*C*, 78); although the Irishmen also seek to escape, the boatman remarks that they never will do so, since "They hang like leeches to the things that others have ... hands which always receive can offer nought" (*C*, 78). The three disembark on the other shore—from which no one ever returns, the boatman claims; Joan notes that "for the first time in our lives we have no turning back" (*C*, 79), and the play ends as Proctor asks whether she can see the light that reputedly exists beyond the darkness that surrounds them.

In an interview with Peter Ansorge when *Cromwell* was first produced, Storey remarked that "the only model for *Cromwell* was Shakespeare,"[1] and in terms of its dramatic structure this seems quite likely to be so. The brief scenes that constitute each act are presented with only the most essential props, and although the light fades at the end of each scene, neither the amount of time that has elapsed between any two events nor the total time that passes during the course of the play is ever specified. Nevertheless, it is clear that, as the Chorus in Shakespeare's *Henry V* remarks, the playwright is freely "jumping o'er times,/Turning th' accomplishment of many years/Into an hour-glass." Similarly, the geographical setting of the play shifts repeatedly, and there are seldom two consecutive scenes in the same place; no particular locale is ever identified by name, no indication of the distances traversed is ever given, and the production notes specify only that the setting is "a stage" (*C*, 7). Indeed, throughout the text of the play, the stage directions are minimal and unadorned (like those in Shakespeare's works but in contrast to the detailed instructions given in *The Contractor* and *The Changing Room*). Although the language is poetic and metrically regular (predominantly iambic), it is printed in prose form and punctuated with ellipses that provide the sole guide for the actors' delivery.

In terms of genre, however, *Cromwell* has little in common with the Shakespearean theatre—least of all with the history plays, since English history is merely the pretext for the action of the play and neither actual events nor "real" personages figure significantly in the plot. Because of the ambiguous closing scene in which the protagonist remains both literally and figuratively lost in almost total darkness, there is none of the definite finality that audiences commonly expect at the end of any work of fiction; Storey's play concludes with neither the celebration of a festive "new beginning" that resolves traditional comedies nor the peripeteia that characterizes tragedy. Like Hamlet, each of Storey's characters (ex-

[1]Peter Ansorge, "The Theatre of Life: David Storey in Interview," *Plays and Players* September 1973: 32.

cept Mathew) must decide for himself "whether 'tis nobler in the mind to suffer/The slings and arrows of outrageous fortune,/Or to take arms against a sea of troubles," but either course is shown invariably to entail a futile sacrifice of both life and property, in exchange for which human sufferings and "troubles" not only remain undiminished but are in fact increased. The action of the play yields no explicit resolution of its central political issue, the relative merits of the vying courses of political action (and inaction) that are advocated by the various characters as they respond to the oppression and warfare that recur throughout the plot. Since no analogues or models for these aspects of *Cromwell* are to be found in Shakespeare, the search for a tradition in which the play might be accommodated (whether exclusively modern or in terms of earlier forms as well) must be conducted elsewhere.

Partly because it lacks both a clear conclusion and a resolution of the issues that it raises, *Cromwell* seems to invite comparison with several plays by Samuel Beckett. In his essay entitled "Insanity and the Rational Man in the Plays of David Storey," Albert E. Kalson suggests that in *Cromwell* Storey has created a "Beckett-like world" in which

> two garrulous Irishmen, sounding much like Didi and Gogo, serve as a chorus throughout. . . . Like Beckett's characters existing in a void, Storey's characters in *Cromwell* are trapped in the limbo-like world of a bare stage. The play's opening [in which the Irishmen await an unidentified companion in the cold alongside a deserted road] is an obvious echo of *Waiting for Godot.* . . . The beginning of the second scene amplifies the Beckettian strain as Proctor joins the Irishmen who are obviously waiting for someone [whom they claim they have never seen].[2]

Nevertheless, the suffering that is depicted in *Cromwell* arises from a surfeit of religious convictions that are politically and militarily enforced; as such, it bears little if any resemblance to the plight of Beckett's characters, whose afflictions result from their pervasive religious doubts, epistemological uncertainties, and physical inertia—with all of which political ideologies are wholly unconcerned and to which they are irrelevant. Furthermore, many of the similarities to *Waiting for Godot* are superficial or coincidental at best: both *Hamlet* and Brecht's *Mother Courage* open with a pair of characters waiting in the cold (beside a road in the German play) before encountering an unknown person, and in fact complaints about being (or having been) cold occur in the opening lines of every one of Storey's plays except his first, *The Restoration of Arnold Middleton*. Even though Beckett is commonly associated with minimalist theatre, few of his plays actually take place on a bare stage, since the

[2]Albert E. Kalson, "Insanity and the Rational Man in the Plays of David Storey," *Modern Drama* 19.2 (June 1976): 123.

settings for *Endgame*, *Play*, and *Happy Days* are stark but carefully designed and quite detailed. In addition to its antecedents in Elizabethan theatre, Storey's use of the bare stage in *Cromwell* has a far greater affinity with the works of Bertolt Brecht than with those of any author in the theatre of the absurd.

Specifically, both the design of *Cromwell* and the treatment of its subject matter so strongly resemble those of Brecht's *Mother Courage* that the similarity cannot be overlooked, although the presence of a number of Storey's recurrent concerns make the play characteristically his own. By presenting the stories of ordinary people rather than heroes or historical characters, both plays portray the multiple afflictions and hardships that warfare imposes on civilians in any epoch; the purposeless destruction of life and property for the sake of strategic advancement in the name of religion is a prominent theme in each work, as the desolation that results from military campaigns is graphically described. Although both plays are set during wars that took place in the mid-seventeenth century, there are few details that limit the actions of either to the specific era in which they occur. Brecht specifies that the events presented in his play occupy the interval between 1624 and 1636 in various countries throughout northern Europe during the Thirty Years' War, but Storey is even less specific, since only the title and the types of weaponry used (swords and pikes) indicate that the characters in *Cromwell* are living in the mid-1600s. The loss or devaluation of traditional values is a primary concern in each play, as the recruiting officer in *Mother Courage* remarks that "there's no loyalty left in the world, no trust, no faith, no sense of honour,"[3] a view that is elaborated further in *Cromwell*:

> PROCTOR. [To the Irishmen, whose actions are governed solely by expediency and who disclaim any irreversible commitment, allegiance, or conviction.] If everyone thought like you there'd be no war ... No principle, honour, virtue ... no cause to raise a man at all.
>
> LOGAN. Ah, but many to celebrate its absence with.
>
> O'HALLORAN. Unmaimed.
>
> LOGAN. Unkilled.
>
> O'HALLORAN. Unblinded.
>
> *
>
> PROCTOR. I see no principle of any sort in that.
>
> LOGAN. Principle, you see, is like a cart: jump on, jump off. * * * No principle, you see, can hold us long. * * * When one cause expires but its opposite begins ... Proctor's flag today ... tomorrow ... this.

[3]Bertolt Brecht, *Mother Courage and Her Children*, trans. Eric Bentley, in vol. 2 of *Bertolt Brecht: Plays* (London: Methuen, 1962) 3.

PROCTOR. * * * Without ideals no man can live.

LOGAN. And with ideals we end like this. (*Gestures round* [at the corpses of those who were slain in battle].)

(*C*, 50-51)

In each play, the major prop is a delapidated cart that must be pulled by members of the respective families, since their draft animals have been confiscated in the war. Storey's use of the cart is primarily functional, since it bears the coffin that the group seeks to bury in consecrated ground, but in Brecht's drama the wagon becomes the central symbol of property—for the sake of which Mother Courage sacrifices the lives of her children as well as her own opportunity for future happiness in a settled, prosperous, and respectable life. In addition to the deaths and deprivations that the family suffers as a result of the war, each is burdened by a mute and mentally afflicted child who, at the time of the play, has achieved adulthood; yet, whereas Katterin in *Mother Courage* remains dependent on others throughout her lifetime, Storey presents Mathew as being capable of considerable independent action within his limitations: he murders the soldier, brings bread to the hostages, enables Proctor to escape, and manages to survive the tumults of war more effectively than most of the other characters. Despite his obvious handicaps, Mathew is shown to be an effective and autonomous member of both his family and his society; like Glenny in *The Contractor*, he contributes to the welfare of others and establishes his "place" through his participation in work (farming, pulling the wagon, etc.), which is another of Storey's recurrent concerns.

Many of the affinities between *Cromwell* and *Mother Courage* suggest that the authors are in fact working in the same genre: each is clearly a "parable play," a dramatic form defined as an allegorical or moral tale designed to illustrate an abstract principle by a concrete instance and necessarily is not restricted to (or delimited by) the historical period in which it is set. The production of Brecht's *Man Is Man* is widely acknowledged as having introduced this form into the modern theatre, and it was followed by his better-known parables—*The Good Woman of Setzuan* (written 1938–42), *The Caucasian Chalk Circle* (1943–45), and *Mother Courage* (1938–39). More closely akin to medieval morality plays than to any subsequent literary form but typically more complex and ambiguous than their medieval counterparts, modern parable plays avoid both explicit moralizing and unduly blatant didacticism. In many instances, their historical settings deliberately preclude narrow references to topical events and contemporary relevance, which can nevertheless be inferred. John Arden, whose *Serjeant Musgrave's Dance* (1960) is the most significant example of the form in modern English drama, subtitled

33

his play "An Unhistorical Parable," omitting not only specific historical references and identifiable "period" details but also the date of the fictional incident. Like Brecht and Storey, Arden specifies that the production should be "realistic but not . . . naturalistic . . . so that the audience sees a selection from the details of everyday life rather than a generalized impression of the whole of it"[4] in any particular era. Storey's purpose in selecting the parable format was revealed in his interview with Peter Ansorge, as he remarked that "If you set this kind of play in the past you can make it poetic, which it has to be really—rather than a political or sociological statement. It can't all be explained away like yesterday's headlines."[5] Nevertheless, by implicitly affirming that the moral truths presented in the parable are universally applicable, such plays often comment obliquely on contemporary concerns in a way that is frequently more effective—and certainly less strident—than the works of the "agit-prop" (i.e., agitation and propaganda) movement in the theatre of the 1960s and 1970s.

Despite their obvious similarities to *Mother Courage*, neither the form nor the content of *Cromwell* was influenced by Brecht's work, Storey insists. "The story of the corpse on the cart was told me by a Second World War soldier who came across such an incident in Flanders," Storey explained in a letter in 1982, "but then (I get your point) *he* may have read 'Mother Courage'!" Notwithstanding their various similarities, a key difference remains between Brecht's approach to the subject and Storey's (and that of other English history plays and parables): the English parables tend to be typically more ambivalent, presenting diverse points of view that are all amply supported. The "defense" that John Arden included in the introduction to *Serjeant Musgrave's Dance* is equally appropriate for *Cromwell*:

> As for the "Meaning of the Play" . . . in view of the obvious puzzlement with which it was greeted by the critics, perhaps a few points may be made. This is not a nihilistic play. This is not (except perhaps unconsciously) a symbolist play. . . . Complete pacifism is a very hard doctrine: and if this play appears to advocate it with perhaps some timidity, it is probably because . . . I know that if I am hit I very easily hit back: and I do not care to preach too confidently what I am not sure I can practise.[6]

During the course of *Cromwell*, an entire spectrum of types of political involvement is exemplified and advocated: Proctor expounds an absolute commitment to the defense of ideological principles early in the play; the Irishmen embody an expedient self-interest that acknowledges no

[4]John Arden, *Serjeant Musgrave's Dance* (New York: Grove Press, 1962) 5.
[5]Ansorge 32–33.
[6]Arden 7.

principle except survival; Cleet advocates an egalitarian Utopia to be achieved by force; Joan proposes a stoical resignation to events that cannot be controlled. Unable to change his allegiance as easily as the captured Irishmen do, Proctor defends his principles but soon discovers that the sufferings inflicted by both sides in the name of such ideology are equally abominable. Repudiating warfare and hoping to find a more peaceable kingdom, he is overtaken by Cleet and the insurrectionists, who advocate a pure form of communism that they hope to achieve by overthrowing the occupying forces, abolishing private ownership of land and property, and establishing "a place where everything is shared" (*C*, 57). After escaping their custody, the family returns to the farm, as suggested by Joan, who has endured more horrors than any other character in the play and advocates a stolid (perhaps benumbed) endurance: "Let leaders lead: direct us as they will—support the good, and fight against the ill ... what can't be taken is our joy in work ... our life, like theirs, is forfeit in the end. (PROCTOR *shakes his head.*) But what you looked for was a kind of death—the uniform, at first, and then a home—inviolable extremes that like a hearse can take you safely to a given end" (*C*, 73).

Proctor remains unconvinced of the value of such an attitude (which too closely resembles the resolution "to tend our garden" that concludes *Candide*), and he advocates a form of self-willed determinism for which Albert Kalson terms him Storey's "existential hero."[7] Thus, disputing the insurrectionists' egalitarian ideals, Proctor claims that "a brave man makes his life. He saves it if he can ... Do you think one bloodied head ... a thousand heads ... a mile of corpses ... will change by one degree the world out there? * * * A dead man is no longer fit for good or ill: a live man, however hard, can be fashioned by his will. * * * I carry the revolution in my head, and heart ... not streaked along a sword, or buried with the dead" (*C*, 65-67). Nevertheless, by the end of the play, Proctor has modified, if not rejected, this view of the self-sufficient human will. Recognizing the deficiencies of ideology, militarism, pacifism, communism, and agrarianism, he at last seeks a spiritual solution to what Storey has termed "the problems within us" through prayer—an action that implicitly acknowledges a preexistent essence and a suprahuman will. Yet, even this solution remains tentative, as the play concludes with Proctor's "partial" vision and a quest for the light that may or may not be there. Like Johnson's *Rasselas*, *Cromwell* ends with "a conclusion in which nothing is concluded"; like Arden, Storey declines "to preach too confidently" any particular social or political theory or system.

Although the absence of an explicit political or social statement in *Cromwell* confounded critics and confused audiences, the avoidance of

[7]Kalson 123.

35

such proclamations has been a characteristic of Storey's work throughout his career. Indeed, as Lindsay Anderson pointed out in the program note for the first production of *The Restoration of Arnold Middleton*, the fact that this playwright's concerns transcend political ideologies (and topical issues) makes him unique among contemporary English writers:

> At that time I still believed, or wanted to believe, that things (society) could become "better." David . . . was not under this misapprehension. Also he was not interested in surface, but in essence; not in what was representative, but in what was exceptional. This made him, and makes him, a very exceptional kind of English writer. David Storey's unique quality . . . seems to me a sort of elemental poetry, a passionate reaching-out, an ambition of concept that carries him beyond neatness, completeness, civilised equilibrium. He seeks to penetrate the soul; yet he never forgets the relevance of the social world in which souls meet, conflict, and struggle.[8]

More than any other of Storey's plays, *Cromwell* exemplifies its author's efforts "to penetrate the soul" and his conviction that "the problems within us" underlie the social and political dilemmas of our time. In the interview with Peter Ansorge, Storey remarked that "life has gotten far too complex for making political gestures anymore [*sic*]. They don't work. That's what Proctor discovers in *Cromwell*,"[9] and for this reason the emphasis on spiritual enlightenment at the end of the play is particularly significant. Storey himself points out that at the end of the play

> political decisions are there to be made whether or not one cares to heed them. So Proctor . . . finds that rather than remain endlessly vulnerable to the world and its comings and goings, he will actually try and change the world itself. This he can only do by becoming a demagogue or Cromwellian figure. He can unify the political and religious in the idea of this totally godlike creation. At the end of the play he lives in a kind of dream or vision—it's a way of making himself invulnerable to life. His progress is a kind of Pilgrim's Progress towards accepting rather than denying his invulnerability. He has to learn to live without preconceptions, to accept life for what it is.[10]

Whether or not the likeness is coincidental, a similarly ambiguous "spiritual enlightenment" concludes Lindsay Anderson's film entitled *O Lucky Man!*, which is also a "Pilgrim's Progress towards accepting . . . life for what it is"; the film was completed and released in 1973, the same year that *Cromwell* was produced, although Storey apparently did not directly influence or contribute to the script, which was written by Anderson and David Sherwin, based on an original idea by the film's star, Malcolm

---

[8]Lindsay Anderson, "David Storey," *Playbill* for *The Restoration of Arnold Middleton*, Criterion Theatre, 1967 (London: Playbill, Ltd., 1967) 13.
[9]Ansorge 35.
[10]Ansorge 35.

McDowell. Nevertheless, given the close relationship of Storey and Anderson as well as their mutual admiration, it seems hardly coincidental that, like the play, the film concludes with an ambiguous spiritual insight by which the central character seems to gain an acceptance of life with all of its diversity and heterodoxy: after managing to survive an entire gamut of forms of modern corruption from corporate graft and chemical warfare to covert "intelligence gathering," imprisonment, inhumane medical research, and even a nuclear blast, the film's protagonist ultimately achieves a spiritual insight in the form of a Zen satori (a slap in the face with the film's script, administered by Anderson himself). Even in the printed version of the script, however, both the significance and the implications of the insight remain as problematical as its counterpart in *Cromwell*: "His look is not thoughtful, but direct, comprehending. . . . A Faint smile begins to break at the corner of his mouth . . . the smile of UNDERSTANDING? or of OBEDIENCE?"[11] Whatever the nature of the spiritual insight that he gains, the final scene of the film specifies that its protagonist is "still reaching out"[12] (reiterating one of the qualities that Anderson most admires in Storey's work), in much the same way that Proctor continues his newly enlightened quest at the end of *Cromwell*.

The relationship between the political and spiritual themes in the play becomes more intelligible when examined in the context of *Radcliffe*, Storey's third novel, which was published a decade before *Cromwell*. Beyond the novel's stale and predictable characterization of Puritans as irredeemably alienated from their own bodies, sexually repressed, and guiltily unable to accept their own physicality and temporality, Cromwell is said to be the last embodiment of an "ambition for some sort of complete action. One that exists simultaneously in both [social and spiritual] worlds. Someone who acts politically and religiously in the same event. The world's grown empty of such men. And such opportunities."[13] The severance of spiritual and political action—a consequence of the desacralization that Eliade and others have described—is thus a basic part of Storey's understanding of the plight of modern (i.e., post-Renaissance) man. Within this context, Cromwell becomes the final tragic figure in English history and literature—a man whose actions united political and religious conviction, while his fall resulted from both a flaw in his character (his Puritan contempt for and distrust of the physical, an imperfect understanding of human nature) and the irreversible trend toward desacralization that characterized his time; ironically, Cromwell was himself the principal *agent* of much desacralization, as he removed many rituals

[11]Lindsay Anderson and David Sherwin, *O Lucky Man!* (London: Plexus, 1973) 188.
[12]Anderson and Sherwin, 192.
[13]David Storey, *Radcliffe* (New York: Coward-McCann, 1963) 26.

from worship and persecuted those who sought to retain their traditional practices. Yet, because *Cromwell* is a parable rather than a "tragical history," its subject is not the life and career of England's last tragic figure; instead, the play portrays the consequences of living in a desacralized world in which political and spiritual actions are no longer necessarily the same, and the fact that its plot takes place during the struggles of the mid-seventeenth century merely enables the audience to see the effects of such desacralization during its emergence as a modern trend. Despite the best efforts of the Puritans to preserve the union of social and religious responsibilities, it soon becomes clear that the tendency toward desacralization is strong among the common people who are the play's characters. The Irishmen who form the "chorus" of it are at best only "nominal" Catholics, and one of them declares to Joan that "there's nothing beyond death, you know" (*C*, 23) and suggests that the family's insistence on burying its dead in consecrated ground is mere "superstition" (*C*, 22); the head of the household implicitly shares this view, since he deliberately substitutes the body of the slain trooper for the member of his family whom the others intend to give a properly religious burial. Clearly, throughout *Cromwell* "The Sea of Faith" that Matthew Arnold described in "Dover Beach" has already begun its retreat, and the efforts of Cromwell himself can have no more effect than those of King Canute four centuries earlier. Accordingly, at the end of Storey's play, Proctor and Joan find themselves in precisely the predicament that Arnold described; having traversed "a darkling plain/Swept with confused alarms of struggle and flight,/Where ignorant armies clash by night," they have learned through their sufferings that "the world . . ./Hath really neither joy, nor love, nor light,/Nor certitude, nor peace, nor help for pain." The sole consolations available to them are the love that they bear each other ("Ah, love, let us be true/To one another!" as Arnold wrote) and the questionable presence of the distant light—"which *seems*/To lie before us like a land of dreams,/So various, so beautiful, so new [emphasis mine]"—though that, too, may be an illusion in the modern world.[14]

Throughout *Cromwell*, concepts of madness and ideology are repeatedly conjoined. The vital distinction between actual madness (i.e., a *derangement* of "normal" faculties) and the "idiocy" of Mathew (a congenital *deprivation* of same) is consistently maintained, even though the word "fool" is applied to each; nevertheless, Mathew—a mute who obviously lacks any ideological orientation—functions more capably than (and outlives) the majority of his "sane" companions. The Irishmen, who also survive the tumults of the play, consider themselves to have been "damn fine fools" for not having fled the town before they were conscripted (*C*,

[14]"Dover Beach," lines 32–36.

13), and when Proctor escapes they refer to him as "the bloody fool" (*C*, 40) but also "a soldier * * * through and through" (*C*, 40) and "a man of action" (*C*, 41), as if all three terms are in fact synonymous. With his "huge shriek" and the deranged appearance of "a wild figure" (*C*, 54), Cleet is also described as a "madman" (*C*, 54) as he takes the captives to the hiding place of his fellow insurrectionists, where (as one of the Irishmen remarks) "manic fools unite" (*C*, 57); yet, later, as Cleet and his men listen to Proctor's self-justifying arguments against further involvement in the wars, one of the rebels says (of Proctor) that "the man's insane" (*C*, 65). Regardless of the nature of the commitment—whether secular or sacred, traditional or anarchic, altruistic or pragmatic, institutional or merely self-interested—the presence of an ideology gives each person a semblance of madness in the estimation of those who do not share his views. As one of the Irishmen notes, the ideologue has "allegiance fastened like a shroud around his head. * * * 'Tis a blindfold, masking common sense" (*C*, 48). Even Proctor's spiritual insight at the end of the play can lead to demagoguery, since he may become another "Cromwellian figure" himself, as Storey has suggested. Accordingly, despite the ambiguous but potentially hopeful ending of the play, it seems that there is no wholly acceptable course of action in terms of which one can cope with the multiple atrocities and assorted sufferings caused by the war—a view that Storey maintained during more contemporary conflicts, as he revealed in the Ansorge interview: "The play took shape when Vietnam and Northern Ireland were at their heights. I wrote it towards the end of 1968 and the beginning of 1969. I felt that there was no position you could take up in the face of those events. The main point of *Cromwell* was that it has become immaterial which side you choose to be on. Political decisions make men destroy the values which they are ostensibly defending. It's that kind of dilemma."[15] Three centuries of military technology have merely refined the means through which sufferings may be inflicted, as it increased the number of casualties that any strategic action can cause; the human dilemma depicted in the mid-seventeenth-century world of *Cromwell* remains essentially unchanged today, as *O Lucky Man!* also makes clear.

The devaluation of traditional forms of ritual is recurrently demonstrated and described as the plot of *Cromwell* unfolds. The most obvious instance is, of course, the attempt of Joan's family to bury its dead in sanctified ground, and she herself notes that the importance of the ritual "depends on how strong you feel" about it (*C*, 22) rather than on its effect on the dead man's soul, and she points out that the proper performance of the rite is essential to her mother's mental stability:

[15]Ansorge 32.

O'HALLORAN. I feel strong enough ... I feel strong enough to put him in the ground myself.

JOAN. My mother can't ... Without a blessing ... Even if there's nothing left but bone: without that he'll find no rest. And without that, she'll find none either.

O'HALLORAN. Superstition ... I'd bury the man myself: put damn stones inside the box ... She'd never know ... And he's too far gone, I think, to bother much himself ... There's nothing beyond death, you know.

(JOAN *doesn't answer.*)

(C, 22-23)

The secret substitution of the corpses further confirms the devaluation of the ritual, since the welfare of the old man's soul has clearly been subordinated to expediency and personal safety. The revelation of the true identity of the body in the coffin devastates Joan's mother, whose "mind has gone" as a result of the shock of the disclosure and the subsequent beatings administered by the soldiers as they seek to learn the truth (C, 36). Convinced that "he'll not enter into paradise without a priest" (C, 41), she dies as a result of her inability to accept (or adapt to) this upheaval of the moral order that she has traditionally known; "her brain was seized," as Joan tells the Irishmen, and her body was buried "beside her father" in unconsecrated ground (C, 53). Proctor also realizes that the secular rituals that had hitherto defined his status and "place" in the world no longer seem valid: "I'm used to having conviction on my side ... badges, stripes, emblems, that tell me who and what and where I am," he remarks (C, 59), but his worldly experiences undermine both the ideologies that such insignia denote and the rituals through which they are bestowed. Even prayer—one of the most ancient and fundamental forms of ritual—seems to have been devalued in *Cromwell*, since none of the characters seek consolation or alleviation of their sufferings through it; despite the surfeit of religious ideologies that ostensibly causes the war, neither soldiers nor civilians are seen to pray, and when Proctor does seek enlightenment by such means at the end of the play the result is both partial and ambiguous. Clearly, if meaningful and significant rituals are to be found in this play, they will not appear in their traditional and institutionally sanctioned forms.

The final scene of the play, in which Proctor, Joan, and Mathew are borne across the river by the boatman to a dark country where a more hopeful and strife-free life may (or may not) be found, stands in marked contrast to the familiar types of ritual that are presented earlier. Fortunately, Storey himself has explained the use of ritual in this scene, which has perplexed viewers and critics alike:

That last scene is just the transference from one kind of life to another. It's not really a movement from life to death. Absolution through passing over water is a king of popular myth and religious rite. Water as in baptism symbolizes some kind of purification. That *might* be happening in the scene. But equally the Boatman might just happen to be a guy who carries people over a river at that particular point in the play. It's got to work on both levels. The purely literal level has to work first. And perhaps work only at that level. Leave the audience to fathom the symbolic level.[16]

Nevertheless, the literal and symbolic functions of the boatman are not fully integrated in the play, and the significance of many details about him remains obscure. John Russell Taylor maintains that "surely the dark river [Proctor] and his family cross at the end must be the river of death, and the Boatman cannot but suggest Charon,"[17] and a number of details support this view: the Boatman ferries his passengers to a dark land from which no one ever returns (*C*, 79), he insists that each passenger must pay his own fare rather than accept it from someone else (*C*, 78), and he tells them that he knows only the stream and shores but nothing of life on either side (*C*, 78). Other details, however, contradict the equation of Charon and the Boatman, since the latter suggests that the Irishmen may never cross the stream (*C*, 78); furthermore, in the second act of the play, he asks whether the Irishmen are "the ones who passed through here before" (*C*, 59) and inquires about their former companions, "the girl" and her family (*C*, 60), which suggests his contact with the group *after* the soldiers have overtaken the family and its coffin-laden cart—although such a scene is not included in the play. Since Storey acknowledges that "that last scene is . . . not really a movement from life to death," such symbolism is a pointless distraction that unnecessarily obscures (and detracts from) the nature of the ritual that he intended to portray at the conclusion of *Cromwell*.

Even though *Cromwell* is Storey's least representative work, it provides a useful paradigm for the examination of ritual in his other works. Despite the paradoxes raised by both the action and the imagery of the play, a number of conclusions about Storey's understanding of the nature and function of ritual may be deduced from this work and his comments on it:

1. Traditional, institutionally sanctioned forms of ritual (e.g., prayer) now seem to lack the efficacy that was attributed to them in former times.

2. Whereas such rituals formerly confirmed an individual's sense of personal significance in a well-defined "place" within a worldly and/or

[16] Ansorge 33, 35.

[17] John Russell Taylor, *David Storey*, Writers and Their Work 239 (London: Longman Group Ltd., 1974) 26. It seems likely that this booklet was already written and in production before Storey's interview with Peter Ansorge appeared; if so, this explains the conflict between Taylor's interpretation of the final scene and Storey's explanation of it.

cosmic hierarchy, such beliefs are increasingly difficult to maintain in a desacralized world, wherein both hierarchies and allegiances are strained by conflict and doubt.

3. Specifically sacred ceremonies (e.g., the funeral mass) are now valued primarily for their worldly effects (e.g., the consolation of the bereaved) rather than for any putative transcendent value (i.e., any effect on the state of the soul).

4. Whenever nontraditional rituals are depicted in Storey's plays, the activity fulfills a "literal" and workaday function with immediate goals that are not inherently related to the value of the act as a ritual. Consequently, participation in such a ritual may often be "unselfconscious" (i.e., the participants may not be particularly aware that the activity in which they are engaged is in fact ritualistic).

5. The desacralized, nontraditional rituals that are depicted in Storey's plays are to be understood *generically*, in terms of broad general categories (e.g., initiation, confirmation); they do not deliberately reenact specific details or archaic or primitive prototypes, although they may implicitly recapitulate the experience embodied in the earlier form (i.e., as Eliade has shown, any initiation is a reenactment of death and rebirth).

In *The Contractor* and *The Changing Room*, these insights about the nature and significance of ritual are embodied in a unique and innovative dramatic form of Storey's own. Yet in order to understand their place within his oeuvre, it is first necessary to assess the devastating effects of the loss or devaluation of ritual, which is shown in its impact on both individuals and their immediate families in a number of his plays set in contemporary times.

"Disintegration Is Inimical to the Soul":

The Restoration of Arnold Middleton

and *Life Class*

As tendencies toward desacralization have accelerated throughout the decades of the twentieth century, increasing numbers of people have found themselves able to cope with neither the stresses that accompany constant and rapid secular changes nor the loss of a personal center— a source of the permanence and stability that were formerly provided by religious faith. In post-1956 English drama, a number of plays have portrayed such personal breakdowns: John Osborne's *Entertainer* (1957) and *Inadmissible Evidence* (1965), Simon Gray's *Butley* (1971) and *Otherwise Engaged* (1975) present the desperate and unsuccessful attempts of beleaguered men to preserve a semblance of coherence and order in their lives. Unlike the heroes of earlier ages, who persevered against (and sometimes overcame) the worldly forces that threatened to overwhelm them, the protagonists in such works typically find that their lives disintegrate as the psychological or social pressures mount; they find no cohesive core of shared beliefs to provide stability amid the worldly flux. Like both of Simon Gray's plays, David Storey's *Restoration of Arnold Middleton* (1967) and *Life Class* (1975) depict the struggles of teachers who confront crises of disintegration and displacement in their personal lives. The figure of the beleaguered teacher recurs throughout Storey's writings, figuring prominently not only in these plays but in *Pasmore*, *A Temporary Life*, *Flight into Camden*, and *In Celebration* as well; typically, their crises are only tentatively or ambiguously resolved, although (as the title of his first play indicates) he is particularly interested in the means whereby a "restoration" (i.e., the recovery of a sense of "wholeness") might be achieved in a secular world. In each play, the protagonist's personal crisis coincides with an act of sexual assertiveness that, because of its outrageousness and its dramatic "shock value," becomes a personal nadir from which the restoration must begin: yet, whereas Arnold Middleton is the perpetrator in his play, Allott (the teacher in *Life Class*) stands by ineffectually as a model in his classroom is raped by two of the students. For too long, both teachers have sought refuge from the problems and pressures of their lives by withdrawing into their academic subjects—history and art, respectively—while remaining cynical about their students, their colleagues, and their careers. Although history affords an appreciation of the stable social and cosmic orders that characterized earlier societies, and although art offers the timelessness of aesthetics, neither can provide protection against personal disintegration nor a solution to "the problems within us" in the modern world, as Storey's plays make clear.

Two distinct strands of plot—one involving domestic conflicts and the other presenting a more subjective, psychological crisis—are interwoven in *The Restoration of Arnold Middleton*. The most sensational (and less thematically significant) of these presents the strained relationships that exist among the title character, his wife, Joan, and her mother, Mrs. Edie Ellis, who is "a rather unconsciously sensual woman in her late fifties" (*RAM*, 11) and who shares the Middletons' home. The nature of the marital problems soon becomes apparent in the opening scene as Mrs. Ellis remarks that her daughter has "never understood" her husband and that—despite his annoying habit of cluttering the house with diverse artifacts that he considers historically interesting—Arnold "doesn't give [Joan] anything else to grumble about. You can't complain about him. Not really" (*RAM*, 13). Nevertheless, Joan's resentment of her husband remains clear, and he seems surprisingly familiar with his mother-in-law, addressing her as "Loved one!" in his first line in the play (*RAM*, 17) and behaving in a noticeably more unrestrained and antic way whenever he is alone with her: he barks like a dog to startle her, beats the floor with his coat as if he were whipping a student who had stolen a piece of chalk, and discusses both his job and his students with a cynical candor that he never extends to his wife (*RAM*, 17–19). In the second scene of the first act, as the threesome returns from a night on the town during which all three have drunk too much, the women's rivalry becomes more explicit. Angered when her husband accidentally calls her by her mother's name, humiliated when he mocks her in an offensive limerick, and hurt when he dances with Mrs. Ellis, Joan decides (using physical force as she finds it necessary) to make Arnold choose which of the women has the more attractive legs:

MRS. ELLIS. Choose, Arnie. Then she'll let you go.

JOAN. Choose!

ARNIE. Edie! She's got the best legs! All the way.

JOAN. What? (*Hiccup.*)

ARNIE. Edie's! Edie's all the way.

(JOAN *has released him.*)

JOAN. You prefer *her* to me!

ARNIE. Completely.

(ARNIE's *still kneeling, clutching his head, still humoured, considering how best to take his revenge.*)

JOAN. (*hiccup.*) You don't love *me!*

ARNIE. No!

JOAN. You've never loved me!

ARNIE. Never!

JOAN. You wanted *that* (*hiccup*) and then it was all over.

ARNIE. Absolutely.

(*RAM*, 36)

Although they later try to conceal the incident from outsiders with excuses and omitted details, the continuing resentment over it is clear throughout the second act, the primary action of which is a party given at the Middletons' home so that Arnold's colleague Jeff Hanson may have an assignation with the gym teacher, Miss Wilkinson. Incongruously, Sheila O'Connor—a student who follows Arnold home from school and has asked him to take her out—joins the group at Hanson's invitation. With more drinks and provocations, animosities that have long been suppressed emerge, culminating as Arnold drunkenly squeezes the trigger of his loaded Lee-Enfield rifle, which he is holding against the head of Hanson (who does not realize that the firing pin has been removed and mistakenly believes the gun to be unloaded). Shortly thereafter, Arnold goes to bed, and the second act ends as Mrs. Ellis—drunk and disheveled, wearing Arnold's pajamas—comes out of his bedroom. During the third act, which is primarily a discussion of the causes of the breakdown and the means of a tentative "restoration," it is decided that Mrs. Ellis will live elsewhere, resolving that aspect of the marital crisis, without of course repairing the damage that has been done.

The domestic crises that form the basic plot of *The Restoration of Arnold Middleton* are merely symptoms of a more general personal disintegration, which provides the more subtle and significant plot that is most developed in the latter half of the play. One of the verses that Arnold recites in the first act effectively summarizes the alienation and displacement that contribute to his emotional breakdown:

> There are things in your life
> Not even your wife

> Would think could pass through your brain.
> But give me a light
> And I'll show you a sight
> That would turn even Satan insane.
>
> (*RAM*, 31)

Clearly, as in many of Storey's other works, the problem is "within us" individually and is seldom communicated in even the most intimate relationships; as in *Pasmore*, for example, the problem surfaces only under duress, during crises that threaten to destroy the marriage itself. The essence of "the problem" is a desperate feeling of personal paralysis, an inability to achieve a "significant" action (i.e., a permanent contribution—or alteration of—one's own life and times). Like J. Alfred Prufrock, Leopold Bloom, and countless others in twentieth-century literature, Arnold Middleton yearns for a personal significance and dignity that, he finds, the modern world cannot provide:

> ARNIE (*abstracted*). I don't know. Life has no dignity, Joan. * * * And death hasn't a great deal to recommend it, either. (*Pause.*) Both of them, when you look at it: they're pretty anonymous affairs. I don't know. I feel I should be able to do something. I feel ... the moment's come ... it's actually arrived. (*He grasps the air.*) And yet it refuses to ... emanate. * * * This is my situation in life.
>
> (*RAM*, 86–87)

Such dissatisfaction taints not only his family relationships but his career and his entire concept of self-worth as well, as he caustically remarks to Joan:

> ARNIE. I live. I go along. I look behind ... And I see ... not achievement towering in my path.
> JOAN. No.
> ARNIE. Ruins. I can see ... wonderful.
>
> (*RAM*, 100–101)

Acutely aware that his "limitations are limitless" (*RAM*, 99), he finds himself unable to fulfill a purposeful and significant role in life. Like Prufrock, he longs "to force the moment to its crisis"; yet, ironically, whereas Prufrock's afflictions are manifested in sexual timidity and abulia, it is Arnold Middleton's sexual *assertiveness* with Mrs. Ellis that ultimately "forces" the crisis in his life.

Because Arnold Middleton is a historian, he is particularly conscious of the loss of personal significance and purposefulness as a uniquely modern phenomenon. In the artifacts that he accumulates in both his home and his classroom, he seeks a means of personal contact with a

46

more meaningful past, as if the objects themselves are tangible verifications of the pattern, purpose, and significance that once characterized individual and collective existences. The central symbol of the play is the full-size suit of armor by which the set is "dominated" at the opening of the first scene—a relic of the lost age of chivalry, a vestige of a world in which the cosmic (spiritual) and worldly orders were clearly aligned and in which the actions of an individual (i.e., the knight who wore the armor) were direct and efficacious, sanctioned by an unambiguous code of conduct, confirmed by ritual, and endowed with both purpose and significance thereby. Nevertheless, however effectively the armor embodies bygone values and systems of belief, it remains an anachronism— a hollow and empty form that can "suit" no modern man. Accordingly, it is now "out of place" (as Arnold soon finds out) and unappreciated by everyone else in the play: Joan resents its presence, hides it in the closet, and wants to throw it out altogether, insisting (rightly) that "these [modern] houses weren't built for things like this" (*RAM*, 13) and that, for reasons that she cannot identify, "it makes me feel terrible just to touch it" (*RAM*, 13); the school's Headmaster, annoyed because it creates a disruption as Arnold drags it across the stage during a convocation, assumes that it is intended to be "a comment upon his own austere regime—perhaps on the strenuous nature of his religious practices— [and] order[s] its immediate seizure and removal from the premises" (*RAM*, 40); even the other teachers suspect that it is "some cheap means * * * of publicizing [Arnold's] subject at the expense of others in the curriculum," and Hanson suggests that it is "perhaps an indication * * * of the kind of company you prefer," an indication that his wife and friends are no longer "sufficient" (*RAM*, 40). As a result, Arnold realizes that the significance that he finds in the armor is misunderstood or unacknowledged by others, and he acquiesces at last to Joan's desire to throw it out—although he keeps its sword as a memento.

While the suit of armor provides Storey's most prominent symbol for the devaluation whereby modern man has lost the sense of dignity and purposefulness in life, other aspects of the play reinforce this theme. History itself seems to have been depreciated, even in Arnold's classroom, as Miss Wilkinson remarks:

MAUREEN (*re-entering*). His classroom's extraordinary. More like the court of King Arthur than a schoolroom. Have you seen his museum?

JOAN (*re-entering*). No.

MAUREEN. The children love it. What it has to do with history I've no idea. They seem to spend all their time building model castles, singing ballads and doing great big pictures of William the Conqueror ...

(*RAM*, 59–60)

In the same way that William the Conqueror has become a bare outline in a coloring book, Robin Hood has been reduced from his mythical-historical status to the lead role of a rather inept school play, although Arnold himself retains an appreciation of the hero's alienation and identifies with his status as "A usurper. An outlaw! * * * Always on the outside of things. * * * Cynical of the established order: disenfranchised, dispossessed. A refugee, if you like, from the proper world" (*RAM*, 95). The pandemic reduction of stature and the loss of individual capacities for significant or heroic action affect the modern political system as well, as Arnold points out:

> Do you know what the greatest threat to the present century is? (*Pause.*) The pygmies. * * * So small, so inconspicuous, they infiltrate everywhere. Not only out there, but into seats of government and power. And, of course, they're disguised. Not as men. Not even as small men. But as conditions of the soul. (*Relaxes.*) You think that's a conspiracy? No. We *choose* the lesser men. (*RAM*, 97)

In contrast to the practical governance of "small" and "inconspicuous" politicians who purport to be no better than the common men, the ideal of kingship retains its historical allure for Arnold—not because he prefers despotism or would supplant democracy with authoritarianism, but because he considers the king to be a symbolic incarnation of the transcendent qualities that modern life lacks:

> ARNIE. *Kings!* * * * They're a sort of receptacle, if you like. Into which flow all the goodness and intentions of mankind: and out of which in turn flow benevolence—and decisions. Authority. Rule. One becomes a king, not by chance, but by right: attributes fed in long before conception. Pre-ordained. * * * Look. A simple arithmetical problem set in all the schools. (*He pulls up a chair and sits facing them.*) Take what we are from everything, and what remains?
>
> HANSON (*pause*). I don't know.
>
> MAUREEN (*as* ARNIE *looks to her*). No.
>
> ARNIE. Goodness and kings. * * * Kings rise above themselves. They become ... inanimate. Formed. * * * Napoleons—they have their day. Usurpers, whether for good or ill. But the king rules not by revolution, but by constitution. He is *born*: He is *bred*: He is created king inside.
>
> (*Pause.*)
>
> His *constitution* makes *the* constitution which makes him king.
>
> (*RAM*, 96–97)

Of all the radical ideologies that have been asserted on the English stage since the mid-1950s, surely this proclamation by Arnold Middleton is the most startling. More appropriate to the reign of Elizabeth I than to that of Elizabeth II, it is clearly "out of place" in the modern world— another vestige of bygone times. It would seem less surprising if it were written in past tense and could be discarded as easily as the play's *material* relic, the suit of armor, but such is not the case. Like the armor, Arnold's paean to kingship is a manifestation of his affinity for the distant past and his yearning for the certainties implicit in a premodern frame of mind. Yet, whereas the physical artifacts are merely reminders of past greatness that imply a standard by which contemporary men and women can be measured and found wanting, Arnold's discourse on the innate superiority of kings reveals the *spiritual* source of his alienation, which transcends the nostalgic attachment to vestiges of a romanticized past. The assertion of a virtual divine right of kings reflects his intense but unfulfilled longing for the security of a spiritual hierarchy and a transcendent worldly order, but in terms of his ability to cope with modern life and his own personal problems, such ideological assertions have only a diagnostic—not a curative—value. They reveal the causes and symptoms of Arnold's malaise, but they will neither achieve practical effects in the society nor contribute to his eventual "restoration." If Arnold Middleton is to regain a sense of "wholeness" and an ability to function meaningfully in the contemporary world, the values and ideologies of the sixteenth century will be of little use in the "brave new world" that he must confront.

Further complications arise in Arnold Middleton's quest for order (worldly, cosmic, and personal) because there is no religious stability in the family, as Joan remarks while under the influence of alcohol:

JOAN. Do you believe in God?

MAUREEN. Well, in a sort of ...

JOAN (*lifting back her hair*). I honestly don't know what to believe in. * * * Arnold actually ...

MAUREEN (*pause*). Yes?

JOAN. Is God.

MAUREEN. Oh.

JOAN. He's only assumed the identity of a schoolteacher in order to remain incognito. Inconspicuous. For a God, you see, who believes in modesty and self-effacement, there are severe doctrinal problems in asserting that he's God at all. Do you understand what I mean?

> (JOAN *watches her for a moment with some satisfaction.*
> MAUREEN *gives no reply at all.*)

It's an enormous privilege, of course. (*Pause.*) Being married to him at all.

(*RAM*, 78)

Beyond the obvious humor in Joan's drunken reflections on her husband's identity, this speech reveals the play's serious concern with the effects of desacralization in modern life. As John Weightman pointed out in one of the few substantial reviews that the play received during its first run, "In the absence of God's will, the human will inflates madly to fill the gap, so that a little man in a suburban villa may come to believe that he is Napoleon or Jesus Christ, *i.e.*, the non-believer turns into his own God and his brain explodes in the process. Clearly, if the world is not to end with a series of psychological bangs before the one big bang, we need some sort of mental hygiene for a godless universe."[1] Such "mental hygiene" would provide the "restoration" and personal reintegration for which Arnold Middleton longs, but it will not be achieved until the encumbering vestiges of outmoded ideals (the armor, the ideology of kingship, the delusions of spiritual grandeur, and the personal heroics) have been discarded.

Both Arnold's classroom and his collection of artifacts at home are refuges against the "godless universe" and the problems that he finds there. Specifically, the school "museum" provides an enclave against domestic turmoil, since it is a place that Joan has never been allowed to see; it is "more like the court of King Arthur than a schoolroom" (*RAM*, 59), a private domain where Arnold's authority—his "rule" and "order"—remains unchallenged, even though he finds the situation artificial and unsatisfying, as his cynical remarks about his students reveal. At home, he is surrounded by his collection of "various objects, mounted and in excellent state of preservation: a stuffed eagle, a sword, a ship, a model aeroplane, etc., which may suggest the rudiments of a museum, but *bereft of any specific human connotation*" (*RAM*, 11; emphasis mine). Accordingly, in the absence of a "human connotation" by which a significant context and continuity could be established, such objects become in effect mere fragments shored against personal ruin and psychological disintegration. Joan, who remarks that (until the armor arrived) the collection contained nothing even resembling a human being, complains that her husband's accumulation of objects is both extensive and diffuse: "It's scattered in every cranny of this building. You can't sit down without finding a stone 'with an interesting mark' on it or a bit of wood that fell from Noah's ark, or a rotten old nail that dropped out of somebody's rotten old chariot" (*RAM*, 15).

Whether Arnold's artifacts really include such detritus or whether (as seems more likely) Joan's frustration and resentment cause her to exaggerate the facts for comic effect, the objects from the collection that are most prominent in the action of the play (the armor, the rifle,

[1] John Weightman, "The Outsider in the Home," *Encounter* 29.3 (September 1967): 44.

and the sword) share one important characteristic: each represents an *individual* and *personal* means of participation in struggles that shape history. Accordingly, the rifle—an individual soldier's weapon, to be wielded against a personally identifiable enemy (unlike the impersonal and collectively operated bomber, for example)—becomes Arnold's example of the lost glories of the empire: "Above the mantelpiece you'll observe a Lee-Enfield rifle, a weapon of historical importance to the British nation. * * * With that weapon we preserved ... (*He gestures airily about him.*) * * * And what are we now? Gropers in the debris of our ..." (*RAM*, 70). Significantly, the more complex and technological artifacts that Arnold's collection includes (the ship, the airplane, the motor) are all *models*—objects built by one person, whereas their "actual" counterparts were manufactured by numerous workers on assembly lines, a more efficient but impersonal means of production. Yet even though this preference for "individual and personal" objects characterizes much of Arnold's collection, it also includes many objects (e.g., the stuffed eagle and the things about which Joan complains) to which these criteria are tangential, if not irrelevant; thus they fail to provide the vital and unifying "human connotation" that the accumulation lacks and needs. When, as one of the steps toward his eventual restoration, the entire collection is thrown out, Arnold keeps only one object—the sword that accompanied the suit of armor. In it, he finds a symbol of permanence that surpasses the flux of history: "Certain things can't be destroyed however much you try. Rifles rust, erode, and fall apart. They become mechanically defunct. But swords, while rusting too, preserve down to their last grain an emblem of truth. Instruments of honour, which the world is a feebler place without! Dignity. (*Draws himself up.*) The past brought to us in swords!" (*RAM*, 99). As an embodiment of permanent values and immutable truth (the exact nature of which remains as ambiguous as the uncertain light at the end of *Cromwell*), the sword becomes in effect a *religious* symbol. Unlike the other artifacts, which were relics betokening change rather than permanence and transcendence, the sword can provide a "rock" upon which a secular faith may be built and in terms of which personal "honour" and dignity (traditionally confirmed by ritual) may be reestablished, thereby "restoring" his soul.

The fact that it is the *soul* that must be restored (rather than the mind or body) becomes clear in Arnold Middleton's lengthy but crucial speech that concludes the first scene of the final act. While reviewing the influences that have shaped his personality and contributed to his present crisis, Arnold reveals the essentially spiritual nature of his problems and reiterates a number of Storey's recurrent concerns:

When I was young, my mother said to me:
'Never drown but in the sea—
Rivers, streams and other dilatory courses
Are not contingent with the elemental forces
Which govern you and me—and occasionally your father—
So remember, even if the means are insufficient, rather
Than die in pieces, subside by preference as a whole,
For disintegration is inimical to the soul
Which seeks the opportunity or the chances
To die in circumstances
Of a prince, a saviour, or a messiah—
Or something, perhaps, even a little higher—
You and me and several of your aunties,
On my side, though working class, have destinies
Scarcely commensurate with our upbringing;
I hope in you we are instilling
This sense of secret dignities and rights
—Not like your father's side, the lights
Of which I hope we'll never see again,
Who have, I'm afraid, wet blotting paper for a brain.

(*Pause.*)

'Please, please my son,
Don't fail me like your father done.'

(ARNIE *stands for a moment regarding the wall.* * * * *His head sinks.
His shoulders droop. His forehead leans against the wall.*)

Oh. Oh. Oh.
When I was young, when I was young,
There were so many things I should have done.

(*RAM*, 87–88)

Although Storey denies any such influence, the images of death by drowning and the disintegration of the soul obviously resemble the poetry of T. S. Eliot, and a number of the stylistic features of Arnold's speech— the unobtrusive rhyme, the varied lengths of the metrically regular lines, the conversational but confessional tone, and even the "Oh. Oh. Oh." (which in "The Waste Land" introduces the refrain of "The Shakespearean Rag")—are strikingly similar as well. As in Lawrence's *Sons and Lovers*, the maternal influence predominates in shaping the protagonist's "spiritual" destiny; the father, whom the transcendent "elemental forces" allegedly influence only "occasionally," has failed to fulfill his wife's expectations (which are both unrealistic and comically grandiose), so that a sense of male guilt is unintentionally "instilled" in the son alongside "this sense of secret dignities and rights."

Such beliefs in "destinies/Scarcely commensurate with our upbringing" in the working class fuel the generational conflicts that recur throughout Storey's works and are most prominent in *In Celebration, Flight into Camden, Pasmore*, and *Saville*: the parents—particularly the mothers—instill in their children a system of beliefs that (however unexamined it may be) has sustained the older generation; the children, on reaching adulthood and entering the professional classes after receiving college degrees, discover that the values and beliefs of their working-class parents are increasingly untenable and that (to the dismay and incomprehension of both mothers and fathers) their personal "means are insufficient" for the significant action that seems to be expected of them. But Storey also makes it clear that the parents are not entirely to blame, since they have merely continued and sustained the beliefs that have prevailed for centuries in various forms; as Arnold himself remarks, he is "caught up in a million abominations, attributes, some of them fed in long before conception" (*RAM*, 86), and he notes that his "ancestry is rooted in action, in events, not causes" (*RAM*, 96). The artifacts that Arnold has accumulated are reminders of the significant "actions" that were accomplished in the past; yet, as in *Cromwell*, it soon becomes apparent that the sacred and secular dimensions of human experience can no longer be united in a single action that is both social (worldly) and spiritual, and the opportunities to achieve the personal grandeur and glory "of a prince, a saviour, or a messiah" are practically nonexistent in the modern desacralized world. As a result, the hope that he might become "something, perhaps, a little higher" than even a messiah is patently absurd—although it gives ironic support to Joan's earlier assertion that her husband "is God." However unrealistic the inculcated expectations may be, the anxiety and guilt that they engender contribute substantially to Arnold Middleton's breakdown. Nevertheless, the *psychological* crisis remains the product of a more fundamental and profound *spiritual* affliction—a feeling of utter spiritual inadequacy, a recognition that his "limitations are limitless" (*RAM*, 99).

As he approaches a confrontation in his various personal crises (domestic, psychological, spiritual), Arnold Middleton finds a certain allure in madness, which—like the collection of artifacts and the classroom museum—affords a refuge from the unpleasant realities of a "godless universe." When his colleague, Hanson, casually remarks to Arnold that "you take to insanity * * * like other men take to drink" (*RAM*, 95), he reiterates an insight that Arnold himself had painfully achieved in the previous scene: "Perhaps I could go mad. Insanity, you know, is the one refuge I've always felt I was able to afford. The insights that irrationality brings. Well, in the end, that's what we're looking for. Cleavages. Cracks. Fissures. Openings. Some little aperture of warmth and light" (*RAM*,

86–87). Madness, which is a recurrent theme in Storey's writings, is thus akin to religious faith in that both provide "insights" that transcend reason (hence, "irrationality"). To borrow the phrases of the hymn by Isaac Watts, madness can provide a "shelter from the stormy blast" if not "our eternal home" in a desacralized world; in the absence of "God, our help in ages past," traditional beliefs afford no firm foundation for "our hope in years to come," and more temporary and immediate recourses are needed. While madness is clearly among the "options" that are available in the play, it (like the refuge of the artifacts) is ultimately rejected during Arnold's crisis, and his breakdown should actually be characterized as "madness" only in the most general sense; unlike the title character of *Pasmore* and the wife of the narrator in *A Temporary Life*, Arnold Middleton displays none of the extreme symptoms associated with madness in Storey's other works (acute withdrawal, unexplained crying, displaced anxiety), and his psychological crisis passes surprisingly rapidly *after* its "spiritual" counterpart is resolved through the discovery of the immutable truth that is symbolized in the sword:

ARNIE. Oh! (*Cries out.*)

JOAN. Arnie!

ARNIE. Oh! There's something coming out!

JOAN. Arnie ...

ARNIE. Oh, dear, Joan.

JOAN. Arnie ... It's all right.

ARNIE. Oh, dear, oh!

>   (*He covers up his head.*)

JOAN. Arnie.

ARNIE. Oh, dear. Oh, dear. There's something. What? Oh, dear. There's something coming out.

JOAN. Arnie.

>   (*He looks up, still holding his head.*)

    Come on now.

ARNIE. Oh. Oh.

>   (*His hands are clasped to the top of his head.*)

    What am I to do?

JOAN. Here.

>   (*She holds out her hand.*)

ARNIE. Oh. *Now!* (*Screams, hugely. Then:*)

JOAN. It's all over.

ARNIE. Oh, dear.

(*After a moment he lowers one hand.*)

Oh, I'm sure ... I think.

JOAN. Yes.

(*RAM*, 103)

As Katharine Worth has observed, "Arnold's recovery of sanity is represented as a 'happening,' in the direct way that Harry's stroke is represented in [Arnold Wesker's] *Chicken Soup with Barley*."[2] Yet even though purely subjective crises and psychological cures or "restorations" are always difficult to depict effectively onstage, this particular instance seems especially abrupt and not entirely convincing, perhaps in part because of the repetitiousness and banality of the dialogue. Reconsidering the ending during our conversation, Storey remarked that

I think it's ambivalent and not in a good way. I think that's one of the many weaknesses of the play. . . . I remember rewriting it; I think I must have put that end on then and changed the title as a hopeful gesture, but I think it didn't work. I think it appeared to work in the theatre simply from the sheer energy of the actor who played the part [John Shepherd]. He gave it a tremendous neurotic energy which isn't the kind of energy in the writing, and he got away with it. I mean, he made it work in that way. But really, . . . he's restored to a very conventional bourgeois life, and that's really awful, a sort of living death. Yet the ambiguity comes in—the audience obviously feels there should be something hopeful in the writing, in the implication that this is rather a turning point. I remember the actor crying out . . . as though he's sort of giving birth to himself. . . . He gave it a lot of energy.

Yet, however unconvincing the sudden restoration may be, the entire theme of personal breakdown and recovery has been skillfully and subtly developed *throughout* the play—particularly since it was the author's first work for the stage. Thus, as John Russell Taylor has pointed out,

The major problem for the writer is that its hero is going mad, and the mad on stage . . . make coherent drama considerably more difficult. Storey solves the problem very neatly, by not allowing us to realize for sure that Arnold is going mad until he is actually on the point of being restored. He is eccentric, admittedly, but then characters who cultivate eccentricities as a defense against the world are by no means unfamiliar in recent English writing, especially when they are school-teachers.[3]

[2] Katharine Worth, *Revolutions in Modern English Drama* (London: Bell, 1973) 38.
[3] John Russell Taylor, "British Dramatists: The New Arrivals, III—David Storey, Novelist into Dramatist," *Plays and Players* June 1970: 24.

A similar technique of deferring the audience's recognition of madness provides much of the dramatic effectiveness and thematic impact of *Home*.

Whether or not the "restoration" is convincingly achieved in a single primal scream and attendant paroxysms, the mundane dialogue of the scene conceals several significant gestures that occur at the conclusion of the play. When Joan extends her hand to Arnold, it is the first sign of genuine forgiveness that she has shown, and her assurance that "it's all over" (*RAM*, 103) suggests a possible reconciliation with her husband—which the tone of Arnold's subsequent "Oh, dear" *could* reinforce. Ironically, the last words of this play about spiritual disintegration in a "godless universe" are "Thank God" (*RAM*, 104). As in *Cromwell*, the exact nature of the spiritual truth that Arnold Middleton has found remains ambiguous, although its tangible symbol (the sword) seems more sustaining than the uncertain light for which Proctor continues his quest in the land of darkness. Although Arnold tells Hanson that "The doctor recommends a long sea-voyage" (*RAM*, 94)—a prescription that seems particularly ironic in terms of Arnold's metaphoric fear of drowning—he assures Joan that he will go "Back to school. Monday! * * * Rest. Recuperation ... Work!" (*RAM*, 102), thereby introducing a theme that will become most prominent in *The Contractor* and *The Changing Room* (in each of which work contributes substantially to the psychological—and perhaps spiritual—well-being of the characters).

Furthermore, it seems that Arnold gains a new acceptance of both the psychological "scars" wrought by his "upbringing" and those that history has inflicted on both the ideal of kingship and the standards that it implied:

> ARNIE (*carried away*). Scars ... (ARNIE *holds out the palms of his hands, looking at them.*) They inhabit the skin. Deformities actually acquire that authority. (*Looks up bitterly at* HANSON.) Did you know? (*Pause.*) Remove them—and you remove life itself. Well?
>
> HANSON. I don't know what you're talking about actually, Arnold.
>
> ARNIE. I'm talking about ... alternatives.
>
> HANSON. Alternatives. I see.
>
> ARNIE. To kingship.
>
> (*RAM*, 98)

In addition to his new acceptance of his own "scarred" life and times, Arnold reconciles his relationship with his wife, addressing to her his final bit of verse—a stark contrast to the coarse limericks and derision spoken about her earlier:

Oh, lovely woman ... feel no obligation.
Beauty is its own salvation.
All the rest is meant to burn.

(RAM, 104)

Nevertheless, the restoration remains tentative, as the final stage direction indicates: *"They stand facing one another, still some distance apart"* (*RAM*, 104). A strikingly similar conclusion—a tentative, guardedly optimistic, and subjective "restoration"—occurs at the end of *Pasmore*:

> In the winter he returned to teaching. Outwardly, despite the events of the preceding year, little had changed. He still had a regular job, a home, a wife and children; the apparatus of his life . . . was virtually the same. Even the despair, it seemed, persisted.
>
> Yet something had changed. It was hard to describe. He had been on a journey. At times it seemed scarcely credible that he had survived. He still dreamed of the pit and the blackness. It existed all around him, an intensity, like a presentiment of love, or violence: he found it hard to tell.[4]

Like Pasmore, Arnold Middleton finds that "outwardly" little has changed (although Mrs. Ellis moves out of the house and Joan finds a job). "Inwardly," however, "something had changed" as he rejected his previous attempts to find "refuge" in the vestiges of earlier times in which each individual's place in a stable worldly (and cosmic) order was confirmed by traditional rituals. The "restoration" that Arnold Middleton achieves is a personal reintegration, an acceptance and affirmation of life with its "limitations" and "scars"; having cast off the accumulated "apparatus of his life" (i.e., the collection) as so much "debris," he has found a more sustaining and transcendent "emblem" of truth in the sword, even though the specific discovery (like the outcome of Pasmore's journey) "was hard to describe."

Despite the subtlety, complexity, and seriousness of its themes, *The Restoration of Arnold Middleton* is a deft and witty comedy—Storey's only comic work except for the farce *Mother's Day* that was produced in 1976. The humor arises primarily from Arnold's interaction with his mother-in-law (who he finally pretends is invisible on the morning after the assault) and from his cynical descriptions of his students and their school. As Michael Billington remarked in *Plays and Players*, "I must stress that the play is extremely funny: for instance, Mr. Storey conveys, with hilarious accuracy, the sort of idiotic bandiage that schoolmasters indulge in when they think they're not being overheard. The ponderous jocularity that teachers love to cultivate is also put authentically across: school prayers, for instance, become '800 spirits about to do obeisance to the

---

[4]David Storey, *Pasmore* (New York: Dutton, 1972) 190.

one and only.' "[5] For these reasons, as John Russell Taylor pointed out, the play seems to invite comparison with Kingsley Amis's *Lucky Jim*, another "anarchic" academic comedy:

> It is tempting to say that Arnold behaves like Lucky Jim for Jimmy Porterish reasons. The surface is all schoolboyish japes, tall stories ... and little academic jokes with other members of the staff. But they arise, not from Lucky Jim's brainless philistinism, but from a real anguish with the world for not being what he wants it to be. He looks for strength, for majesty; he asks too much of people, and they fail him. So he seeks refuge in a shell of his own choosing.[6]

Noting that Storey had worked on the play for "eight years, on and off," Michael Billington found it "only natural that the themes and styles of other writers should have rubbed off on him."[7] Storey pointedly denies all such suggestions, remarking that he had seen very few plays in his entire life up to that time and *none* by the authors to whose works his own might most readily be compared, Harold Pinter and Edward Albee. The theme of incestuous rivalry also predominates in Pinter's *Homecoming* (1965), although in Storey's work the sexes have been reversed so that two women (or three, including the student Sheila O'Connor) compete for the attentions of one man. Nevertheless, the alcohol-induced revelations and vitriolic recriminations that dominate the first two acts of Storey's play bear a striking resemblance to those in Albee's *Who's Afraid of Virginia Woolf?* (1962), which also takes place in the home of a teacher, and *A Delicate Balance*, for which Albee won the Pulitzer Prize in 1967. Specifically, the opening lines of *A Delicate Balance* establish a tone and theme that also characterize Storey's play:

> AGNES (*Speaks usually softly, with a tiny hint of a smile on her face: not sardonic, not sad ... wistful, maybe*). What I find most astonishing—aside from that belief of mine which never ceases to surprise me by the very fact of its surprising lack of unpleasantness, the belief that I might very easily—as they say— lose my mind one day, not that I suspect that I am about to, or am even ... nearby ...
>
> TOBIAS (*He speaks somewhat the same way*). There is no saner woman on earth, Agnes.
>
> AGNES. ... for I'm not that sort; merely that it is not beyond ... happening; some gentle loosening of the moorings sending the balloon adrift—and I think that is the only outweighing thing: adrift; the ... becoming a strange in ... the world, quite ... uninvolved, for I never see it as violent, only a drifting.[8]

[5]Michael Billington, "First Nights: *The Restoration of Arnold Middleton*," *Plays and Players* June 1970: 30.

[6]Taylor, "New Arrivals" 24.

[7]Billington 30.

[8]Edward Albee, *A Delicate Balance* (New York: Atheneum, 1966) 7.

During the course of the play, the six characters of *A Delicate Balance* confront the unnamed, seemingly inexplicable "terror" of the collapse of traditional values and the resultant emptiness of their selfish, affluent, and hitherto complacent lives. In much the same way that Arnold Middleton seeks refuge in his collected artifacts, history, and outmoded ideals, Albee's characters seek solace and reassurance variously in alcohol, family ties, and friendship (the latter pair of which is severely strained in the crisis); in each play the resolution is a tentative "restoration" of the "delicate balance" that constitutes sanity, after a long time during which each has been unknowingly "adrift."

Despite its wit, its careful construction, and its thoughtfully developed themes that marked an auspicious beginning for Storey's career as a playwright, *The Restoration of Arnold Middleton* is in some ways recognizably a "first play," containing certain features that the author carefully avoided in his later works. Specifically, according to John Russell Taylor, Storey feels that is was "a mistake" to "direct his audience's attention very specifically to what he wanted them to see," so that (like *Radcliffe*) the play "is scattered with great big notices saying 'Pay attention now, this is significant,' and I think that spoils the book. I did a bit of the same with the play. It was at this point that the suit of armour . . . first appeared. I don't know that that was an improvement; I think it's just that bit too much pushing something right under people's noses."[9] In effect, as his career has developed, Storey has retained the physical symbols while making them less obtrusive and explicit (e.g., the tent in *The Contractor*) and omitting the abstract discourses that they might prompt, so that they retain both more ambiguity and more resonance. Certainly, his later plays lack the lengthy and meditative speeches that occur as Arnold holds forth on kingship, drowning, pygmies, and the aspirations of the soul; in Storey's first play, however, the suit of armor provides a necessary object on which these speculations may be dramatically focused. Arguably, the presence of Sheila O'Connor is a more significant flaw in the play: her presence at the party is incongruous (since it seems implausible that Hanson would include a student in a party that is actually an assignation that he wants to keep secret at the school where he teaches), and she has no dramatic function other than to mislead the audience's expectation of a sexual dalliance in which Arnold will engage, so that the revelation of his assault on Mrs. Ellis will be all the more surprising. Nevertheless, such imperfections do not substantially detract from the overall effectiveness of the play which—as Michael Billington suggested in his review of it for *Plays and Players*—"ranks with *The Workhouse Donkey* [John Arden], *A Patriot for Me* [John Osborne], *Afore Night Come* [David

---

[9]Taylor, "New Arrivals" 22–23.

Rudkin], and *Serjeant Musgrave's Dance* [Arden] as one of the richest and most exciting plays of [its] decade."[10]

When juxtaposed against *The Restoration of Arnold Middleton, Life Class* (1974) reveals Storey's growth as a playwright and his increasingly sophisticated dramatic techniques, despite fundamental similarities between the two plays. In each, the protagonist is a teacher whose marriage is failing, whose students are (with few exceptions) unappreciative, whose values and beliefs are not shared (indeed, not comprehended) by those around him, and whose recourse becomes an increasingly untenable withdrawal into his subject and a cynical disparagement (often in doggerel) of the outside world. The sources of each man's personal disintegration are revealed in crucial scenes near the ends of their plays, but whereas Arnold Middleton offers a virtual soliloquy, Allott's self-revelation is disclosed while he is temporarily out of the classroom, as two of his students read aloud one of his poems they have discovered in his sketch pad:

MATHEWS. "Poor old Allott ..."

PHILIPS. "Dirge on a forgotten planet ..."

MATHEWS. "Allott is the palette ..."

PHILIPS. "On which my sins began ..."

MATHEWS. "First ..."

PHILIPS. "He was a saviour ..."

MATHEWS. "Secondly ..."

PHILIPS. "A saint ..."

MATHEWS. "Thirdly ..."

PHILIPS. "Lost his chances ..."

MATHEWS. "Fourthly ..."

PHILIPS. "Learnt to paint ..."

MATHEWS. "Fifthly ..."

PHILIPS. "Came to pieces ..."

MATHEWS. "Sixthly ..."

PHILIPS. "Showed his hand ..."

MATHEWS. "Seventhly ..."

PHILIPS. "Set the creases ..."

MATHEWS. "Eighthly ..."

PHILIPS. "Joined the band ..."

[10]Billington 30.

MATHEWS. "Ninthly ..."

PHILIPS. "Went to heaven ..."

MATHEWS. "Tenthly ..."

PHILIPS. "Rang the bell ..."

MATHEWS. "Eleventhly ..."

PHILIPS. "Thought he'd better ..."

MATHEWS. "Twelfthly ..."

ALLOTT (*having entered*). "Go to hell" * * * .

(*LC*, 72)

Allott's candid and guilt-ridden verses are certainly less evocatively poetic (and less reminiscent of T. S. Eliot) than Arnold Middleton's, but the same fundamentally religious preoccupations recur in each: the concern with "sins," a role as "a saviour" or "a saint," "lost chances," and an ultimate self-condemnation—although Allott referred to himself earlier in the poem as "the apotheosis," "the amenuensis," and "the polarity from which the world began" (*LC*, 71–72)—reveal a spiritual alienation that is practically identical to that depicted in the earlier play. Nevertheless, Arnold Middleton's lengthy soliloquy seems less dramatically effective than the scene in *Life Class*, which gains suspense (and heightens the audience's interest) as Allott's self-revelatory verses are read clandestinely during his brief absence from the scene. As in *The Restoration of Arnold Middleton*, the personal guilt of the central character originates in the unrealistically high expectations that were set by his mother; because these aspirations and ideals were in fact unattainable, the ensuing crisis involves a loss of "the significance of life," as another of Allott's poems (written on the wall of the classroom) reveals:

MATHEWS (*reads*). "O where has the significance of life gone to ..."

ALLOTT (*without looking up*). "My mother said."

MATHEWS. "... If it's not where we might expect it, it must be in some other place instead."

(*LC*, 69)

Compounding his guilt and his feelings of inadequacy, Allott's perception that he has entered the "time of life * * * [when] inspiration often falters" (*LC*, 37) suggests that his withdrawal into art no longer provides the certainty and creative conviction on which he formerly relied, so that his traditional solace is less secure. Whereas the classroom in *The Restoration of Arnold Middleton* remained the unseen refuge from domestic strife and the problems of an unhappy marriage, in *Life Class* the school-

61

room is the sole setting, and the marital turmoil (which formed one of the two strands of plot in Storey's first play) is described in some detail but not portrayed onstage. As a result, while *Life Class* lacks the fierce wit and mutual recriminations that fill *The Restoration of Arnold Middleton*, the latter work is more unified in its construction and more sustained in its tone.

Even though Allott's wife never appears onstage, her deteriorating relationship with her husband contributes substantially to the personal crisis that culminates during the second act of the play. Like the title character in *Pasmore*, Allott has separated from his wife, and a divorce seems imminent:

> ALLOTT. We've been separated, you know, for some considerable time. She's coming, I suspect to give me news of a very significant nature ... or, in the terminology of the employment exchange, my cards.
>
> CATHERINE. Oh. I'm sorry, sir.
>
> ALLOTT. One of those things. The artist, after all, has no real life outside his work. Whenever he attempts it, the results, Catherine, leave—to say the very least of it—a great deal to be desired.
>
> (*LC*, 42)

Characteristically, Allott seeks to use art as a refuge from—and an excuse for—the failures of his personal life; nevertheless, it is clearly a type of ratiocination, since he later admits having become an artist only "because I thought that way I'd be of least trouble to anybody else" (*LC*, 66), and he repeatedly refers to his works as "invisible events which only I can see" (*LC*, 64)—a classification in which he includes the marriage itself. Indeed, the breakdown of the marriage presages both Allott's fear of madness and his feelings of martyrdom, as he remarks to Philips:

> ALLOTT. * * * My wife * * * said, "You're going crazy." And the fact of the matter is, at times, I really think I am.
>
> PHILIPS. Baudelaire ... Dostoyevsky ... Nietzsche ... you have to bear them all in mind ... men who teetered on the very brink of human existence and had the privilege—the temerity, even—to gaze right over the edge ...
>
> ALLOTT. I've gazed over the edge, Philips, long enough ... it's the staying there that worries me ... I'm beginning to think I'll never get back ... How does one live as a revolutionary, Philips, when no one admits there's a revolution there?
>
> PHILIPS. Prophet in his own country, old boy ... Think of Christ.
>
> ALLOTT. I think of nothing else ... I'm even beginning to think, Philips, that it's not my duty to resurrect mankind.
>
> (*LC*, 56)

Whereas *The Restoration of Arnold Middleton* ended with a tentative and guarded marital reconciliation as well as an abrupt apparent "recovery" (as a part of which the embedded desire to function as a "messiah" was at least partially overcome), the final scene of *Life Class* offers no such reassurance as Allott loses both his wife and his job.

However grandiose Allott's unattainable aspirations may be and however seriously he entertains them (like many of his remarks, these are tinged with irony and sarcastic exaggeration), he surely finds little to sustain them in his classroom. His students are at least a decade older—but scarcely more mature—than Arnold Middleton's pupils. Demonstrating neither particular aptitudes for art nor a serious interest in it, Allott's students maintain a recurrent—almost constant—chorus of crude remarks, sexual innuendos, double-entendres, and coarse references to the model who poses before them and to each other as well. As Allott himself observes while consoling the model in her remorse over being no longer "youthful young," the students are "myopic ... disingenuous ... uninspired—* * * pubescent excrescences on the cheeks of time" (*LC*, 15-16). Without particular concern, he points out that their priorities (in obvious contrast to his own) place "mass before beauty, excrescence before edification ... [and] salaciousness before refinement" (*LC*, 40). Yet, while such an assessment is both accurate and insightful, it exceedingly objectifies the problem and neglects both the cruelty and the dehumanization that are implicit in the students' classroom behavior. These, in turn, result in the two students' deliberate sexual assault of the model, which Allott—with characteristic detachment and indifference—does nothing to prevent.

Facing the unavoidable fact that his marriage is crumbling and realizing that his students lack both ability and interest, Allott sustains himself with a belief in the transcendence of art itself as an ideal. Allott's classroom, like Arnold Middleton's "history museum," becomes his privately sanctified space, in which each individual can align himself within the artistic tradition as he discovers or explores the creative process. Thus, he reminds his students, the classroom is "not a clinic, you know. It's not a haven of rest. It's where the embryonic artist may experience—perhaps for the first time in his life, Brenda—the faint flutterings of his restless spirit" (*LC*, 28). Despite the shortcomings of his students, he reminds them of the importance of the purpose for which, in theory if not in fact, they have convened—a purpose transcending the present moment and subsuming the cares of the workaday world: "Art is above sex," Allott insists (finding there a refuge from the failure of his marriage), "... and it's above politics, too. That's to say, it absorbs sex, and it absorbs politics" (*LC*, 33). The class is itself in fact a ritual—a patterned (regularly scheduled) event, the purpose of which Allott eloquently summarizes as "to pursue a beautiful and seemingly mysterious object [the human body], and to set it down—curiously—as objectively as we can" (*LC*, 33). This wonder-filled "perusal"—an appreciation of the complexity and beauty of the "life" before them—is more important than the actual lines that the students commit haltingly and tentatively to paper. As Allott makes clear in encouraging the students to overcome their paralyzing fear of imperfection, the essential concern is the *process* of art rather than its *product*, the finished drawing, however unskillful it may be:

ALLOTT. Draw. Draw. That's all you're here to do.

CARTER. What if we make a mistake, sir?

ALLOTT. Draw round it, underneath it. Makes no difference in the end ... *What is true will last* ... What is real—Gillian and Mooney—is eternal.

(*LC*, 21)

Participation in the "process" of art thus enables the transcendence of space and time through a direct and personal experience of "what is true" and "eternal" through an appreciation of the "mysterious"—all of which were traditionally the essential concerns of religion. Accordingly, art has become—for Allott, if not for his students—the surrogate religion of a desacralized world, and the classroom is the "sanctified space" in which the celebrants convene for an exalted purpose: "The lesson that we've been convened, as it were, to celebrate ... [is] that we are life's musicians ... its singers, and that what we sing is wholly without meaning ... it exists, merely, because it is" (*LC*, 30). Within the religious context of the "life class," the nude model replaces the idol as the object on which the ritual observance is focused; Allott, as the teacher, becomes a virtual priest of art, extolling its virtues and presiding over the novices' performance of a ritual (i.e., a patterned, purposeful, and significant event) that surpasses the temporal reality. Unfortunately, however, Allott's novices neither appreciate their teacher's beliefs, nor understand his values, nor share his priorities—a fact that is made unmistakably, graphically clear as Mathews and his friend Warren enact an appallingly brutal rape of the nude model who poses defenselessly before the class.

Even when considered within the context of violent acts of deliberate cruelty that occur in much contemporary drama, contemporary fiction, and contemporary life, the rape depicted in *Life Class* is a shockingly vile and outrageous act. Yet, clearly, it is neither gratuitous nor sensationalistic, since with unmistakable impact it embodies the central problem and theme of the play: symbolically, the rape is the ultimate, destructive assertion of the most crude physical and temporal reality over the transcendent one, a vile and violent disruption of art by the most brutish form of life. As such, it is also the ultimate profanation of Allott's "temple," an outrage revealing the unworthiness of the priest as well as the novices—and causes the former to lose his job. Yet, with typical cynicism and detachment, Allott accommodates even the act of violation itself within his theory, as he lamely tries to explain to Stella, the victim: "Violation, they tell me, is a prerequisite of art ... disruption of prevailing values ... re-integration in another form entirely. What you see and feel becomes eternal" (*LC*, 89). Yet, virtually before the stunned audience on stage (or its counterpart in the theatre) has had time to recover from the shock of the event that has just been observed, an equally surprising fact is suddenly revealed: amid raucous laughter and gibes at their fellow students, the perpetrators of the rape reveal that it was in fact a *simulation*—a calculated hoax, a convincingly realistic deception, an "imitation" of "life," a work of artifice if not of art, and (the ultimate irony of the play) an "act of theatre" performed before the shocked onstage "classroom" audience; it is, in effect, Storey's play-within-the-play. The extent of Stella's complicity in the hoax remains unclear, though the fact that she does resume posing shortly after the incident implies that she too was aware of the students' ploy. In any case, ironically, Allott is dismissed because of an event that never *actually* occurred.

Like the meeting of the class itself, the act of posing is also a ritual—a patterned activity (with its various classic stances) that has as its purpose the facilitation of art, the means of individual contact with "what is true" and "eternal"; the significance implicit in the act of posing is that it places the model within the entire tradition of art, whereby countless models throughout the ages have been immortalized—transfigured, indeed—in paintings, drawings, and sculptures. However, for Allott this *process* of transfiguration—of posing—remains more important than the *products* that commemorate and depict the action that has taken place; such is the point of the incident in which Allott makes Mathews pose (clothed) while he solemnly sketches for a long time until the student collapses, although it is later revealed that the sketch pad has remained blank. "There isn't any drawing," Allott explains, "... or rather, the drawing was the drawing ... perhaps you weren't aware" (*LC*, 73). More than just another of the teacher's "small cruelties" (as Edith Oliver alleged in her review in the *New Yorker*),[11] the incident not only parodies the activity of most of the students—whose drawing papers also remain blank in most cases—but also encapsulates the ritualistic aspect of the classroom activity. Insofar as the purpose of the class is "to peruse a beautiful and mysterious object and to set it down * * * as objectively as we can" (*LC*, 33), the body of each model is transfigured as its beauty and mysteriousness are

[11]Edith Oliver, "The Theatre: Off Broadway," *New Yorker* 29 December 1975: 43.

celebrated—whatever the quality of the artistic "product"—as the attention of the artists is focused and directed through ritual. By this process—an "act of attention"—the model is idealized, celebrated, and even revered, transcending the mundane reality of ordinary life. For these reasons, Allott reveals *his* intention of posing for the class (*LC*, 77) just as he is most beset by his domestic problems and least able to find solace or transcendence in his traditional role as a teacher, presiding as others are idealized and revered through the classroom ritual. The name that Storey selected for the model—Stella—ironically suggests that she is as remote and inviolable as a star (a standard symbol of transfiguration and transcendence); "Stella's real," Allott remarks, "... Then again, in another sense, you could say she's quite unearthly" (*LC*, 16). The students' constant coarse familiarity with her throughout the play—as well as the rape that provides its climax—reveals that, like her beauty, such idealization is exclusively "in the eye of the beholder." Such transcendence is a product of the ritual of posing rather than a consequence of mere nudity (there is no counterpart for it in *The Changing Room*, for example, in which nudity is more casual and incidental, rather than the object of an act of attention); there is no *inherent* transcendence in the body itself. As Saunders (another of Allott's students) remarks while Mathews removes some of his clothing prior to the rape, "It's the dividing line, you see, between life and art ... Stella represents it in its impersonal condition ... Mathews represents its ..." (*LC*, 77–78). Accordingly, the model herself becomes the central symbol of the play—the exact counterpart of the suit of armor in *The Restoration of Arnold Middleton*, occupying center stage for much of the play, embodying the "impersonal" and idealized state for which each protagonist yearns, but disrespected and defiled by those who fail to realize the symbolism, the transcendence, and the ritual that each represents.

These rituals—the class meetings and the posing—constitute the "invisible events" that are discussed at length in *Life Class*, though Allott alone recognizes their value. Although Allott was allegedly "one of the leading exponents of representational art in his youth" and (according to his colleague Philips) comparable to Michelangelo, he has become "an impresario ... purveyor of the invisible event ... so far ahead of its time you never see it" (*LC*, 70). Explaining why he no longer paints or sculpts, Allott tells Catherine that he believes in a more "public" art, which can nevertheless be understood within the artistic tradition:

> ALLOTT. It's my opinion that painting and sculpture, and all the traditional forms of expression in the plastic arts, have had their day, Catherine ... It's my opinion that the artist has been driven back—or driven on, to look at it in a positive way—to creating his works, as it were, in public.

CATHERINE. In public, sir?

ALLOTT. Just as Courbet or Modigliani, or the great Dutch Masters ... created their work out of everyday things, so the contemporary artist creates his work out of the experience—the events as well as the objects—with which he's surrounded in his day to day existence ... for instance, our meeting here today.

(*LC*, 42)

The "event" taking place in the classroom subsumes the "realities" of the mundane world in which, as Allott remarks,

We all sail, to some extent, under false colours. * * * I mean, you may not see yourself as an artist ... I may not see myself as a teacher. * * * Stella earns her living; I earn my living ... you earn your living * * * but between us, we convene ... celebrate ... initiate ... an event, which, for me, is the very antithesis of what *you* term reality ... namely, we embody, synthesize, evoke, a work, which, whether we are aware of it or not, is taking place around us * * * all the time. (*LC*, 46)

The essential function of this "invisible event" is, the teacher points out, "to incorporate everything that is happening out there into a single homogenous whole" (*LC*, 38)—which was, of course, the role of religion in earlier times, fulfilled through traditional rituals before modern desacralization rendered them ineffective. Still, Allott's students fail to grasp his meaning:

CATHERINE (*gazing at* STELLA). There's nothing happening, sir.

ALLOTT. There's a great deal happening ... Not in any obvious way ... nevertheless several momentous events are actually taking place out there ... subtly, quietly, not overtly ... but in the way artistic events *do* take place ... in the great reaches of the mind ... the way the leg, for instance, articulates with the hip, the shoulders with the thorax; the way the feet display the weight ... the hands subtend at the end of either arm ... these are the wonders of creation, Catherine.

(*LC*, 38–39)

Infatuated with his theory of "invisible events" and with rituals that he alone recognizes, Allott overconfidently assumes that his belief—his surrogate religion—can accommodate all aspects of life:

ALLOTT. There are certain ungovernables in life, but even they can be incorporated into a general pattern—into a single, coherent whole ... other things, of course, don't have to be guided.

CATHERINE. Such as, sir?

ALLOTT. Natural impulses. Feeling creates its own form, form its own feeling.

(*LC*, 44)

67

Simulated though it turns out to have been, the rape of the model remains, obviously, the ultimate assertion of unrestrained "natural impulses" as the most "ungovernable" and primal of urges "creates its own form" before the shocked members of the class. Allott's "spiritual" reality of transcendent art and invisible events is violated by the intrusion of its "antithesis" (*LC*, 46), the most base and sordid of worldly "realities." Accordingly, Saunders's ethereal reflections on "the dividing line between life and art" and on what "Stella represents" are interrupted by Warren's shouts of the coarsest and crudest possible form of encouragement for Matthews: "Get your prick out ...! Here ... here, then! Go on. Grab her!" (*LC* 77-78).

Allott's remark to Stella that "Violation * * * is a prerequisite of art" (*LC*, 89) represents his final attempt to accommodate the "ungovernable" into his theory, but the attempt fails as his comments degenerate into nebulous (and rather trite) musings on the growth of flowers and the passage of time. The incidence of the rape—and the consequent dismissal of Allott from his job—betoken the "disintegration" that is, as Arnold Middleton remarked, "inimical" to both "the soul" and the spiritual reality in which both teachers believe.

The ultimate "purveyor of the invisible event" (*LC*, 70) is, of course, David Storey himself, and much of *Life Class* seems to offer a defense and explanation of his dramatic technique—particularly in his allegedly plotless plays, *The Contractor* and *The Changing Room*. As Allott expounds the value of "the experience—the events as well as the objects—with which he's surrounded in his day to day existence ... for instance, our meeting here today," the point that Storey emphasizes is equally applicable to the theatre itself:

> ... the feelings and intuitions expressed by all of us inside this room ... are in effect the creation—the re-creation—of the artist ... to the extent that they are controlled, manipulated, postulated, processed, defined, sifted, *re*fined ...
>
> CATHERINE. Who by, sir?
>
> ALLOTT. Well, for want of a better word—by me.
>
> (*LC*, 42)

Implicitly, this speech affirms the presence of the author's controlling consciousness in selecting and portraying the episodes of the play itself; ironically, the fact that Allott does *not* "control" the events taking place in the classroom is clearly demonstrated during the rape scene. The action of *Life Class*—and by extension the "invisible events" that constitute *The Contractor* and *The Changing Room*—are not merely random "slices of life" or the theatrical counterpart of unedited *cinéma-vérité*. Their action—a detailed and naturalistic "imitation of life"—has been "controlled, manipulated, postulated, processed, defined, sifted, [and] refined" toward the affirmation of the author's thematic concerns. Clearly, too, Storey wishes to differentiate himself from those whom Allott describes as "the poseur, the man masquerading as the artist ... the *manufacturer* of events who, in his twentieth century romantic role, sees art as something accessible to all and therefore the prerogative not of the artist—but of anybody who cares to pick up a brush, a bag of cement, an acetylene welder ... anyone, in fact, who can persuade other people that what he is doing is creative" (*LC*, 30). Such is particularly Storey's view of contemporary "fringe theatre," which he described during our conversation as "very parochial," adding that "its dynamic is amateurish. It's basically a subsidised form. If you took the subsidy away, its artistic life wouldn't be sufficiently vigorous to run a theatre there at all." Unlike various types of undisciplined and free-form "happenings"—but like Allott's "invisible events"—Storey's "plotless" plays are deceptively simple, enabling both theatregoers and critics to overlook the significance of the actions (and rituals) that are taking place onstage.

Allott's lecture to his snickering students on the appreciation of the complexity of the human form is equally applicable to the understanding of any work of art, whether on canvas or on the stage:

> It's merely a question * * * of seeing each detail in relation to all the rest ... the proportion—the width as well as the height * * * the whole contained, as it were * * * within a single image. Unless you are constantly relating the specific to the whole * * * a work of art can never exist ... It's not merely a conscious effort; it is, if one is an artist and not a technician—someone disguised, that is, as an artist, going through all the motions and creating all the effects—an instinctive process (*LC*, 29–30).

The selection of the graphic arts as a metaphor for his playwriting seems particularly appropriate for Storey (who, earlier in his career, worked as both an artist and a teacher), since his most important and innovative plays—like paintings—have no plot, as the term is commonly understood. Instead, both *The Changing Room* and *The Contractor* present "a single image" (i.e., an "invisible event") within which "the whole" of the play is contained.

Whereas in *The Restoration of Arnold Middleton* only the title character voices the thematically significant statements of the play, in *Life Class* such statements are distributed among a number of characters—a clear indication of refined dramatic technique. For example, Foley—Allott's eccentric headmaster—collects broken plaster statues and stores his urine in large jars in the closet of his office (as if to confirm Auden's observation that "excretion is . . . the primal creative act");[12] yet he also upholds the importance of regionalism in the arts: "Fact of the matter is, all the profoundest art is regional. It takes time for its universal principles to be revealed. For instance, who would have thought that a meticulous and obsessive interest in the Auvergne countryside would have made Cézanne one of the greatest—if not the greatest—painter of the present age" (*LC*, 63–64). A similarly meticulous interest in regional detail is evident throughout Storey's writings but is most prominent in the use of regional dialect in *The Changing Room*, as Storey remarked in 1976: "In New York [when] they put on *The Changing Room* ... all these people goggling at all these characters on stage talking broad Yorkshire ... couldn't understand a word of it."[13] Yet, in the same interview, Storey also acknowledged that he also tends "to work the same thing over from different angles ... it's a bit like Cézanne or someone painting the same thing over and over again in different versions"—exactly as Foley remarked in assessing the greatness of his works.

Surprisingly, many of the most abstract thematic statements in *Life Class* are given to Saunders—the student who reports the rape incident and causes Allott to lose his job:

> SAUNDERS. The human condition ... is made up of many ambivalent conditions ... that's one thing I've discovered ... love, hatred ... despair, hope ... exhilaration, anguish ... and it's not these conditions themselves that are of any significance, but the fact that, as human beings, we oscillate between them ... It's the oscillation between hope and despair that's the great feature of our existence, not the hope, or the despair, in themselves.
>
> (*Pause.*)
>
> STELLA. It's a wonderful observation ...
>
> (*Pause.* SAUNDERS *settles himself: gets out his equipment.*)
>
> I like people who think about life.
>
> SAUNDERS. I don't think about life. I'm merely interested in recording it.
>
> STELLA. I see.
>
> (*LC*, 74)

In addition to Stella, Allott himself endorses these views of "the nature ... the ambivalence—as Saunders so aptly described it—of all human responses" (*LC*, 80-81). Meanwhile, Storey—like Saunders—maintains

---

[12]W. H. Auden, "Greatness Finding Itself," *Forewords and Afterwords by W. H. Auden*, selected by Edward Mendelson (New York: Random House, 1973) 86.

[13]Victor Sage, "David Storey in Conversation with Victor Sage," *New Review*, October 1976: 65.

his own preference for "recording" rather than "thinking about" life, claiming that "Intellectualism, it's the English disease * * * All these attitudes towards experience ... it's the English Tradition, isn't it? (laughter) ... in the end, there's no experience *there*."[14] Nevertheless, earlier in the play, Saunders offers another observation on dispassionate realism (which is surely an "attitude towards experience" itself) as a technique in art:

> There's something dispassionate in human nature ... that's what I think ... something really dispassionate that nothing—no amount of pernicious and cruel experience—can ever destroy. That's what I believe in ... I think a time will come when people will be interested in what was dispassionate at a time like this ... when everything was dictated to by so much fashion and techniques. (*LC*, 49)

Whatever its artistic antecedents, the *literary* forebears of this credo obviously include Flaubert, Zola, and their followers in the late nineteenth and early twentieth centuries. Yet, despite the meticulous detail and realistic portrayal of the subject, as Allott points out, "The essence of any event * * * is that it should be ... indefinable. Such is the nature ... the ambivalence * * * of all human responses" (*LC*, 80–81). Similarly, in discussing his own works, Storey maintains that "the best things I do, I don't know what they're about when I've finished them. When I have the ideas first, they're usually no good ... At best, the illustration of a thesis, at worst pretentious bullshit."[15] He is equally chary about reading sustained critical analyses of his works, as he indicated in a letter to me, "on the basis that what the plays and novels are supposed to be about will only get in the way of what I thought they may have been about (usually erroneously—but then, that's only a device to get me to write any)."

Certainly, the "thesis" is more explicit in *Life Class* than in *The Changing Room*, *Home*, or *The Contractor*, but even so, the great majority of thematic statements in *Life Class* concern *how* the play is to be understood (a technique that is also applicable to his other plays) rather than specifically *what* the action of the play means. "The artist sings his song," Allott remarks, "but doesn't contemplate its beauty, doesn't analyze, doesn't lay it all out in all its separate parts ... that is the task of the critic" (*LC*, 30)—a position that Storey has also maintained in his interviews. Nevertheless, with so much instruction being offered to the audience, it is appropriate that the setting for *Life Class* is a classroom—and the subtle irony of the title (that the play instructs the audience in understanding the author's other works) becomes clear.

[14]Sage 64.
[15]Sage 63.

Throughout its latter half, there are a number of indications that *Life Class* was intended to be a farewell to a certain *type* of theatre—if not, as was suspected by a number of reviewers at the time, a farewell to the theatre itself. In a reference to his series of "invisible events" that seems equally appropriate to the author's series of naturalistic but allegedly plotless plays, Allott declares that his work to date has been "Ahead of its time ... impossible to perceive ... the pagaent is at an end now. * * * The process, as you can see, is virtually complete" (*LC*, 88)—as if Storey felt a certain discouragement that his plays had been neither properly understood nor recognized for their innovativeness. Despite Allott's assertion that "I've achieved some of my best work, I think, in here" (*LC*, 90)—a statement that is equally true of Storey's relationship with the Royal Court, where *Life Class* and his other works had been produced—he (Allott) foresees no continuation of it in his career: "My next work may be something altogether less commendable ... That's to say, more ... substantial ... if not altogether more extravagant than what I appeared to have achieved today ... I shall have to see ... sans means ... sans wife ... sans recognition who's to know what I ... might rise to ..." (*LC*, 88). There is also little hope that his works will be better understood in the future, as his conversation with his colleague Philips reveals:

> PHILIPS. Posterity, old son. If they don't see it now, they'll see it later. We're building up an enormous credit ... (*Gestures aimlessly overhead.*) somewhere ... You with your ... events ... me with my designs ... book-jackets, posters ... Letraset ... singular embodiments of the age we live in.
>
> ALLOTT. Sold anything lately?
>
> PHILIPS (*shakes his head*). ... You?
>
> ALLOTT. How do you sell an event that no one will admit is taking place?
>
> (*LC*, 55)

Whatever value might later be recognized in Philips's graphics, his remarks are irrelevant to Allott's "invisible events," which leave no artifacts for posterity to judge. Such is not entirely the case with Storey's plays, of course, since a number of them have been recorded on film and videotape, and the texts of all except *Phoenix* have been published. The apparent implication that he has been unable to "sell" his works could be easily refuted by citing the success of his productions at the Royal Court and the lengthy list of favorable reviews and awards that his plays have received (though relatively few have been revived since their initial productions). Nevertheless, the analogy between Allott's "invisible events" and the live performance of Storey's plays in the theatre (as opposed to their filmed or videotaped counterparts) remains clear.

Like John Osborne and Edward Bond, Storey has expressed a deep dissatisfaction with both critics and audiences who, he feels, have neither understood nor recognized (i.e., have not "bought") the ideas that his works embody. Even Katharine Worth's incisive *Revolutions in Modern English Drama* (1973) discusses Storey's work only briefly and in terms of the realism of the 1930s, noting that he "moves between novel and drama with Maugham-like ease" rather than attributing to him any innovations in form.[16] "How does one live as a revolutionary," Allott asks, "when no one admits there's a revolution there?" (*LC*, 56). Yet, whereas Osborne and Bond have repeatedly and contentiously explained and defended their plays, proclaiming their social and political beliefs at the same time, Storey seems relatively resigned to the lack of comprehension that he detects. He has maintained a rather taciturn endurance of what he perceives to be the state of affairs in contemporary theatre, and he issues neither prefaces nor manifestoes to explicate his plays. Even so, as he recalled his anger "at the reception—or rather lack of reception—of [his] first two novels," he remarked (during the interview with Victor Sage in 1976) that in the early stage of his career he had not

> learnt that there's nobody out there ... nobody knows what the hell you're doing. * * * It's no use telling everybody: "Look, this is what I'm doing." It's no use beating a fool about the head ... you've got to find other, more subtle ways. * * * There's no audience, even at the Royal Court ... every time you do a new play, you have to whip up an audience ... they're all so bloody bourgeois ... they sit there like this (laughter). * * * I can't go to the theatre myself, it's the audience, they put me off.[17]

Like Storey, Allott finds himself surrounded by those who do not comprehend the meaning of his works: his students maintain that "there's nothing happening" as he describes the "invisible events" that are taking place before them, and when he quotes a Latin epigram (which summarizes a major theme of both *The Changing Room* and *The Contractor*) to encourage their efforts, his audience—predictably—fails to understand:

ALLOTT. Good ... good. That's the spirit ... Labor Ipse Voluptas Est.

WARREN. Rest, sir?

ALLOTT. No, no ... Just carry on.

(*Fade.*)

(*LC*, 57)

---

[16]Worth 26.
[17]Sage 63, 65.

The students in Allott's classroom and the audiences for contemporary plays are apparently identical, in Storey's view, in both their lack of appreciation of art and their priorities, preferring "excrescence before edification ... salaciousness before refinement" (*LC*, 40), as the record-breaking runs of such anodyne fare as *Oh! Calcutta!* and *No Sex Please, We're British* reveal. The latter—London's longest-running comedy—is a particularly significant example to Storey, as he revealed during my conversation with him:

> When we opened *The Contractor* in the West End, we were in competition with a play called *No Sex Please, We're British.* We were in competition because we both went to the same theatre [the Strand], and in the end our management panicked and went to a much smaller one round the corner, the Fortune. They didn't think we could get sufficient reviews to fill it, and it was a much larger theatre. We opened within a week, and that play got absolutely diabolical reviews. . . . They said it was absolute unmitigated rubbish and insulted the intelligence of the audience. It's been running ever since . . . a roaring success! We in *The Contractor* ran absolutely ecstatic reviews from all the critics, the popular and the highbrow, and it survived—but just—for about a year, and it came off.

Arguably, the rape in *Life Class* may even provide a sole concession to those members of the audience who complained that "nothing happened" in Storey's previous plays. Yet, whether or not such speculation is warranted—and Storey has given no indication that it is—a recognition of the analogy between the students in the classroom and the audience in the theatre (both of which are being instructed in the appreciation of "invisible events" at the same time) counters the seemingly valid criticism of the students that was noted by John Weightman in *Encounter*: "There is never any indication that they are specifically art students, *i.e.* people who, in addition to their randiness and bowel-movements, are genuinely interested in the problems of art. They are all perfectly philistine. * * * In the most benighted educational institutions—and I have seen a few—there are always one or two teachers and pupils who save the honour of the place."[18] Ironically, insofar as anyone "saves the honour of the place," it is Saunders, who reports the rape incident, "taking the part of public decency and order in this matter" as Allott himself remarks (*LC*, 84); among all of the students in the class, Saunders seems to be the most conscientious and capable artist, setting up plumb lines and carefully measuring the portions of Stella's body. Allott also suggests that a "genuine" interest "in the problems of art" is no longer a prerequisite for becoming an artist (much less an art student), since, as he tells

[18]John Weightman, "Art Versus Life," *Encounter* September 1974: 57–58.

Warren, "it's not even a discipline because, if you presented me with a straight line and told me that's what you saw—under the absurd license of modern illusionism—I'd have to accept it" (*LC*, 46). However, the most significant reason why the students "are all perfectly philistine" seems to be the suggestion that they are, in Storey's view, exactly like the audience for his own "invisible events": "there's nobody out there * * * [who] knows what the hell [he's] doing."

Life Class was not in fact Storey's final play to be produced at the Royal Court—nor was it the last play that Storey wrote, despite its numerous valedictory implications. *Mother's Day*, Storey's only attempt at farce, was produced there in 1976 and was written within days of *Life Class*, as he disclosed in my interview with him:

> *Life Class* and *Mother's Day* were written in the same week, shortly after I came back from the opening of *The Changing Room* on Broadway [in 1973] * * * When, at the end of *Life Class* I said "I'm going to do something which is mind-boggling," I thought when I sat down to write *Mother's Day* that that was going to be the mind-boggling [thing]. I thought it was going to be a murder play but it came out as a kind of black farce. But [in *Mother's Day*] I saw the kind of anarchy of the life class with the students and the rape and so on as very much the sort of the anarchy, as if a kind of photostat, * * * the reverse of every traditional practice. Everything which was against the rule and totally unacceptable in family life was the norm in this family.

Mother's Day met with nearly universal critical opprobrium, however, and even the apparent valediction in *Life Class* was greeted with approval in some reviews, particularly by W. Stephen Gilbert in *Plays and Players*: "The valediction . . . is to the life class, to the careful portrayal of 'that incredible miasma we call life,' which has made Storey's name and about which he has surely said all he's got to say. . . . God, I hope so. . . . This tantalising suggestion . . . lit up the last 40-odd minutes of the play . . ."[19] In fact, Storey has indeed included within *Life Class* a final summation of his views of life and art—a statement surpassing the discussion of impersonal methodologies and the technique of avant-garde "invisible events." The most poetic of these summary statements occurs near the end of the play, as Allott muses that art traditionally

> leaves objects—certain elements of its activity—behind ... stone, paint, canvas ... bronze ... paper ... carbon ... a synthesis of natural elements convened by man ... whereas we, elements as it were of a work ourselves, partake of existence ... simply by being what we are ... expressions of a certain time and place, and class ... defying hope ... defying anguish ... defying, even, definition ... more substantial than reality ... stranger than a dream ... figures in a landscape ... scratching ... scraping ... rubbing ... All around us ... our rocky ball ... hurtling through time ... singing ... to no one's tune at all. (*LC*, 82)

[19]W. Stephen Gilbert, "Life Class," *Plays and Players* May 1974: 26.

In much the same way that Arnold Middleton sought refuge and security among "objects" that were left behind from previous ages, Allott recognizes the value of the traditional heritage, even as he seeks to explore beyond it and to open new frontiers. As at the end of *Cromwell*, Storey's protagonist in *Life Class* resolves to pursue his visionary goal amid the darkness and uncertainty of life, wherein past experience (both his own sufferings and those that, recorded and collected, constitute the cultural tradition) provides the sole available guide. Accordingly, Allott reveals that

> I've always seen myself as something of a pilgrim ... a goal so mystical it defies description ... not gates, exactly, I see before me ... more nearly * * * a pair of eyes. * * * We are all, I've come to realize, *brothers* ... even if some, it transpires, have to be more brotherly than others ... Michelangelo's David and Carabaggio's Disciples at Emmaus—to name but two—were not easily come by: they were the process [*sic*] of a great deal of mental pain. I shall let that anguish * * * go before me ... Go before me and—if the past is anything to go by—light my way. (*LC*, 87)

Characteristically, the end of Storey's play is both ambiguous and tentative; the conditional clause ("*if* the past is anything to go by") echoes the questioned existence of the "light" at the end of *Cromwell*. Whereas *The Restoration of Arnold Middleton* concluded with the first hesitant signs of a marital reconciliation, Allott's condition "sans means ... sans wife ... sans recognition" (*LC*, 88) is far more desperate, and there is neither a suggestion of a "restoration" nor an indication of what his "next work" might be.

But to the extent that the play corresponds to Storey's own career as an artist who abandoned his vocation as a teacher in order to become a novelist and playwright, *Life Class* may contain a final irony: at the end of Storey's seemingly "valedictory" play, his central character has reached the time in his life that corresponds exactly to the point in the author's own life at which his career as a writer began. Conceivably, in the same way that Stephen Dedalus at the end of *Ulysses* might be prepared to begin a novel remarkably like *Ulysses* itself, Allott may be on the verge of a career as a playwright; his first work, like Storey's, might be expected to portray the domestic crises of a beleaguered teacher, and he might even subsequently develop a way of presenting "invisible events" on the stage.[20]

[20]An additional parallel for this interrelationship between the plays may be found in the best-known films of Storey's director and mentor, Lindsay Anderson: in both *If...* (1968) and *O! Lucky Man* (1973), the central character (called Mick Travis in each, though they are not necessarily the same person) is played by Malcolm McDowell, who was co-author of the screenplay for the later film and incorporated into it many autobiographical details. At the end of the ostensible sequel, Mick Travis/McDowell undergoes a successful

In writing *Life Class*, therefore, Storey returned to the subject matter of his first play and recast it, incorporating and defending the refinements of dramatic technique that he developed during the interim years. Accordingly, his "valedictory" play is best regarded as the completion of a cycle of plays, during the course of which a new dramatic form—the theatrical "invisible event"—was developed, refined, and ultimately defended. For the final play of the cycle, Storey returned to the subject of a teacher beset by marital failure, appreciated or understood by neither his students nor his family nor his colleagues, cherishing the values that his academic subject traditionally has afforded, longing for the security and solace provided by the "eternal verities" (and the traditional rituals whereby they were instilled) in earlier times, but finding that these can offer no haven from the problems of life in the modern desacralized world. Although the action of Storey's first play takes place entirely in the home of the protagonist and his final play of the cycle is set exclusively in the classroom, the implication of each is clear: whatever the means whereby one copes successfully with the inevitable crises of life in a desacralized world, there can be no withdrawal from life into a personal "surrogate religion" and no retreat to the sureties of more simple—and more stable—times.

screen test before Lindsay Anderson himself who is about to film *If...*; the later film ends at the point of the author's career at which his then-new career began, and—as in Storey's plays—a cycle has been completed.

CHAPTER 4

"Other Refuge Have I None":

Home and Family in

In Celebration, The Farm,

and *Mother's Day*

After listening to Jimmy Porter harangue his wife and family with the now-famous vehemence that startled theatregoers in 1956 and heralded a new era in English drama, one of the characters in John Osborne's *Look Back in Anger* comments that "I've never seen so many souls stripped to the waist since I've been here."[1] In retrospect, the remark seems to have been particularly prophetic; certainly, it is no less applicable to the English and American drama that was written during the ensuing decades than it is to the Porter household. Throughout the years since the debut of *Look Back in Anger*, the souls of a seemingly endless array of characters have been bared with remarkable candor, although the stripping—both literal and metaphorical—seldom stopped at the waist. At times, as in *The Restoration of Arnold Middleton* and *Life Class*, such personal revelations are voluntary or at least self-induced—confessional admissions that are offered in anger or in anguish. More often, however, they occur as a result of strife within a family, as long-suppressed memories and latent hostilities prompt painful and sometimes violent confrontations in which the defenses and pretenses maintained by others are relentlessly torn away in the midst of the family, which is ideally (in Christopher Lasch's phrase) the ultimate "haven in a heartless world."[2] Whatever the shortcomings of other refuges—including those sought by the protagonists of *The Restoration of Arnold Middleton* and *Life Class*— the home has traditionally remained a source of sustenance and solace amid the turmoil and tribulations of the world. Yet because the home—

[1]John Osborne, *Look Back in Anger* (1957; New York: Bantam Books, 1965) 87.
[2]Christopher Lasch, *Haven in a Heartless World: The Family Besieged* (New York: Basic Books, 1977).

like Sartre's Hell—is essentially "other people," it too often becomes a battlefield of conflicting desires, long-held resentments, and an intimate knowledge of others that can be menacingly employed. Among Storey's plays, such is particularly the case in *In Celebration* and *The Farm*, while *Mother's Day* deliberately reverses every conventional standard and expectation of family life.

The theme of familial relationships recurs throughout Storey's novels and plays, and he readily acknowledges its importance in his work. Replying to a remark by Victor Sage that he "seem[s] to look at the world . . . through the lens of the family" throughout his writings, Storey told the interviewer that "I don't think it's possible to describe a community, the way the world is today. I'm trying to get at the roots of organic experience in my work. . . . The family . . .—and the way people relate to one another in *work*—is important to me because most of my [formative] experience of life . . . was with the family."[3] Despite its universally acknowledged importance as the basic social unit, the modern family is often comprised of isolated and lonely individuals who are united by common experience and shared loyalties, yet whose communication may be inhibited and whose relationships are frequently strained. For the narrator of Storey's *Flight into Camden*, for example, the home becomes the site of "the only battle left for me to fight [,] as if our love were only there to drive us to greater and more outrageous tests of its strength."[4] Similarly, one of the sons in *In Celebration* remarks that one can "Trust the Shaws ... Not two minutes together—and out it comes ... Fists all over the place" (*IC*, 85). An even more extreme assessment is offered by another character in *Flight into Camden*, who tells the narrator that "Families to me are just like vicious animals, radiant with solicitude and affection until you touch them. Then they rear up like crazed beasts. They seem to be the worst parasites of the lot, living off everything around them that they can: neighbors, jobs, friends, anything. * * * In my experience, they've destroyed far more than they ever created."[5] Although this description seems more applicable to families portrayed by Albee, Pinter, O'Neill, and Williams, many of Storey's characters are encumbered by the potentially destructive guilt and anxiety that their family relationships impose: both Allott in *Life Class* and Arnold Middleton feel that they have failed to fulfill the expectations of their parents (particularly the unreasonable and unattainable ideals that their mothers have nurtured), and each of Storey's novels contains at least one scene of generational conflict and confrontation.

[3]Victor Sage, "David Storey in Conversation with Victor Sage," *New Review* October 1976: 64.

[4]David Storey, *Flight into Camden* (New York: Macmillan, 1961) 53.

[5]Storey, *Flight* 64.

Reviewing the first production of *In Celebration* in 1969, Benedict Nightingale described the theme that would be elaborated in Storey's later works, and he associated it with the theories of R. D. Laing:

> As Storey seems to see it, we're subject to appalling pressures almost from birth. Each preys, morally, on each, generation after generation. Parents and educators, as spouses and employers later, force their acquired values and habits on us, until 'by the time the new human being is 15 or so, we are left with a being like ourselves, a half-crazed creature, more or less adapted to a mad world.' It's worth remembering that Storey . . . is an admirer of guru Laing, whose words these are.[6]

In fact, Storey denies any influence—or admiration—of Laing, describing himself during my interview with him as having "always been indisposed" toward the "romantic view of society" represented by *The Politics of the Family*, for example. In discussing *Saville* with Victor Sage in 1976, however, Storey reiterated his opinion (although he increased the "formative" age by seven years) that "by the time you're twenty-one, you've hardened your attitudes towards your experience ... once your ego, or rather your superego, is formed."[7] Yet even though Storey recognizes the predatoriness of family relationships and the pressures that they imply, there are in his works no "crazed beasts" as savage as those in *Who's Afraid of Virginia Woolf?*, *The Homecoming*, or even *Look Back in Anger*. Despite the long-suppressed but simmering hostilities and the "hardened" adult attitudes that have shaped their personalities, Storey's characters retain poignant memories of home and family as well, allaying some of their more predatory impulses and deflecting the psychological blows that they might otherwise inflict. Thus, throughout the second act of *In Celebration*, tensions build as the three sons exchange numerous recriminations and reveal (in the presence of their father) their long-repressed resentments and their disillusionment with their ostensibly successful lives. But the expected climax—a confrontation between the mother and her most vehemently iconoclastic son—never takes place. Instead, guardedly but by mutual tacit assent, the essential stability of the home is preserved.

The importance of the home and family as a source of permanence and stability amidst worldly flux is reiterated by a number of characters throughout *In Celebration*. Each of the sons remarks on the absence of change in their parents' home, with its "solid, heavily furnished living room" and its "heavy and provincial" furniture that has "no particularly distinguishing features, either of period or 'character' " (*IC*, 11). The

---

[6]Benedict Nightingale, "Three Sons," *New Statesman* 2 May 1969: 632.
[7]Sage 64.

familiarity of both the human and physical relationships constitutes the predominant impression that the first of the sons to arrive home receives:

SHAW. * * * What's it like to be back home, Steve?

STEVEN. Home ...

SHAW. After all this time.

STEVEN. Well. I don't know, Dad ... Very much the same.

(*They laugh.*)

(*IC*, 23)

Clearly, the sameness is not merely a matter of familiar furnishings unchangingly arranged, as Mrs. Shaw points out to another son:

ANDREW. Like a museum, is this. Hasn't changed in five thousand years.

MRS SHAW. We've just had it decorated. A few months ago.

(*IC*, 24)

Instead, it is the product of the "character" and stability of its inhabitants; one of the neighbors mentions that Shaw himself "never changes" (*IC*, 34), and his marriage has endured for forty years. In fact, the enduring bonds of family relationships have been the most important priority in the father's life:

STEVEN. * * * I don't think ought's changed here since I was last up.

SHAW. * * * Family, lad. Family. There's nothing as important as that. A good wife: children. God's good grace. (*Looks briefly up*) If you have good health and your family, you don't need anything else.

STEVEN. Aye ...

SHAW. Sixty-four years next month. If I haven't learnt that I've learnt nothing.

(*IC*, 12)

During the second act of the play, Shaw again asserts the primacy of family ties, declaring that "A car, money, a big house ... They're nowt. A family like this. That's all that counts" (*IC*, 73). Yet, as the Shaws' neighbor explains, such families are now the exception rather than the rule:

ANDREW. How are your lads, then, Mrs. Burnett?

MRS BURNETT. Oh, well enough. Half a dozen kiddies. Not two minutes to come up and see their mother ... Still. That's how it is. (*To* MRS SHAW) That's where you're lucky, love. Your lads come home. Don't disown you. Don't forget you as you're getting old.

81

SHAW. Aye. We've been damn lucky.

(*IC*, 37)

Clearly, neither the family nor any other institution commands the loyalty that its counterpart in earlier times received; as Mrs. Burnett resignedly admits, "That's how it is." Nevertheless, while it commands less overt allegiance in successive generations, it remains—particularly for the parents' generation—a source of solace and a refuge in a crisis-laden world.

The absence of visible change in the area surrounding the house seems less reassuring than the constancy of the home, however, and Shaw tells his son that "Nothing changed out there either, you can see. Houses ... houses ... houses ... as far as the eye can see ..." (*IC*, 13). Indeed, as the opening and closing scenes of Lindsay Anderson's film of this play (for the American Film Theatre series in 1975) make clear, the Shaws' residence is indistinguishable from thousands of identical row houses in the industrial midlands. Like its counterpart in *This Sporting Life*, the Shaws' home "amongst all that mass and detail was a fleck, a speck in the hundred thousand landscape, a smudge on the lattice of all those streets."[8] Yet behind the unchanging and grimy facades, abandonment and desuetude have begun to take a toll that Shaw movingly describes:

> SHAW. * * * Miles of nothing, this place. Always has been, always will be. The only thing that ever came out of here was coal. And when that's gone, as it will be, there'll be even less. Row after row of empty houses, as far as the eye can see ... It's starting ... I pass them on the way to work. I stop sometimes and look in—holes in the roof, doors gone, windows ... I knew the people who lived there ... All this was moorland a hundred years ago. Sheep. And a bit of wood ... when they come in a thousand years and dig it up they'll wonder what we made such a mess of it for ... (*Gestures at the walls.*) Look at these foundations and think we all lived in little cells. Like goats.
>
> STEVEN. We did (*He laughs* * * *).

(*IC*, 18)

Such transformations, the growth and decline of the industrial economic base, are (of course) generational changes, becoming evident only over long periods of time and seldom altering the continuity of the residents' day-to-day lives. The three generations of the Shaw family—like their counterparts among the Ewbanks in *The Contractor*—recapitulate these socioeconomic changes that have shaped modern Britain and the rest of the Western world: Mrs. Shaw's unseen (presumably deceased) father was a "small-holder" or, as her husband less flatteringly refers to him, a "pig-breeder" (*IC*, 22); Shaw, a miner, works for the industrial system

[8]David Storey, *This Sporting Life* (New York: Macmillan, 1960) 190.

that supplanted such agrarianism; his sons—the recipients of university degrees and the beneficiaries of their parents' economic and personal sacrifices—have become "professionals," pursuing careers in law, teaching, and industrial relations (all of which involve services rather than goods and require none of the physical exertion that their father's job demands). Within this single family, the changes that have transformed the English economic system (if not its society's class-conscious traditions) are embodied.

The occasion of the Shaws' fortieth anniversary prompts the sons' return home, but the celebration that provides the play's title seems to be undertaken more as a duty than a joy. When one of the sons declares cheerfully that "this time tomorrow we'll all be back home," his brother quickly reminds him that "We're here to give them a good time. Something they'll remember. God alone knows they deserve it" (*IC*, 39–40). Within these modest ambitions, the family outing—a "night on the town" at an expensive restaurant in an elegant hotel—is an apparent success; Shaw reports to his inquisitive neighbor that their evening has been "Grand! Grand! Lovely ... Couldn't have been better!" and that it was in fact the "best night of my life!" (*IC*, 61). Nevertheless, the subsequent acrimony among the sons and their father reveals that the celebration has failed to *unite* the family by overcoming the isolated grievances of its members for even a single day and night. Accordingly, the most fundamental purpose of any celebration has not been fulfilled, since traditionally (as Ferdinand Tönnies points out)

> the concept of *celebration* is commonly related to the ideas of cult and veneration. Festivities bring together those who become separated and who live apart, and they feel themselves reunited in the exaltation of the ceremonies. Quarrels cease and community comes into its own. Thus the festival recalls belongingness and gives it renewed validity. The convening of the clan has something festive about it *as does the contemporary family reunion* [emphasis mine]. Fellow-clansmen and countrymen . . . feel united through common usage and common duty in honoring the ancestor, god or saint. The same thing is true of fellow-workers and friends. Just as festivals are to this day celebrated to honor men, so, at all times, festivals were celebrated to honor the gods. And custom fixes certain days as holidays.[9]

As a result of the desacralization of modern life, however, there are no broadly based cults, little veneration of anything, and no occasions "to honor the gods." Ironically, in *In Celebration*, the most iconoclastic of Shaw's sons refers contemptuously to the others' reverence toward the mother—who, they hope, will not hear their quarrels:

[9]Ferdinand Tönnies, *Custom: An Essay on Social Codes*, trans. A. Farrell Borenstein (New York: Free Press of Glencoe, 1961) 52.

ANDREW. * * * What's she to be protected from?

SHAW. What?

ANDREW. I mean ... that ... Goddess, we have up there. * * * Dad. Wise up. You've enshrined that woman in so much adoration that she's well-nigh invisible to you as well as to everybody else.

SHAW. What ...?

ANDREW. You owe her *nothing*. What're you trying to pay off?

SHAW. What ...?

(SHAW *stands, blinded, in the centre of the room.*)

(*IC*, 81)

When obligations and "adoration" are heatedly denied, when the "Goddess" becomes an object of derision and resentment rather than love and veneration, the "celebration" inevitably becomes a hollow form, a gratuitous exercise, a *devalued* ritual. Yet such is the case not only in the Shaw household but in the larger society that it represents, as Peter Brook observed in *The Empty Space*: "We have lost all sense of ritual and ceremony—whether it be connected with Christmas, birthdays, or funerals—but the words remain with us and old impulses stir in the marrow. We feel we should have rituals, we should do 'something' about getting them, and we blame the artists for not 'finding' them for us."[10]

Although Storey's unique way of "finding" modern rituals in everyday life (and depicting them onstage) is the crux of *The Changing Room* and *The Contractor*, it is ironic that in *In Celebration* the loss of the "sense of ritual and ceremony" afflicts primarily the younger, highly educated generation; Shaw himself remains content with the celebration despite the subsequent disruption, of which his wife remains unaware. During the first act, he remarks that "Moments like this you begin to think it was all worth while" as he reflects on the sacrifices he and Mrs. Shaw made throughout the years of educating three sons and "setting them up in life" (*IC*, 36), and at the end of the play he admits that he has no idea what the altercation was all about:

SHAW. Well, then ... that's that, eh?

MRS SHAW. Yes ...

SHAW. Did you enjoy it, love?

MRS SHAW. I did. Yes ... And you?

SHAW. Aye ... Aye.

MRS SHAW. They never change.

[10]Peter Brook, *The Empty Space* (New York: Atheneum, 1968) 45.

SHAW. Aye.

MRS SHAW. What was all that about, then?

SHAW. Nay, search me, love ... Now then. Where do you want me? Here. Look. Let me give you a start.

(*Goes to help her.*)

(*IC*, 103)

Like the central events in many of Storey's other plays (the wedding in *The Contractor*, the rugby match in *The Changing Room*, the confrontation between Allott and his wife in *Life Class*), the celebration itself takes place offstage so that, in effect, the rituals *surrounding* it are more evident in the play. Careful preparations are made for the "parade" down the street to the car so that all of the neighbors can see their departure (and the successful sons of whom the Shaws are so proud), and Mrs. Shaw has purchased a new hat and "wants to make 'an entry'" (*IC*, 53), which itself is a ritual, for the approval and admiration of the men in her family. During the few moments that these and other such rituals occur—including the toasts of champagne on their return home and the dinner itself (as described for two of the neighbors)—the entire family *is* united, fulfilling the essential purpose of the celebration. Yet, even though the parents are well satisfied with the entire event and fail to understand their sons' anguish, the fact that the *entire* celebration does not unite the family for even a single night reveals the devaluation of both traditional rituals and family ties in the modern world.

Whereas the long-planned celebration becomes the occasion of much discord among the sons, their memories of the domestic rituals and habits that shaped their childhood provide the brothers' most amicable—and most poignant—moments together. Many of these reminiscences reveal the poverty that the family endured, and although the sons no longer suffer such deprivations, having joined the "professional classes," there have been few improvements in their parents' lives:

ANDREW. You forget, don't you, what a primitive place this really is. Do you know, the other morning we ran out of toothpaste * * * and I suddenly remembered: we never had toothpaste at home. Do you remember? We all used to clean our teeth with salt. (*Laughs*) Three little piles on the draining board every morning, when we came down.

STEVEN. We never had any cakes either. Do you remember that? There was a jam tart, or one piece of sponge roll, for tea on Sunday.

COLIN. And old Steve there had to stand at table because we only had four chairs.

ANDREW. I remember. Would you believe it. (*They look round at the room.*)

(*IC*, 40)

85

According to the definition offered by Bossard and Boll in *Ritual in Family Living*, any such routine constitutes a ritual; more precisely, however, the preparation and use of the piles of salt—like the other practices that earned Mrs. Shaw her "Proficiency in Human Hygiene" when she was in school—are habits, since they are patterned and purposeful activities but convey neither status nor significance. In contrast, the fact that Steven invariably "had to stand at table" repeatedly affirmed his "place" as the youngest child (i.e., confirmed his status in the family), making it a ritual of sorts, and the presence of the tart or sponge roll helped make Sunday tea a part of that day's secular but ritualistic observances. The family's poverty also marred more formal rituals and continues to haunt the sons' dreams:

> ANDREW. * * * Do you remember when old Shuffler came to see my Dad about going to the university?
>
> STEVEN. Shuffler?
>
> COLIN. He'd left by the time you'd got there.
>
> ANDREW. Sixth form. Careers. Came here one night to talk to my Dad about 'the pros and cons' of going to university. Sat in a chair: we had it there. Put his hands out like this and ... ping! Bloody springs shot out.
>
> COLIN. Nearly dislocated his elbow! (*They laugh.*) * * * After he came here old Shuffler never talked to us again. Whenever we met in the school corridor he used to gaze at some point exactly six inches about your head. Talk about the pain of poverty. I still dream about that look. I do ... I often wake up trying to convince him that we're not as poor as that any longer.

> (*IC*, 41)

Despite financial support from their unmarried son (who, on the morning after the celebration, reveals to them that he intends to marry), their parents are, of course, still "as poor as that." For them, much more than for any of their sons, very little has changed.

Despite the sons' ability to laugh together about the conditions of their childhood, the effects of the family's dire circumstances are evident in their scarred emotional lives. As the reviewer for *Plays and Players* remarked, Andrew, Colin, and Steven (in order of birth) are respectively "the Revenger, the Crippled, the Crucified."[11] Colin, the unmarried industrial-relations negotiator, is the most complacent and conventional of the three—and the most supportive of his parents, buying their new furniture and providing other financial assistance; yet he is also, as Benedict Nightingale remarked in the *New Statesman*, "insensitive, arrogant,

[11]John Holmstrom, "Keep It, Mum," *Plays and Players* June 1969: 29.

and a bit stupid,"[12] having few interests outside his work and few goals except financial security. As his elder brother remarks,

ANDREW. You are listening to a man whose life—believe it or not—is measured out in motor cars.

COLIN. In blood! In men! In progress!

(IC, 43)

Clearly, Colin is one of the "pygmies" about whom Arnold Middleton complained—a professional compromiser and negotiator rather than a "man of action," a believer in absolutes, a "king." Echoing Arnold Middleton's allegation that in politics "we *choose* the lesser men" (*RAM,* 97), Andrew taunts Colin about his suitability for holding political office: "I hope they make you Chancellor, or Prime Minister. And I hope it gives you something to do, fills your time, infects [*sic*] your life with a certain feeling of significance and meaning ... for if it doesn't, I hold out for you, Colin, *brother,* no hope of any kind at all" (*IC,* 84).

The absence of "a certain feeling of significance and meaning" in life is, of course, a recurrent concern throughout Storey's writings, but (as *Cromwell* explicitly demonstrates and as Andrew himself recognizes) the political system and its laws provide no satisfactory recourse. Realizing that laws are the result of compromise, conciliation, and capitulation to "special interests," Andrew has abandoned his career as a solicitor in order to become an artist—a vocation in which personal values may be individually, directly, and uncompromisingly expressed. Predictably, the parents have no idea why their son became dissatisfied with his career; the father confides his amazement that Andrew "chucked up his job to be an artist. * * * With two children to support. * * * A career as a solicitor, that he's worked at ... that I worked at * * * at the table with him: fractions, decimals, Latin ..." (*IC,* 17). Similarly, his mother admits her bewilderment—and receives a startlingly frank and cynical reply:

MRS SHAW. I can't understand why you gave it up. After all the years you spent studying. It seems a terrible waste. You were never interested in art before.

ANDREW. No ... I'm not now, either.

(IC, 27)

To his parents—and to his wife and children as well—his art works are no less puzzling than the decision to abandon his career:

ANDREW. * * * Lo and behold. Triangles.

MRS SHAW. Triangles?

---

[12]Nightingale 632.

ANDREW. Or very nearly. The fact is, I'm not very good ... Subtle indentions on either side. Bit here ... Bit there ... Each one a different colour ... the variations in which would almost deceive the eye ... beautiful. If you like triangles, that is ... Abstract.

MRS SHAW. Abstract?

ANDREW. Not a sign of human life.

MRS SHAW. Oh.

ANDREW. Just the first. After that: squares.

MRS SHAW. Squares ...

ANDREW. Rectangles. *Rhomboids.* Sometimes, even—nothing.

MRS SHAW. Nothing?

ANDREW. Well, I say nothing ... there'd be a little ... spot ... of something, here and there. * * * Still ... old-fashioned.

MRS SHAW. Old-fashioned?

ANDREW. Absolutely. Don't use paint now, you know.

(*IC*, 26–27)

Attracted to the unmitigated self-expression that art affords but lacking the discipline that (in Storey's view, so evident in *Life Class*) it demands, Andrew is the virtual embodiment of the worst traits of "the poseur, the man masquerading as an artist * * * anyone in fact, who can persuade other people that what he is doing is creative" (*LC*, 30). Cynically, Andrew *uses* his new vocation to escape his responsibilities to his wife and sons—a fact that (naturally) seems unconscionable to his parents, an action that they would never have considered themselves. Yet, paradoxically, the ultimate reason for Andrew's abandonment of his obligations to his family—as well as his cynicism, the dominant trait in his personality—is that he remembers having felt abandoned and forsaken during his own childhood; "I've never been in * * * this family," he complains (*IC*, 81). Specifically, when he was five or six years old, he was put out of the family home and housed with one of the neighbors, as Mrs. Shaw explains:

MRS SHAW. * * * We put him out with Mr Reardon, you know, when Steven was born.

COLIN. Why was that?

MRS SHAW. Nay, love. To save me work ... Saved my life, you did, you know. We kept you at home. You were only two. (*Kisses his head.*) I don't know where we'd have been without ... I don't think he's ever forgiven me.

COLIN. What? ...

88

MRS SHAW. Andrew ... He was away six weeks. He used to come to the door, crying, you know. I don't know. I tried to tell him. If he'd have been here we'd have had a terrible time.

(IC, 89)

Shortly thereafter, Andrew confirms that this incident scarred a personality and shaped his later development:

ANDREW. The harm that I was done, was done a very long time ago indeed.

MRS SHAW. He's nearly as bad as he was last night.

ANDREW. I am bad. I am ...

STEVEN. Andy ...

ANDREW. Do you remember when I used to cry outside that door ... "Let me in! Let me in!"

MRS SHAW. Oh, now ...

ANDREW. Why wasn't it ever opened? *Why?*

STEVEN. Andy ...

ANDREW. Why wasn't it ever opened, Steve?

(IC, 99)

As a consequence, Andrew admits that "ever since I was turned out I've been able to look after myself" (*IC*, 93), developing a protectively cynical wit, a deliberately "iconoclastic" attitude (a term that he has proudly applied to himself since adolescence), and a conviction that family ties are more tenuous than they seem. Feeling that he was excluded from his own family, he readily excludes serious consideration of his wife and children as he pursues his new self-indulgent but unremunerative career as an artist. Whether or not a single childhood episode shapes the entire adult personality as the play strongly implies (although a number of critics have maintained that the motivations of both mother and son are insufficient and unconvincing), the incident provides a clear illustration of Storey's views on the effects of family interaction—and of exclusion therefrom.

Neither as complacent as Colin nor as iconoclastic and irresponsible as Andrew, Steven suffers in silence, seems torn in his allegiances, and shows signs of an imminent nervous breakdown. Long acknowledged by both his parents and his brothers as the most intelligent of the sons, Steven has become a teacher and writer, although he has recently abandoned a long-planned book on modern social trends:

COLIN. What was it all about then, Steve?

STEVEN. Oh ... (*Shrugs.*)

89

ANDREW. Modern society. To put it into words.

STEVEN. I don't know. (*Shrugs.*)

ANDREW. Indicating, without being too aggressive, how we'd all succumbed to the passivity of modern life, industrial discipline, and moral turpitude.

MRS SHAW. Don't mock him.

ANDREW. I'm not mocking him. * * * He let me read a bit of it once. What? Four years ago. He's been writing it nearly seven. I don't know why he's packed it in. I agree with every word.

(*IC*, 33–34)

The reasons for Steven's abandonment of the project are never explicitly revealed, as he remains surprisingly inarticulate throughout the play. As Storey himself remarked in his interview with Ronald Hayman, the actor playing Steven "has to sit virtually in silence for the whole play, not because the author doesn't think he's important but because he hasn't got anything to say, or if he has he can't express it and that's his dilemma."[13] Nevertheless, Steven has lost the fiery determination of his youth, as Andrew remarks:

Admittedly you were—for ever—silent. But even when at school—the school we have, only a moment before described, fit only for the sons of Christ—and then only after the most rigorous scrutiny—your arrogance, your disdain ... your *contempt*—were there for everyone to see ... I know. * * * Where, oh where has all that venom gone to? Where, for Christ's sake, Steve, is the spirit of revenge? (STEVEN *shrugs.*)

(*IC*, 42–43)

Like Colin (who, to his mother's surprise, is revealed to have been a member of the Communist party while attending the university), Steven appears to have become less radical as he gained financial security, a respectable profession, and—unlike Colin—a wife and four children as well. In fact, however, because he feels allegiances toward the beliefs of both of his brothers, he is unable to adopt the attitudes of either:

ANDREW. What's happened to that re-vitalizing spirit? To the iconoclast, to use my mother's word.

STEVEN. I don't know.

ANDREW. Steve!

STEVEN. Look. There's no hard and fast rule. The world's as real as anything else: you don't ... compromise yourself by taking part in it.

ANDREW. No? ... Not even with *this* world, Steve? (*Gestures through at* COLIN.)

STEVEN. No. It's not essential.

ANDREW. And that's why you look as sick as you do, because that's something you believe?

[13]Ronald Hayman, "Conversation with David Storey," *Drama* 99 (Winter 1970): 48.

In Celebration, The Farm, Mother's Day

STEVEN. I look as sick as I do—if I look sick—because I'm not a moralist like you. In the end, attitudes like you've described are easily adopted. All you have to do is throw over what's already there. You're like an evangelist. You both are. You forget there's another kind of temperament.

ANDREW. Well ...

STEVEN. I don't know what the word for it is. (*Turns away.*)

(*IC*, 44-45)

Even though the exact nature of this "temperament"—and the precise causes of Steven's crisis—are never specified in the play, Storey emphasizes (even more than in *Life Class* and *The Restoration of Arnold Middleton*) that the problem is not merely (or exclusively) psychological. References to the lost "re-vitalizing spirit," a "spirit of revenge," suggest the nature of the crisis but fail to encompass its true nature and cause, in part because they are beyond the comprehension of *secular* "evangelists." Like Andrew, however, Steven recalls a childhood incident that seems to have presaged—if not predetermined—his adult crisis: "He [Andrew] came home and devastated all of us—me certainly, without a shadow of a doubt—with all the reasons why it was no longer tenable—a belief in God. As if belief were a kind of property, like a limb, which you could put on or take off at will ... Believe me: remove any part and all the rest goes with it" (*IC*, 46). "Devastated" by the loss of his religious beliefs, Steven has neither substituted the worship of industrial mammon (as Colin has done) nor adopted the narcissistic "moralism" of Andrew; like Proctor in *Cromwell*, he has become disillusioned with efforts at social reform. Gropingly and inarticulately, he searches for essential spiritual values in a desacralized world—a yearning that, despite tears and exhortations, remains by definition unfulfilled. Accordingly, he is unable to complete his book because "the passivity of modern life, industrial discipline, and moral turpitude" are symptoms of a spiritual crisis that he intuits (and, indeed, feels acutely in his personal life) but remains unable to communicate, lacking a language to describe a "religious" world. Appropriately, he bears the name of the first Christian martyr.

In contrast to Steven's spiritual desolation, his father's faith—while neither profound nor particularly devout—is reaffirmed daily as he emerges safely (the result, he feels, of God's protective presence) from his dangerous work in the mines. Although the conditions in which the miners toil could amply fuel both Andrew's iconoclasm and Steven's social criticism, Shaw seldom complains, refuses to retire, and takes pride in both his endurance and his almost half century of labor in the mines:

SHAW. * * * Do you know how high it is where I work?

(*He looks round.*
They shake their heads.)

91

SHAW. Thirteen inches.

COLIN. It can't be.

SHAW. Thirteen inches. (*Stoops and measures it off the floor with his hand.*)

REARDON. He's right. The Rawcliffe seam.

SHAW. Thirteen inches. If I as much as cough, the whole damn roof'll come down on top of me. Two hundred yards of rock above, the centre of the earth beneath. Why you're nothing but a piece of stone yourself, propped up between one bit and the next. You lie with your belly shoved up against your throat. * * * You can't know what it's like unless you've been down ... And not even then. It takes a few years of going down before you get a glimmer ... You get a view of life you don't get anywhere else. You really get a feeling of what God's good protection means. (*Coughs.*)

(*IC*, 66–67)

Like Steven, Shaw recalls the incident in which Andrew "proved" that a belief in God is (in Steven's phrase) "no longer tenable," but it had little if any impact on the father's life or his practicality-based faith. "He could make it fit any set of facts he wanted," Shaw recalls; "... I remember him coming home when he was about thirteen and proving to me that God no longer existed. He's never looked back since then" (*IC*, 17). For the father, the episode was merely an intellectual exercise performed by a son whose education surpassed his own; in Andrew's manipulation of facts to support a syllogistically valid conclusion, Shaw finds evidence for Andrew's aptitude for a career in law—but no dismemberment of his own beliefs. Shaw's practical faith in "God's good protection" is complemented by his wife's conventional religious beliefs and practices; she is, as Andrew remarks, "conscientious, devout of temperament, overtly religious ... sincere." Nevertheless, Shaw on occasion makes light references to his own religious beliefs, confident that the world proceeds according to God's inexorable plan:

SHAW. * * * I'm good for lifting if I'm good for nowt else. When I come again I think they'll make me into a donkey. Reincarnation. It's stamped all over me from head to foot.

STEVEN. You better be careful. Somebody might hear you.

SHAW. Oh, she knows me. Ought to. Well enough.

STEVEN. I meant up there. (*Points up.*)

SHAW. Oh ... He goes His own way. Nothing I say'll alter that.

(*IC*, 21)

Neither, he might add, will his convictions be altered by anything his "iconoclastic" son might say, however intellectually sound and logically irrefutable it might be.

Throughout his adult life, Shaw's faith in education has remained as staunch as his belief in God—although on this subject, too, his sons have become disillusioned. "Education, lad: you can't get anywhere without ..." (*IC*, 22), he reminds Steven, ironically citing Mrs. Shaw as an example, since she graduated at age sixteen with a certificate affirming her " 'Proficiency in Domestic Science, Nature Study, and the English Language.' All done out in copperplate script" (*IC*, 22). Having worked in the mines since he was fifteen and having received little formal education himself, he devotedly prepared his sons for college so that they might escape the manual labor that he himself performs. Accordingly, he both envies and idealizes the jobs that his sons hold:

> SHAW. * * * I wish I got half of what you got, I can tell you: and for doing twice as much.
>
> STEVEN. It's got its drawbacks.
>
> SHAW. Drawbacks. It could draw back as far as it liked for me ... Teaching. Good God ...
>
> (*IC*, 13)

Similarly, he feels (with much justification) that Andrew has wasted the opportunities that uncomplaining sacrifices at home and in the mines made possible:

> SHAW. You've got a career you have. I spent half my life making sure none of you went down that pit.
>
> ANDREW. I've always thought, you know, coal-mining was one of the few things I could really do. (*Looks at his hands.*) One of the few things, in reality, for which I'm ideally equipped. And yet, the one thing in life from which I'm actually excluded.
>
> SHAW. You're ideally equipped to be a professional man. Or owt you want. But that place: an animal could do what I do. And I can tell you, most of them are.
>
> ANDREW. Aye. You're right. (*Snarls at* STEVEN.)
>
> (*IC*, 32)

Nevertheless, to Andrew the entire educational process seems to have been futile, conveying a hollow respectability and token amenities:

> When I think of all the books I've had to read. When I think of all the facts I've had to learn. The texts I've had to study. The exams I've had to ... with that vision held perpetually before me; a home, a car, a wife ... a child ... a rug that didn't have holes in, a pocket that never leaked ... I even married a Rector's daughter! For Christ's's sake: how *good* could I become? The edifice of my life—of his life—built up on that ... We—we—are the inheritors of

nothing ... totems ... while all the time the Godhead ... slumbers overhead. (*IC*, 83)

Like traditional rituals, the educational process has been devalued in the modern world and subordinated to efficient industrial production, as Storey noted in 1963 in a brief essay entitled "What Really Matters": "Education is a social process, one which seeks to persuade those uninformed elements of our society to recognize and adopt the disciplines essential to an industrial economy. Its diplomas, certificates, and degrees, once the incidental framework of enlightenment, are now the components of the machinery itself; patterns of behaviour and instruction vary only within the limits determined by a common end."[14] Describing the same process in American education, Christopher Lasch remarked in *The Culture of Narcissism* that since the first decade of the twentieth century, the school has been "a major agency of industrial recruitment, selection and certification," preparing an efficient labor force through the "inculcation of industrial discipline, vocational training, and selection . . . 'fitting the man to the job,' in the jargon of educational reformers at the time of World War I."[15] Despite the vaunted differences in the educational systems and methodologies in the United States and Britain, the purposes underlying them remain the same. Indeed, the education that Shaw's sons received has prepared them only for the more "respectable" and remunerative jobs, which require little actual exertion but provide neither the satisfaction nor the pride that their father has found in his manual labor.

Shaw's belief in education as the means to an ideal life seems—particularly to Andrew—to have been a delusion, and he reproaches his parents for "projecting him into a world they didn't understand. Educating him for a society which existed wholly in their imaginations ... philistine, parasitic, opportunistic ... bred in ignorance, fed in ignorance ... dead—in ignorance" (*IC*, 51). In the play's most searing confrontation, Andrew seeks to show his father the futility of his years of toil toward his particular goal:

ANDREW. * * * What is it, Dad? What image did you have ... crawling around down there at night ... panting, bleeding, blackened ... What world was it you were hoping we'd inherit?

COLIN. Shurrup [*sic*]. For Christ's sake, shurrup.

ANDREW. These aren't your sons, old man ... I don't know what you see here ... But these are nothing ... less than nothing ... has-beens, wash-outs, sem-

[14]David Storey, "What Really Matters," *Twentieth Century* 172 (Autumn 1963): 96.

[15]Christopher Lasch, *The Culture of Narcissism: American Life in an Age of Diminishing Expectations* (New York: Norton, 1978) 135.

blances ... a pathetic vision of a better life.

(*IC*, 84)

Nevertheless, as Andrew concedes to Colin (and as Steven concurs), the parents themselves are not personally to blame for this state of affairs, since there is (Andrew notes) "No blame. No bloody nothing" (*IC*, 83). Although Shaw "sits dazed" by the revelation of his sons' resentments and is stunned by the vehemence with which they are expressed, by the following morning he has returned to the security and orderliness of his daily routines; it seems likely that the previous night's outburst will have no more effect than his son's "disproof" of the existence of God many years before. The father remains untainted by the "intellectualism" that Storey has termed "the English disease"[16] and that Andrew denounces as "obscene" (*IC*, 45), even though the son's *Angst* is clearly a product of it. Such a theme is hardly new, of course: "In much wisdom is much grief," the author of Ecclesiastes recorded, "and he that increaseth knowledge increaseth sorrow" (Eccl. 1:18). As Shaw concedes at the end of the play, he has no idea what all the shouting was about; oblivious to the intellectually nurtured doubts that have incapacitated two of his sons, wrecking both their careers and their personal lives, he remains secure in his faith, his work, and his home—all of which have their familiar rituals and routines.

Whereas Shaw has sustained his ideals of the life of a "professional man," his sons recall another ideal that their father's library fostered in them. Among his paperback westerns (the details of which Shaw can never recall), his sons found an image of freedom and individualism, as Steven remarks:

STEVEN. One of the first things I ever remember was a picture in one of them. A cowboy with a hat out here and trousers flapping like wings, mounted on the back of a rearing horse. Somehow, it still sums it all up.

ANDREW. What?

STEVEN. Dunno ... Freedom. (*Pause.*)

(*IC*, 32)

Such cowboys were, of course, typically men who were unencumbered by families. To Andrew, his father's reading habits represent a congenial escapism that requires neither critical analysis nor intellectual retention of detail (in obvious contrast to the books that he studied in school):

ANDREW (*picks up paperback*). *Battle at Bloodstone Creek.* I used to marvel at that. My dad's reading age hasn't risen beyond when he was ten years old.

[16]Sage 63.

MRS SHAW. We can't all be educated, you know.

ANDREW. No. No. Thank God for that.

(IC, 24)

Steven recognizes the ultimate irony of their father's ideals for his sons and his resultant endeavors on their behalf, preparing them for work that is less meaningful than his own: "The funny thing is that he (*gestures up*) raised us to better things which, in his heart—my dad—he despises even more than Andrew ... I mean, his work actually has significance for him ... while the work he's educated us to do ... is nothing ... at the best a pastime, at the worst a sort of soulless stirring of the pot ..." (*IC*, 86). The result, as Steven mentions to Colin, is a feeling of psychic "disfigurement," which he further defines as "this crushing, bloody sense of injury ... inflicted * * * by wholly innocent hands" (*IC*, 86). This paradoxical plight of being "wronged" by the innocent is the antithesis of the western hero's more simple and solvable problems. Andrew advocates an unheroic retreat, declaring in one of his jeremiads that "You can't be *for* this crummy world and at the same time be for your own psychic ... spiritual ... *moral* autonomy, any longer. It is now the season of the locusts, and if you have anything to save then save it"—lest, like Steven, "you're *overrun*" (*IC*, 52). Nevertheless, Andrew's views—and the personal irresponsibility that they provoke—do not seem to prevail in the play; instead, like Arnold Middleton and Colin Pasmore, Steven returns to teaching and (as Benedict Nightingale concluded in his review) "accepts the claims of jobs, wife, children, parents while, at the same time, believing that the Laingian diagnosis is probably just: an uneasy, unhappy reconciliation that Storey himself may be presumed to endorse."[17] Because rugged individualism has become an anachronism (reduced to the heroics of pulp westerns, in much the same way that the great men of history have become mere outlines in coloring books in Arnold Middleton's classroom), because traditional religious beliefs seem to many to be no more intellectually tenable than superstitions, because both traditional rituals and the educational process have been devalued in the desacralized world, such an "uneasy, unhappy reconciliation" with life is perhaps the most that can be reasonably expected—or responsibly achieved.

Although she is absent during the most bitter confrontations, Mrs. Shaw in many ways represents another form of "reconciliation" that has exacted its toll from the other members of the family. Shaw repeatedly pays tribute to her, acknowledging her years of love and uncomplaining devotion: "She's had a hard life. She's worked very hard. Kept this place

---

[17]Nightingale 632.

like a palace ... One woman in a house of men. She'd have given aught, you know, to have had a daughter. You know, somebody to talk to ..." (*IC*, 53). Early in the play, however, he acknowledges that she found it a "bit of a let-down, marrying me," although his wife was "never one to grumble" (*IC*, 23). The reason for the marriage, which Steven has discovered and disclosed to Andrew, was the child (Jamey) who was born three months after the ceremony. With this fact in mind, Andrew gains new insight into his mother's life, noting that she "... Didn't leave school until she was sixteen ... religious ... raised up by a petty farmer to higher things ... ends up being laid—in a farm field—by a bloody collier ... hygiene ... never forgiven him, she hasn't ... Dig coal he will till kingdom come. Never dig enough ... Retribution" (*IC*, 47). Like the firstborn son in Storey's *Saville*, Jamey Shaw died in childhood—a fact that introduces the theme of atonement, which is also prominent in *The Restoration of Arnold Middleton*. Although all members of the family have been affected by the death, which caused Mrs. Shaw to attempt suicide during the period of grief and depression that followed, the father may in some ways have borne a greater burden, as Andrew suggests: "Forty years of my father's life for a lady like my mother, conscientious, devout of temperament, overtly religious ... sincere ... for getting her with child at the age of eighteen, nineteen, twenty ... I've forgotten which ... on the back of which imprudence we have been borne all our lives, labouring to atone for her sexuality ... labouring to atone for ... what? Labouring to atone ..." (*IC*, 83). An inability to make sufficient atonement is implicated in Jamey's death as well, since Andrew maintains that Jamey's presence was a continual reminder of "guilt. Subsequent moral rectitude. They fashioned Jamey—as a consequence—in the image of Jesus Christ" (*IC*, 47), which makes his death seem a sacrifice for the sins of others:

STEVEN. Andrew thinks Jamey died because he could never atone ...

COLIN. Atone? For what?

STEVEN. I don't know ... Whatever my mother felt ...

COLIN. He died of pneumonia, according to the certificate. I remember seeing it myself, years ago. * * *

ANDREW. He died from a bout of galloping perfection.

(*IC*, 48)

As in *The Restoration of Arnold Middleton* and *Life Class*, the parents in *In Celebration* stand accused of having established unattainable ideals and unachievable aspirations for their children. For the Shaws' first son, the results were fatal, but the others—like the teachers in Storey's other plays—also bear the psychic scars that were inflicted, albeit innocently, in this way.

Even when the brothers talk among themselves, each always refers to "*my* dad" or "*my* mother"—never "our"; this detail (however common it may be in actual usage) further demonstrates that each son remains isolated from the others and that any feeling of unity among them is at best only rarely and temporarily achieved, despite the bonds of family and the occasion of the celebration. But during the brief moments in which they actively participate in the family's familiar rituals, this isolation and alienation *are* overcome. One such moment (which embodies many of Storey's major themes in the play) occurs shortly after the family returns from the "night on the town," while the Shaws and two of their neighbors reminisce about the hardships that they shared during the Second World War:

> REARDON (*to* MRS BURNETT). No warning, now, the next time. Liquefaction will be the order of the day.
>
> SHAW. Aye. It doesn't bear thinking of.
>
> REARDON. No. No. Thank God we've reached the twilight.
>
> SHAW. In one piece. You're right.
>
> (*They're silent.*
> MRS SHAW *humming, then at the third line:*)
>
> MRS SHAW (*sings quietly*).
> While the tempest still is high:
> Hide me, O my Saviour, hide,
> Till the storm of life is past;
> Safe into the haven guide,
> O receive my soul at last.
>
> (COLIN, ANDREW *and* STEVEN *exchange looks,*
> ANDREW *turning away to hide his laugh.*)
>
> MRS SHAW (*sings*). Other refuge have I none ...
>
> (REARDON *starts, then* SHAW, *to sing too.*)
>
> Hangs my helpless soul on Thee,
> Leave, ah! Leave me not alone,
> Still support and comfort me ...
>
> (MRS BURNETT *has started to sing too, they sing strongly.*
> *At the last,* ANDREW, *then* COLIN *and* STEVEN, *join in.*)
>
> All my trust on Thee is stay'd,
> All my help from Thee I bring;
> Cover my defenseless head
> With the shadow of thy wing.

(*IC*, 69–70)

This hymn—Charles Wesley's "Jesus, Lover of My Soul," written in 1740—embodies the parents' traditional faith that the sons do not share, and it reiterates the need for a spiritual "haven" and "refuge," a role that was fulfilled by the church in earlier times and, more recently in the desacralized world, by the family. "The tempest sill is high"—today more than ever, as the discussion of nuclear war reveals—but neither religion nor the family now provides the certain "haven" into which the soul of the beleaguered individual may be surely and unfailingly guided. Without "other refuge," each of the Shaws' sons is indeed left "alone," seeking "support and comfort" that are unforthcoming from traditional sources. Nevertheless, temporarily their isolation is overcome as they join in the ritual of hymn singing (a patterned, purposeful, and significant event that momentarily reaffirms their status in both the family and a community of believers), briefly setting aside the reservations and cynicism that they cannot permanently waylay.

In the family celebration, there remain the last vestiges of what Mircea Eliade terms "festal time"—the "time of celebrations and spectacles" that is differentiated from "the comparatively monotonous time of . . . work" in the lives of members of essentially "religious" societies.[18] Although the elder Shaws are at best only "overtly religious" (in Andrew's phrase) and their celebration is entirely secular, it remains a "special occasion" that they will long remember and with which they are well pleased. As such, it fulfills the traditional role of celebration insofar as any event can do so in a desacralized world. The difference between "festal time" and "work time" provides the thematic center of *In Celebration*, and the importance of this theme has been eloquently summarized by Stuart Hampshire in an essay entitled "The Future of Knowledge":

> The essence of work, or of mere work, is, and always has been, repetition. But over most of known history the repetitions have been given significance by recurring celebrations of seasons and of work done, in feasts, ceremonies, . . . and public manifestations of all kinds. If the repetitions of work are not given any kind of seasonal rhythm or pattern, because the beliefs, principally religious, associated with such rhythms have largely disappeared, then they remain mere repetitions, leaving a blank, an empty aging, an undifferentiated stretch of days and months, as in a prison before death. Under these conditions a lifetime cannot naturally be envisaged as having any significant form; it becomes undecorated and bleak . . . practical but desolate.[19]

Such is, of course, the life to which Shaw's sons (and, to a lesser extent, Shaw himself) return at the end of the play. Their celebration having ended and their strife having been at least temporarily allayed, they return to the routines of their families and their respective workaday

[18]Mircea Eliade, *The Sacred and the Profane: The Nature of Religion*, trans. Willard R. Trask (New York: Harcourt, Brace & World, 1958) 68–70.
[19]Stuart Hampshire, "The Future of Knowledge," *New York Review of Books* 31 March 1977, 18.

99

worlds, despite the sons' forcefully expressed complaints about both. "One sometimes feels that Storey, like Laing, is railing against inevitability," observed Benedict Nightingale at the end of his review, adding that "man is, after all, doomed to work for his bread and to depend on relationships, and both are likely to be less fulfilling and more inhibiting than he'd wish. Only the very innocent and idealistic will suggest anything else. But perhaps that's the very conclusion that after all the rage and railing, Storey himself reaches at the end of this unusually stimulating play."[20] An equally important conclusion to be drawn from *In Celebration*, however, is that, amid the spiritual "crisis within us" and the problems of desacralized life, traditional rituals and institutions have been strained to the limit, offering neither permanent solace nor a haven from the "heartless world"—even on the occasion of a celebration and family reunion.

Whereas Mrs. Shaw has uncomplainingly and faithfully borne the burdens of her life as the lone woman in a houseful of men, the central character of *The Farm* has neither such resignation nor such restraint. A coarse and drunken farmer named Slattery, he has for several years been the sole man in a house full of women—his wife and three adult daughters, all of whom continue to live at home. His son, who yearns to be a writer but has published only a single poem, left the farm as a young man (in part to escape the tyranny and scorn of his father), although he returns home for a visit during the play. As in *In Celebration*, the homecoming reveals that very little has changed and that the family relationships are as strained as ever; the elder Slattery's abusiveness remains unabated with age, and the intended celebration of a ritualistic occasion (the son, Arthur, has planned to introduce his fiancée to his family) never takes place.

Like the elder Shaw in *In Celebration*, Slattery embodies a number of traditional values that are recurrent concerns in Storey's works—particularly the sanctity of work and the primacy of the family—and he tirelessly complains that his children neither share nor appreciate the virtues that he holds dear. Yet, unlike Shaw, Slattery expounds his views in alcohol-fueled harangues, raging not only against the metaphoric "dying of the light" that Dylan Thomas deplored but also against the personal shortcomings of the members of his family and—most important of all—against the demise of the values and the way of life that he has literally labored to sustain. Certainly, Slattery is an abusive, embittered, vituperative man with penchants for excessive drink and for self-pitying, self-proclaimed martyrdom. Yet, in many ways, such terms are equally applicable to Jimmy Porter and countless other alienated protagonists who

[20]Nightingale 632.

have appeared on the English stage since the premiere of *Look Back in Anger*. For all his many faults and all his offensive behavior, Slattery is not merely a bigot; despite his unrefined ways, his abrasiveness, and his profanity, he remains a surprisingly complex and sympathetic character. His declamations express a frustration that is intensely felt if sometimes rudely expressed, and he poignantly describes a number of significant transformations of contemporary society that he deplores but is powerless to affect. Neither a stolid embodiment of the status quo like Colonel Redfern in *Look Back in Anger* nor a pathetic "burnt-out case" like Archie Rice in Osborne's *Entertainer* and Blakely in Storey's *Radcliffe*, the elder Slattery is an anomaly in contemporary English drama: declaiming *against* virtually every change that has been advocated by cadres of *youthful* iconoclasts and working-class rebels since the mid-1950s he quickly establishes himself as an Angry *Old* Man.

Within the Slattery household, the father finds ample targets for his anger; like the protagonist of Storey's 1984 novel *Present Times* (an aging sportswriter and former footballer who finds himself bewildered in middle age by the diverse demands of his children's generation and by his wife's resolution to leave him for a wealthier man), Slattery claims that all of the members of his family have resolutely "gone their own bloody ways ... Gi'en no bloody attention to me ... Never ..." (*TF*, 54). Like the three sons in *In Celebration*, Slattery's daughters represent distinct (and easily characterizable) personality types that one reviewer summarized as "one repressed, one promiscuous, [and] one a would-be revolutionary."[21] Wendy, who is the oldest daughter (aged thirty-three) and the only one who has been married, points out that each of them is engaged in a personal battle that none of the others share: "Brenda battles with her social ideals ... entirely unrealistic ... I battle with my sense of inferiority in being a woman ... Jenny battles with ... I don't know what she battles with ... lasciviousness ... indolence ... sexuality ... acquisitiveness ..." (*TF*, 73). Clearly, Brenda and Jenny are the products—and, to their father at least, the casualties—of the "consciousness-raising" movements of the late 1960s and early 1970s: political radicalism and sexual "new morality" respectively. The nature of Wendy's own "battle" is never made explicit in the play, and although she uses a phrase associated with the feminist movement (on the deplorability of perceptions of "inferiority in being a woman"), it remains unclear whether she is particularly sensitive to this perception in the men around her (including her former husband) or whether she feels this inferiority within herself and is paralyzed by self-imposed restraints. All three types of ideological battles confound the father, whose traditional values are irreconcilable with

[21]Clifford A. Ridley, "Oops—The British Are Coming," *National Observer* 2 November 1974: 23.

those of his daughters, and he admits that he cannot comprehend their conflicts and their resultant behavior:

> SLATTERY. O'der I get, less I understand. Fathered three and married one: I know less now than when I started.
>
> WENDY. Could be said of all of us, I think.
>
> (*TF*, 14)

As Wendy thus acknowledges, the net results of all forms of "consciousness-raising" in the Slattery home have been an increase in both personal dissatisfaction and generational conflict; the certainties and values that they formerly accepted are no longer secure, but there is no consensus on new values with which the old might be replaced.

Slattery's essential complaint about his children's behavior (which diverts them from establishing families of their own) is that it is *unnatural*. Yet, typically, he expresses his view in a crude, blunt, demeaning, and offensive way, making frequent references to the behavior of animals as a standard by which his own brood may be measured and found wanting. "If I married again," he remarks, "I'd bring up half a dozen bloody goats ... Bloody hosses ... Damn sight more rewarding ..." (*TF*, 14). But Slattery's inability to understand his daughters' alienation merely exacerbates the problem:

> BRENDA. Your trouble is ... You see me ... and Jenny. And our Wendy ... Like some sort of primeval cattle. Cows.
>
> SLATTERY. Nay, coos [*sic*] know what they're bloody after ... I don't think any one of you know one end of a man from bloody t'other ... Look at Wendy ... Married sixteen months ... Then leaves ... A bloody doctor. God Christ: I'd almost marry the man meself ... As for bloody Jenny. By God: I've heard of flitting from flower to flower ... She never even stops to rest.
>
> (*TF*, 18)

The consequence of the daughters' struggles—and the fact that most vexes Slattery himself—is their failure to establish families of their own, although they clearly value their own home (despite the constant bickering that takes place there) and use it as a refuge from both the outside world and the "battles" that each fights there. Accordingly, Slattery complains that he hates "to see something going to rot" and proceeds to explain the remark with another reference to "natural" behavior:

> JENNY. *What's* going to rot?
>
> SLATTERY. When your mother was your age she'd had all four of you.
>
> WENDY. You think if we all had children you'd feel a bit easier about us, dad?

SLATTERY. I'm not saying nowt ... If a woman can't have babbies [*sic*] when she's young, I don't know what else she can have. I don't ... Comes as naturally as bloody breathing ... Your own nature's enough to tell you that.

JENNY. You've lived on a farm too long, old lad.

(TF, 14–15)

The implication that women should breed like sows or cattle and that procreation is the sole means of a woman's fulfillment are patently offensive, and Slattery admits that he has "no great opinion of women much, meself ... what wi' the examples I have around me here ..." (*TF*, 62). Nevertheless, he recognizes that his daughters' various preoccupations provide them frustration rather than fulfillment while dissuading them from establishing families of their own, thereby (in his view) undermining the family as a social institution. Certainly, as the quarrels of the Slatterys and the Shaws make clear, the family often provides as much frustration and as little fulfillment as any social "cause." Yet, as Slattery seems intuitively to recognize (although he could never articulate it himself), the family offers one all-important attribute that Mrs. Shaw's hymn in *In Celebration* epitomizes: it provides the sole secular haven of last resort when "other refuge have I none."

Surprisingly, Slattery's assessment of the fundamental problem in his household is corroborated by the rather simple workman with whom Brenda has a liaison after the other members of the family have gone to bed. Even though he is unsophisticated and somewhat inarticulate, he intuitively recognizes that the Slatterys' situation is "unnatural," although Brenda must provide him with the word:

ALBERT. My sister got married when she was seventeen ... Got three kiddies now ... She's not much o'der than you ... hasn't been back home since the day she was wed ... not for long enough you'd notice ...

BRENDA. Well?

ALBERT. Tisn't as if your dad's an invalid or ought ... or your mother needs looking after.

BRENDA. It seems unnatural?

ALBERT. Unnatural ...

BRENDA. Not quite right?

ALBERT. Dunno ... I've never heard of it afore.

BRENDA. Lots of things, I imagine, you've never heard about before.

(TF, 26)

Despite his provincialism and the lack of education for which Brenda belittles him, Albert's dim insight seems more valid than the more respectable views of Slattery's daughters (two of whom are teachers themselves) and of his wife, who he claims

> spends all her spare time in town ... Evening classes ... Sociology ... Psychiatry ... *Anthropology* ... Trying to find out what went wrong, lad.
>
> ARTHUR. Wrong?
>
> SLATTERY. What went wrong. In here. This house.

(TF, 60)

As in many of Storey's other works, "intellectualism" thwarts rather than facilitates such an understanding: Mrs. Slattery's academic disciplines, like Steven's in *In Celebration*, fail to provide even an adequate vocabulary to discuss—much less to resolve—the "problems within us" that are essentially "spiritual" and manifest themselves in such "unnatural" behavior.

As Slattery himself points out, the problem affecting the family is not confined to his household alone, and its causes are to be found in the social trends of the times; it is, in effect, a product of life in the desacralized world. The younger Slatterys are thus "emblematic of the modern age ... Free and easy. Responsible to bloody nowt" (*TF*, 76), and they have adapted to a "computerized, mechanized, de-humanized, antiseptic bloody lot" (*TF*, 76) in a world that is increasingly unlike the one that their father has always known. In fact, the farm itself is threatened by the encroachment of modern civilization, as Slattery notes in his most poignant speech in the play:

> SLATTERY. * * * All gone now ... motor-car factory, Temple Bank. Used to be a lovely bloody farm did that. Could pot rabbits theer any day of the bloody week * * * Shepherd's Nook ... municipal bloody housing. Had some lovely fields, had that. Woods ... Did our courting there, remember?
>
> MRS SLATTERY. I remember.
>
> SLATTERY. S'likely not forget. (*Laughs.*) Be our turn bloody next ... where we're sitting ... two years' time: six-lane bloody highway.
>
> BRENDA. Probably worth it.
>
> SLATTERY. I reckon to you it would.

(TF, 75–76)

Even agriculture has become increasingly mechanized through the years, as basic skills (and a willingness to perform the physical labor that farming requires—and required even more in the past) have been lost:

> SLATTERY. I better get out ... Mechanization ... get just like the bloody machines out theer ... if you don't tell 'em, direct 'em, switch 'em on, tell 'em when

to stop and start, reckon they can't do it by the'selves ... By God: had nothing but hosses here when we first came ... I'n't that right? Bloody 'osses know more about bloody farming than any man you can hire today ...

(*TF*, 54)

In such a world, Slattery maintains, "S'not worth bloody living ... Mek people in bloody factories next. You see. Bloody laugh. They will. Get rid o' bloody ones like me. Old. Out of bloody date. No good ..." (*TF*, 76). Albert, who is employed at the local factory, typifies the new "mechanized" man: his work is a monotonous routine that lacks even the most basic challenge, and his life (according to Brenda) is based on a fear of layoffs that renders all of the workers "immobilized" and "reconciled" to their plights (*TF*, 29). When Brenda tried to incite the workers to take over the company's management, she soon found that the men would only "strike ... to show they're as mean-minded as everybody else: small, mean, bigoted, cheap, materialistic" (*TF*, 28). Clearly, Brenda shares Arnold Middleton's remorse that the world is now dominated by "lesser men," although as a confirmed leftist she could never abide Arnold's longing for "kings." Just as Proctor in *Cromwell* could finally support neither of the warring forces that ravaged the nation, Brenda has come to detest the proletariat as well as the bourgeoisie, since (as she explains to Albert) the values of the two groups are increasingly indistinguishable: "Your entire existence * * * your philosophy of life: *Nothing ventured, nothing lost.* All of you: you're about as mean-minded as the people who exploit you. Between the two of you—I couldn't make a choice" (*TF*, 29). Whereas Proctor continues a quest for spiritual enlightenment at the end of the play, Brenda can conceive of no such goal, since, unlike the hero of *Cromwell*, she lives in a wholly desacralized world. The product of a twentieth-century militancy rather than seventeenth-century oppression, this politically disillusioned contemporary woman turns instead to a prospective career in writing "lewd" fiction (*TF*, 54).

Even though Slattery has "no great opinion of women much" (*TF*, 62), he is equally scornful of younger men in general and his son—the other aspiring writer in the family—in particular. "Maybe we should've all been sons," Wendy remarks, to which Slattery replies, "Aye ... Well, example thy's had, I shouldn't think you'd get very much from that" (*TF*, 14). Specifically, the father complains that his son is a wastrel who has never done any actual work (i.e., physical and productive labor) in all of his life: "Not that I give a damn. I don't. I want you to know that, lad. I mean that sincerely. It teks all sorts to mek a world ... I might work like a bloody animal meself ... no reason why you or anybody else should do the same ... T'only trouble is ... them that do the bloody work get no attention ... them that do damn all get nowt but bloody praise ...

105

Not blaming you. S'human nature" (*TF*, 59). Even one of Arthur's sisters admits that he does "nothing" and that she has "no idea" how he earns a living (*TF*, 27). Their mother reveals that he has "had jobs"—including stints on a farm (a suggestion at which Slattery scoffs) as well as in hotels and in a classroom. The father particularly disparages his son's job as a teacher, noting that "Thy sisters teach. Bloody woman's job is that * * * I could teach as much as they do and still run this entire bloody farm meself" (*TF*, 59). As in many of Storey's other plays, the shortcomings of the son are blamed on the mother, who is alleged to have imposed unreasonably high expectations on him while exalting his slightest achievements. Accordingly, Slattery claims that his wife

> Bloody immortalized that lad afore he was even born ... that's been [his] trouble all along ... Set him up ... Good God ... Thought he was bloody Shakespeare before he'd even opened his bloody mouth * * * Thought we had a new Messiah ... Believed half on it me bloody se'n * * * Slave me bloody gut out and there he was, twiddling his bloody thumbs and rhyming bloody moon with June ... Seen nothing like it. Never have. (*TF*, 63-64)

Furthermore, Slattery alleges that he has in fact been supplanted by his son, who usurped the love and affection that his mother should have shown to her husband:

> SLATTERY. * * * [To *Arthur*] Done sod all in your life ... Whereas me ... worked every bleeding minute ... Never loved me ... It's true. She'll bloody tell you ... Never has ... Idolised you, lad. Been your bloody ruin ... Been my son you'd never have turned out like that ...
>
> MRS SLATTERY. That's not true. You know it.
>
> SLATTERY. Nay, if you don't know when you're not bloody loved, then you'll never know bloody owt. As for him ... God Christ.
>
> (*TF*, 60)

Although Slattery's accusations are brutally stated and probably exaggerated in his alcoholic duress, the charges are not as groundless as they might seem: Wendy discloses to her sister that their mother's "extramural course is leading her into very deep waters," a liaison with the recently divorced, forty-four-year-old instructor of the sociology class that she attends at night (*TF*, 10), and in Arthur's announcement of his engagement to a divorcée who is old enough to be his mother, Slattery finds confirmation of his suspicions about his son's maternal fixation. In short, every member of the Slattery household, with the exception of the father himself, seems—in Slattery's view—to undermine the family as an institution, and the seriousness of the problem is summarized in Jenny's obviously apocalyptic image of the family unit:

JENNY. It's like one huge, corporeal mass ... I often dream of it at night ... a sort of animal with seven heads.

WENDY. Seven?

JENNY. Don't know why. Only six of us at present.

(*TF*, 44)

In terms of the action of *The Farm*, however, such an image seems gratuitous, since the expected domestic Armageddon—a confrontation between the father and the newly engaged couple—does not take place. Instead, the play ends with a return to the status quo that prevailed at the beginning: Arthur, the couple's own son, has been driven out of the family and away from home yet again, and Albert—the workman whose views on family matters and on the nature and necessity of work are compatible with Slattery's opinions, as those espoused by his own "flesh and blood" are not—is welcomed at the family table as if by right, as if indeed *he* were a member of the family itself. Thus, *The Farm* is a specific inversion of Christ's parable of the prodigal son: there is neither forgiveness nor a joyous welcome for the wastrel who returns to the fold, and there will be no feasting in his honor, since the wedding that he planned to announce will not take place. Instead, the "son" who toils every day, albeit in a factory rather than in the fields, is made welcome at the family's ordinary repast.

Like the elder Shaw in *In Celebration*, the farmer Slattery is "ostensibly religious," and he often refers to his beliefs (which are neither subtle nor profound) as a means of rhetorical abuse as he rails against the outrages in his family. His discovery that Arthur's fiancée is the divorced mother of two children provokes a typical outburst that affirms, in its comically profane way, his belief in an impenetrable but divinely directed cosmic plan:

Jesus in his holy heaven ... (*Looks up.*) I hope He's bloody listening. I hope to God that He can hear ... Have I ever done ought to deserve a family ... the likes of the bloody one I've got? ... Have I *transgressed*? ... Have I *overlooked* ...? Have I *condoned* ...? Have I sinned? Have I done *ought* ... at any time ... in any place ... Said all this before ... I know ... Maybe when I bloody get theer [*sic*] ... He'll tell me what it was all about ... (*TF*, 65)

Similarly, Slattery invokes God during an argument with his wife, much as Job must have been tempted to have done, urging her to "Ask *Him* ... *He*'ll tell you ... (*Looks up beseechingly, raising his hands.*) He knows ... He knows everything I've been through. He's been my one true witness all these years" (*TF*, 61). Nevertheless, the farmer's ultimate recourse—if not salvation—is to be found in work rather than faith, and he is determined despite the tribulations of family life to "go on. Like a bloody engine ... Get to bloody work ... Hand to the plough: never look back. Truest words He ever spoke ... 'Dead bury the bloody dead ...' He's right ... All I've bloody looked for ... *always* ... all I've ever looked for ... all my bloody life ... (*Goes.*)" (*TF*, 65–66). Indeed, for Slattery work has become the secular gospel that he would teach to his daughters' pupils in school:

SLATTERY. Work. Work's the only bloody thing that's real.

JENNY. I think he means it.

BRENDA. I think he does. I don't see any reason why he shouldn't.

(*TF*, 76)

Even Mrs. Slattery attests that her husband embodied certain qualities that can no longer be found, as she confides in Brenda early in the play:

MRS SLATTERY. * * * I was only twenty when I married him ... He was very much the sort of man, you know, who, if he saw a thing, went out and got it ... There don't seem to be many people like that nowadays ...

BRENDA. Nowadays?

MRS SLATTERY. Well, I don't know ... Everybody seems so uncertain ... The ones who do seem confident ... you'd dismiss as stupid, I expect.

BRENDA. I don't know. It depends what they're confident about.

(*TF*, 22)

Such uncertainty and loss of confidence are, of course, two of the essential characteristics of the anxiety that accompanies life in an utterly desacralized world.

In much the same way that *Mother Courage* provides a key precedent for *Cromwell*, a number of Chekhov's plays provide the best context for assessing *The Farm*—although Storey typically insists that there was no such direct influence on the work. Nevertheless, the play contains a number of distinctly Chekhovian elements in both the characters' motives and their domestic situation. The most obvious of these is the presence of three sisters whose prospects for an escape from their home in the countryside (and from the dreariness of their lives) seem ever more remote:

BRENDA. * * * Why do you stay here, Wendy?

WENDY. Stay?

BRENDA. Why don't you go away? Get off. Do anything ... clear out.

WENDY. Don't know ... Used to worry about it, a bit, myself ... Doesn't seem a problem any more.

BRENDA. You ought to be a nun.

WENDY. Could almost say I am.

BRENDA. Why has Jenny never married?

WENDY. Don't know.

BRENDA. I'm beginning to feel the same. Don't think I ever will.

(TF, 31)

While Slattery's daughters are in some ways the modern English counterparts of Chekhov's *Three Sisters*, his son Arthur strongly resembles
Konstantin Treplev in *The Sea Gull* in a number of details: each is an
aspiring young writer whose works are neither understood nor truly
appreciated by members of his family (nor, since the audience for his
works is miniscule, is it appreciated by anyone else); each is rejected by
the woman he loves; each endures a strained relationship with an aging
actress (Arthur's fiancée and Konstantin's mother); and each is finally
driven out of the family in an act of despair (Konstantin's suicide, Arthur's
abandonment of hope for a reconciliation within the family), after which
routine household activities (the card game in *The Sea Gull*, the breakfast
in *The Farm*) continue without interruption as the play ends. Like Madame
Ranevskaya's estate in *The Cherry Orchard*, the Slattery's farm is threatened
by "progress" (the encroachment of the highway), and Slattery's description of his wife seems applicable to Madame Ranevskaya as well: "Your
mother's not disillusioned ... She's just not got much bloody common
sense ... No great failing, that, in my book ... She's got a heart as big as
that bloody door ... It'll alus see her through" (*TF*, 17). Even if such
parallels are coincidental, as Storey insists, one of the foremost distinctions of *The Farm* is its portrayal of contemporary, specifically English
experience within the familiar contours of the characteristically Chekhovian form.

Unlike the most prominent of Storey's plays, however, *The Farm* features no central "invisible event" *onstage*, as there is, for example, in *Life
Class*, *Home*, *The Changing Room*, and *The Contractor*. Nevertheless, as Alan
Rich remarked in *New York* magazine, "*The Farm* is full of dark, brooding
counterpoint, of a lean, spare treatment of dissonance, and of broad,
intricate rhythms that summon up visions of Bach—not the cold mon-
umentality of the *B Minor Mass*, but the deep, bitter suffering of the
Saint John Passion."[22] Like its Chekhovian counterparts and most of Storey's other plays as well, *The Farm* does not "generate a great deal of
dramatic movement," as Rich noted.[23] Less charitably, Clifford Ridley
of the *National Observer* complained that "although you discover certain

---

[22]Alan Rich, "Rocky Life on the Farm," *New York* 1 November 1976: 75.
[23]Rich 75.

things about these characters that you didn't know at the outset, you also discover that nothing has happened. * * * And in the theatre, something *ought* to happen. That * * * is what theatre *means*. But if *The Farm* isn't theatre exactly, it's an interesting something-or-other."[24] This recurrent accusation of "plotlessness," which has been leveled at nearly all of Storey's plays, is equally applicable to those of Chekhov. However frequently they are voiced and however widely they are held, such objections are based on a conception of theatre that is not only restrictively narrow but also a century out-of-date—the equivalent of a belief that all contemporary poetry should rhyme and contain regular metrics, that all novels should contain a cleverly constructed and intricate intrigue, or that all music should have a hummable tune. By focusing the audience's attention on unique and autonomous images rather than on traditional machinations of a plot, such plays demand new standards that are comparable to those that seemed so revolutionary in the other arts nearly a century ago when narrative verse, representational painting and sculpture, and intricately plotted fiction were the conventional order of the day—and the modernist movement was soon to be born. Much more than "an interesting something-or-other," *The Farm* is a skillfully written, carefully constructed, distinctly Chekhovian play, whether by coincidence or design.

Certainly, no one can complain that "nothing happens" in *Mother's Day*, Storey's 1976 farce that was written during the same week as *Life Class*. Its plot, like that of Joe Orton's *Entertaining Mr. Sloane*, involves the attempted sexual exploitation of a lodger by various members of the landlord's family. Yet whereas the title character of Orton's work is no less venal and iniquitous than anyone else in the play (and is no less willing to exploit others than to be exploited himself), Judy—the young tenant in *Mother's Day*—remains an innocent but unreproving object of the blatant advances of two generations of male Johnsons. Unlike the sham rape in *Life Class*, the sexual violations that preoccupy the characters in *Mother's Day* occur offstage—if, notwithstanding the graphic descriptions that are vaunted throughout the play, they ever really occur at all. The semblance of illicit sexual activity where none has in fact taken place is surely among the world's oldest dramatic devices, and it is at least possible that—after shocking theatregoers with the ostensible rape that does not take place in *Life Class*—the successive play convinces the (again shocked) audience that the alleged but unconfirmed sexual exploits of this unabatingly lecherous family have actually taken place. The most lecherous of the family members is Gordon, the Johnsons' youngest son, who, like so many other adult sons in Storey's works, is idealized by his

[24]Ridley 23.

mother. Specifically, she extols his sexual prowess and the jotted thoughts (monotonous, vulgar, and trite though they are) that he hopes eventually to publish as a book. Amid Gordon's wildest claims (in a speech that may set the world's record for the most repetitions of the word *fuck* in the fewest lines), he describes his alleged intercourse with Judy before her startled fiancé (whom he mistakenly believes to be her husband); in the aftermath of that, some of the key lines of the play might be easily overlooked:

GORDON. I've just been fucking your wife upstairs. I fucked her everywhere I could. I fucked her up the front, then I fucked her up the back, then I fucked her in the throat, then I fucked her between her breasts, then I fucked her between her thighs. She's resting now. It's been quite a night.

MRS JOHNSON. Gordon always was active as a child.

GORDON. Not too late for breakfast, ma?

FARRER. I say ... *Is this true?* Your son's been with my wife?

MRS JOHNSON. Gordon has a room of his own in town ...

GORDON. In Clarendon Street.

MRS JOHNSON. In Clarendon Street. It's one of the older parts of town.

GORDON. Georgian.

MRS JOHNSON. Georgian. Immediately beneath the walls of our cathedral. You can see its spire from the station when you arrive.

FARRER. Is Judy up there?

GORDON. I shouldn't disturb her. Needs time to recover. *My mother—God bless her—is a little eccentric. I wouldn't believe everything she says.*

MRS JOHNSON. *Gordon's always had a disposition, Mr. Farrer, to use his imagination.* He has a notebook in which he keeps his secret thoughts.

(*MD*, 207-8; emphasis mine.)

Significantly, Farrer's question "Is this true?" is never answered by *anyone*; despite all the uninhibited descriptions of unrestrained lust, there is no *credible* confirmation that *any* of the alleged acts have indeed occurred. Furthermore, the play provides ample reason for *dis*belief: Gordon, whose claims about his own sexual prowess are patently incredible, *is* acknowledged to have a highly active imagination; his mother—who is also his most uncritical admirer—cannot be considered a reliable source of confirmation about what is alleged to have occurred offstage; and Judy—the sole character who *could* reliably recount the night's events, if any—neither confirms nor denies Gordon's outrageous claims. Like Stella in Pinter's *Collection* (1961), Judy remains enigmatically silent about a much-discussed liaison that may or may not actually have taken place. Similarly, there is no reason for the audience to believe the allegation that Gordon has, on various occasions, raped his eldest sister in the cupboard where the "simple if not actually defective" woman frequently secludes herself (*MD*, 176). If the charge *is* true, however, the Johnsons would hardly object, since they welcome the proposed marriage of their other son and daughter at the end of the play.

Whereas the first two acts concern Gordon's sexual exploits, the third develops his announced intentions of murdering his father, who undauntedly accepts this prospect, since "a son has to kill his father, son. It's what life is all about" (*MD*, 218). Like Christie Mahon in Synge's *Playboy of the Western World*, however, Gordon is persistently unsuccessful in his attempts at parricide. When a private investigator (reminiscent of Inspector Truscott in Joe Orton's *Loot* and Sergeant Match in his *What the Butler Saw*) enters the house seeking Judy and her abductor/lover/alleged husband, he is mistaken for Mr. Johnson and knocked unconscious momentarily; he is subsequently persuaded—primarily by Gordon—that he is a criminal lunatic (much as Old Mahon is so convinced by Widow Quin in *The Playboy of the Western World*), although of course Mr. Johnson, the alleged victim, is not dead. Despite the clamor and confusion that the various escapades in *Mother's Day* cause, all of its characters emerge unscathed (unlike the ending of *What the Butler Saw*, with its multiple gunshot wounds). Yet, at the end of the play, an unresolvable ambiguity remains about whether the alleged multiple sexual assaults did actually take place—even though the question probably never occurs to the vast majority of theatregoers (or readers of the play), who have become more or less accustomed to finding every form of sexuality being portrayed (or at least explicitly described) in contemporary comedies and revues. More disconcerting, however, is the fact that this ambiguity was not noted by the reviewers of the play, who were almost unanimously contemptuous of this play. Nevertheless, it is at least possible that the obsessive and rampant sexuality that earned the play its notoriety and its hostile reviews is in fact just "much ado about nothing"—to borrow the title of a play in which both the allegations and appearances of sexual debauchery are equally disruptive but more demonstrably false.

Each of the Johnsons in *Mother's Day* is characterized by an idiosyncratic obsession, tirelessly reiterated in stock phrases throughout the play—and, indeed, throughout their lives. Although such monomania and recurrent patterns of language are traditional means of characterization in comedy, the preoccupations of Storey's characters are much more personal—and more peculiar—than those of the stock characters of traditional farce. In fact, the Johnsons comprise one of the most comically eccentric families in English literature since Stella Gibbons's *Cold Comfort Farm* (1932). Like that novel's Great Aunt Ada Doom, whose life was abruptly and radically altered by the childhood trauma of seeing "something nasty in the woodshed,"[25] Mrs. Johnson is obsessed with the consequences of an early sexual experience: she was seduced by the house painter whom she married shortly thereafter, causing her to be disinherited from the family's vast estate. "Mr. Johnson * * * seduced me when I was only sixteen," she explains, "discovering me one morning lying naked and inexperienced on my single bed. Two nights later we absconded, stopping on the way while he seduced me once again" (*MD*, 211). Repeatedly chiding her husband for the "reduced circumstances" in which she has lived ever since that day (*MD*, 192), she deplores the fact that he "was an inexperienced and vulgar man when he deflowered me, and vulgarity has flourished, vigorously, in the manure of his existence" ever since (*MD*, 198). Accordingly, like the fathers in *In Celebration* and *The Farm*, Mr. Johnson can never redeem himself in his wife's estimation, and he is in effect "martyred" for his sexual indiscretion and unable to make sufficient "atonement" for his past.

As in many of Storey's plays, the mother is the dominant and domineering member of the family, and—even though Mrs. Johnson has not broodingly withdrawn into her own thoughts—Gibbons's description of Aunt Ada Doom is otherwise entirely appropriate for the central character of *Mother's Day*: "She was the core, the matrix; the focusing-point of the house ... and she was, like all cores, utterly alone. * * * All the wandering waves of desire, passion, jealousy, lust, that throbbed through the house converged, web-like, upon her core-solitude. She felt herself to be a core ... and utterly, irrevocably alone."[26] Mrs. Johnson scorns her children as well as her husband; although she idolizes her youngest son, Gordon, her contempt for the others is entirely unconcealed: "[Lily] should have been put to sleep before she was born. She's a living reproach to me, that woman. I can't believe I ever gave birth to her ... Nor to you [Edna] if it comes to that ... It's only Gordon I can believe I ever gave birth to" (*MD*, 183). Their father, meanwhile, is obsessed with genealogy and consoles himself with the realization that "in the great aeons of time by which we are surrounded, the anguish of Doctor Johnson—not to mention the deJohns * * * and very much else—will seem to have been very small beer indeed" (*MD*, 269). Owning no ancestral estate of the sort that his wife forsook by eloping with him, Mr. Johnson nevertheless claims a distinguished lineage, which his wife summarizes (having, no doubt, heard it described on countless occasions): "My husband's antecedents can be traced back by even the most casual enquirer to Doctor Samuel Johnson of Lichfield, the first compiler of an English dictionary: similarly, my own background is that of the landed aristocracy, namely

[25]Stella Gibbons, *Cold Comfort Farm* (1932; London: Penguin, 1977) 113.
[26]Gibbons 112.

the deJohns, whose ancestors were notorious for the wide-spread introduction of the water-closet" (*MD*, 223). The reason for Storey's selection
of these surnames is revealed in the final lines of the play, as the mother
exults that "we leave behind us ... a united family ... its two great progenitors—initiators, each of a different kind—holding above us our
mutual heritage—the great canopy of civilization: one the inventor of a
book, the other of a means by which we might dispose of it" (*MD*, 269).
Notwithstanding Mrs. Johnson's proud claims, the family is "united"
only temporarily—by the prospect of a marriage (the standard device
with which traditional comedies conclude); yet, typically, in the Johnson
household the wedding is—to say the least—unconventional, since it is
Harold (a member of the Royal Air Force who, after eighteen years of
service, has never flown in an airplane or advanced beyond the lowest
rank) and his sister, Edna, who intend to wed.

Unlike Gordon and Harold, who have developed their own obsessions
(sex and gliders, respectively), Edna and Lily are never allowed to assert
themselves. Instead, they are continually imposed upon by other members of the family. More than any other character, Lily is *defined* by the
identity that others impose on her, particularly through their language:
constant abuse and recriminations are inflicted on her, and she is continually berated as a "liar" by her mother. Consequently, Lily's characteristic speech pattern is negative—a recurrent denial of actions alleged
against her ("I didn't") or of information that she is alleged to withhold
("I don't know"), although all such protests are to no avail. More than
any of Storey's other plays, *Mother's Day* sets forth the various means
whereby language—both our own (reflecting our interests and obsessions) and that of others when applied to us—defines and shapes each
person's individuality.

Storey was genuinely surprised by the intensity and near unanimity
of the hostile reviews that were given to *Mother's Day*—which, according
to J. W. Lambert in the *Sunday Times* "would have been better consigned
to the wastebasket"[27] if not to the means of disposal that Mrs. Johnson
mentions for books at the end of the play. Despite such disparagement,
and even though he has been quite critical of a number of his earlier
works (particularly *Radcliffe*, *Cromwell*, and *A Temporary Life*), Storey continues to insist that the farce is substantially consistent with—and not in
any way inferior to—his other works. During his conversation with me,
for example, he maintained that it is quite similar to *Life Class*, which
was written during the same week:

> I saw the kind of anarchy of the life class with the students and the rape and
> so on as very much the same sort of the anarchy, as if a kind of photostat,

[27] Jeremy Brooks and J. A. Lambert, "David Storey Week: Triumph and Disaster," *Sunday Times* 26 September 1976, 13.

because everything in *Mother's Day* was supposed to be a family where every traditional value was carefully inverted and the obverse was true of everyday reality. The family lived out a life which was the reverse of every traditional practice. Everything which was against the rule and totally unacceptable in family life was the norm in this family. [Laughter.] The critics all reacted like members of a normal family would do, precisely with these people as next door neighbors. It was extraordinary; I found it very strange; it beats me. Every time I've reread the play, and I have read it over a period, it seems a very good play to me. The end of it's got problems—it goes on too long—but it's a very funny play.

Furthermore, he insists, the play was much more well received during the previews before the critics came:

It's very strange [that] it had a very long preview, something like two weeks, and every night there was a queue for returns, and the audiences used to applaud at the end of every scene, which never happened with any other play I've had produced, and they roared with laughter and thought it was absolutely outrageously funny. We opened, and the first night the critics came, the play was seen in absolute stony silence. I mean, I knew. [Pause.] What did it I have no idea. It was absolutely extraordinary. And the reviews reflected the stony silence in which it was seen. The reviews were uniformly bad, and the next night the theatre literally was less than a third full and never had more than a third. After being sold out every night of the previews, it was a total disaster. . . . I've never seen a play the audience so genuinely enjoyed, roaring with laughter and applauding; it was a real pleasure to watch the play with them, and within twenty-four hours it was a complete write-off.

Attempting to salvage it from being "a complete write-off," the Royal Court's ads for *Mother's Day* quoted the most damaging of the reviews (exactly as the ads for Joe Orton's *What the Butler Saw* had done)—in order to tantalize prospective audience members with something so outrageous that it had scandalized even London's "critical establishment."

In fact, however, as Storey told John Higgins of the London *Times*, there is a fundamental consistency between this play and his other works, though he insists that the similarities have gone generally unrecognized: "Some [people] have even said that I picked the text up off the street and put my name to it. I can't see it myself: a constant theme runs through all my work, and *Mother's Day* is no exception. Perhaps they find the sexuality different. It should be vulgar in the fine sense of the word; it needs to be played with vulgar energy and directness."[28] The "constant theme" is, of course, the effect of desacralization on modern life in general and on the family in particular. Among the Johnsons in *Mother's Day*, neither religion nor secular norms constrain the most primal and

[28] John Higgins, "David Storey: Night and Day," *Times* (London), 16 September 1976: 13.

anarchic urges of the characters, and there are no rituals to unite (and to confirm the relationships among) the various family members. Even the daily afternoon tea—the central custom of every English home—is devalued in the Johnsons' home, where the teakettle and other provisions are frequently hidden and sometimes mislaid. As a result, all family members prepare their own tea whenever and however they can, and the ritual value of the occasion is lost. In the absence of the stability that rituals of all sort help to provide, Mrs. Johnson's cry at the end of the first scene of the third act seems to summarize the plight that is Storey's persistent theme: "Oh. What it is to have a family. What it is to be a woman: what it is to be a mother. What it is to have no redress. (*Weeps.*)" (*MD*, 252). Like Mrs. Shaw in *In Celebration*, Mrs. Johnson has been scarred by the death of her first son, which reintroduces the theme of "atonement for sexuality" that is prominent in Storey's other "family" plays. The dead child, like Jamey Shaw, has been enshrined in the mother's memory, and his siblings suffer in comparison; the sole exception is her youngest son, whom she identifies—and sometimes confuses—with the brother who died. Like Steven Shaw and Arthur Slattery (who were also youngest children), Gordon Johnson is an unpublished writer and his mother's favorite, in whom she vests incredible and disproportionate expectations. The complaints made by the aged Slattery about his children in *The Farm* are even more applicable to the Johnsons and their tenants, all of whom are certainly "free and easy. Responsible to bloody nowt" and therefore "emblematic of the modern age" (*TF*, 76). The Johnson household offers no haven from the chaotic modern world, since anarchy prevails within the home as well as outside it, as Storey himself has acknowledged: "They are a family who intrinsically invert every decent value. But I think they're genuinely a microcosm of English life with their delusions, illusions and fantasies, and their inveterate capacity to live in the past. * * * Everybody involved in it is screwing everybody else, which is a reflection of the world we live in."[29] The Johnsons' obsession with lineage, peerage, and antecedents fulfills—albeit in a weak and ineffective way—a major function of traditional religion: it places the individual's current situation within the perspective of transcendence, if not of eternity.

The juxtaposition of "great progenitors" and modern "lesser men" was a prominent theme in *The Restoration of Arnold Middleton*, in which (more subtly than in *Mother's Day* with its deJohns and Johnsons) the central character's name also achieved an ironic effect: the beleaguered history teacher of Storey's first play bore the name of the most notable English educators of the nineteenth century (Arnold) as well as the name

[29]Quoted in Oleg Kerensky, *The New British Drama: Fourteen Playwrights Since Osborne and Pinter* (London: Hamish Hamilton, 1977) 12.

of the Earls of Monmouth (Middleton), great military "progenitors" of the sixteenth through eighteenth centuries. There is, of course, no such subtlety in *Mother's Day*—and it would in fact be inappropriate in a farce, since the genre is seldom conducive to subtlety or substantial thematic development. Accordingly, *Mother's Day* reiterates a number of Storey's central themes without exploring new implications or additional dimensions of them. Insofar as a new theme is developed on the significance of language as a means of self-definition, it tends to be overwhelmed in the clamorous and scandalous developments of the plot, and it has gone unnoticed by reviewers of the play.

Oleg Kerensky, who is one of the few critics to have praised *Mother's Day*, has claimed that "if it had been a hitherto undiscovered piece by Orton, it would probably have been hailed as another of his comic masterpieces."[30] Yet, despite its superficial similarities to several of Orton's plays, it seems highly unlikely that *Mother's Day* could be mistaken for an unknown work by Orton, since Storey's play lacks both the epigrammatic wit and the satiric iconoclasm that were Orton's most distinctive characteristics. Yet, even though the play suffers in comparison with almost any of Orton's farces, it is not a play that should be "consigned to the wastebasket" either. More than any of Storey's other plays, *Mother's Day* sets forth the consequences of the devaluation of the modern family, wherein "every decent value" is beleaguered if not subverted as a result. The play also demonstrates anew the author's willingness to attempt a variety of literary modes, exploring and reshaping his subject matter by adapting the conventions of traditional dramatic forms. Although not all of these efforts have been equally successful, Storey's versatility and his willingness to accept the risks inherent in such experimentation are noteworthy in and of themselves. Accordingly, *Mother's Day* is at least a creditable experiment—a significant attempt to extend the playwright's abilities and the already substantial range of traditional dramatic forms that he has mastered. Within his canon, however, it remains at best a minor work.

[30]Kerensky 12.

CHAPTER 5

"Ordinary People, Really":

Home, Sisters, and *Early Days*

Whereas *Mother's Day* depicts the disintegration of the family and the inversion of its traditional values, the subject of *Home* is the void that is left by the family's disappearance. Despite their chats about assorted (usually eccentric) relatives, the five lonely characters in *Home* have no real families: they have been abandoned by their spouses and their children, confined in an asylum, and forsaken, left to their own meager—if not deficient—resources, passing their time idly and awaiting death. *Home* is the most elegaic of Storey's plays and in many ways the most evocative, as the plight of its characters becomes a metaphor not only for contemporary England but for the human condition as well.

The nature of the "home" in which the characters reside is revealed only gradually as this entirely plotless play proceeds. The opening scene of the first act consists of a lengthy and rather mundane conversation between Harry and Jack, two well-dressed and congenial men who meet at an outdoor table and pass time discussing the weather, their health, their relatives, and various acquaintances who pass into their view (though unseen by the audience). In the following scene, two women occupy the table as the men stroll the grounds, and the nature of the "home" becomes clear: one of the women has had her belt and shoelaces taken from her lest she attempt suicide again, and the other smashed every breakable object in her family's house. During the second act in which the foursome is occasionally joined by a partially lobotomized former wrestler who obsessively lifts the iron furniture to prove his strength, various secrets and unconfronted truths are willfully exposed among themselves, albeit without effect, for the characters themselves are already near despair.

The title of the play reveals a fundamental irony that becomes clearer as the work is juxtaposed against Storey's "family" plays, even though the characters' families are conspicuously absent: because they have no "home" wherein they could find the support and refuge that the family traditionally provided, these men and women have been placed in an institutional "home." No longer a "haven in a heartless world," the "home"

118

has become an agency of the society from which the traditional "family home" formerly provided refuge. Administered and regulated by the state through its impersonal and dehumanizing bureaucracy, the very *meaning* of the word "home" has been transformed: the home no longer merely *offers* asylum but *is* an asylum—a wholly secular institution, a manifestation of the desacralized world, the ultimate product of the stresses, pressures, and strains that rend the families in Storey's other plays.

As Carol Rosen has shown in her study entitled *Plays of Impasse: Contemporary Drama Set in Confining Institutions* (Princeton, 1983), *Home* is one of a surprisingly large number of recent plays that depict life within a mental asylum (or other such place of involuntary confinement) as a metaphor for the larger society of which it is a part. Often, in their various and disconcerting ways, such plays "hold the mirror up" *not* so much to "nature" as to the ostensibly "normal" culture, whose outcasts and discards inhabit the confined world, forming there a community of sorts and a subculture of their own. Yet, in contrast to Peter Weiss's *Marat/Sade* or Bernard Pomerance's *Elephant Man*, for example, in which the reasons (mental and physical, respectively) for the confinement are apparent from the outset, Storey's play relies on an unusual method of deferring the disclosure of the actual nature of the "home" that is being portrayed; that is, in order for the play to be effective, the audience's recognition of the characters' situation must be only gradually revealed.[1] Consequently, as Storey remarked in a conversation with Ronald Hayman, the numerous critics who disclosed the nature of the "home" in their reviews

did a disservice to the play in saying that it was about a nuthouse. In fact it's not the material of the play itself and to say it's a mental home is a way of distancing the critics and audience from the play. It sets you away from the emotion, from the suffering, whereas the characters, I would think, are what you might see in the street any day. I mean they really are with us, rather than apart from us, and to stress the metaphor of the mental home rather distorts the play. I wouldn't think any of the characters are actually mad. . . . There is a sort of disclaimer really when it becomes firmly a play about a mental home.[2]

[1]As Carol Rosen points out, however, Storey's use of the deferred disclosure of the nature of the asylum is not unique: "A suggestive parallel to Storey's setting in *Home* may be found in Ibsen's last experimental play, *When We Dead Awaken*, as well as in Marguerite Duras's new-wave novel of elliptical reality, *Destroy, She Said*, trans. Barbara Bray (New York: Grove Press, 1970). Terrence McNally's play, *Bad Habits* (1974), parodied this kind of sanatorium" (*Plays of Impasse: Contemporary Drama Set in Confining Institutions* [Princeton: Princeton University Press, 1983] 291, n. 47). A similar strategy of deferred disclosure is also featured in Robert Weine's film *The Cabinet of Dr. Caligari* (1919).

[2]Ronald Hayman, "Conversation with David Storey," *Drama* 99 (Winter 1970): 49, 52.

Before the establishment of the welfare state and the disintegration of the family, such people *would* have been "outside," their care being considered the responsibility of their families, since his characters are not, as Storey points out, dangerously "mad."

In another way, the casting decisions for the English and American productions of *Home* may also have provided a "disclaimer" for the play, without actually having done a "disservice" to it. In the roles of Harry and Jack, respectively, Sir John Gielgud and Sir Ralph Richardson received virtually unanimous critical acclaim, and their consummate skill and personal rapport brought out the full poignancy of Storey's deliberately mundane dialogue. The accolades accorded them in London were equaled, if not surpassed, when they appeared in the New York production, and the play was included in the Public Broadcasting System's "Great Performances" series, further establishing theirs as the definitive version of the play. Yet because both actors were nearing seventy years of age when the play was first performed in 1970, audiences might plausibly have inferred that the "home" in which the characters reside is an "old-age home" as well as an asylum—and that the men's melancholy reveries and lachrymose silences are symptoms of senescence. Such is clearly not the case, however, as the published script reveals: Harry is described as "a middle-aged man in his forties" (*H*, 9), and Jack seems to be approximately the same age, since their memories of events (like their opinions and attitudes) virtually coincide. Certainly, the presence of markedly younger actors in the central roles would have a tremendous impact on the overall effect of the play, making the characters and their problems far more "like us" (for most of the audience) than like one's parents or grandparents. During my interview with him, Storey agreed that such casting would lead to "a completely different interpretation," adding that

> I would have thought they [Gielgud and Richardson] made their sadness more accessible, being elderly, because you can say "Well, that's the end of the line" and they look back, and so on. With middle-aged men it might have been more difficult. I've never seen a production like that. There've been a lot of productions of it, but I've never actually seen one where it was played by much younger actors. Actually, I've never seen any other production except that one. I can't relay what one looks like. It must be basically quite different.

Like the protagonists of *Pasmore*, *Life Class*, and *The Restoration of Arnold Middleton* (and like the institutionalized wife of the narrator of *A Temporary Life*), the characters in *Home*—both the men and the women—reached the crisis in their lives while still "in their prime." For them, however, there can be no sudden "restoration" in the company of a spouse (as there was for Arnold Middleton), no imminent return to the workaday world (as there was for Steven Shaw), and no consolation in the postures and pretenses of avant-garde art (as there was for Andrew Shaw and Allott). Instead, the characters of *Home* have been vanquished in their efforts to cope with life, isolated from—and forsaken by—family and friends who remain outside the institution, and abandoned to a monotonous confinement ending only at death, to which they are resigned.

The plight of the characters in *Home* is hardly less bleak than any in Samuel Beckett's plays, though the causes of their anguish are primarily social rather than cosmological—and its depiction is realistic rather than "absurd." Even though the play typifies the "poetic naturalism" that Storey established as uniquely his own style in *The Contractor* and *The Changing Room*, a remarkable number of Beckettian themes and motifs recur throughout *Home*—although Storey characteristically denies any familiarity with Beckett's works at the time that he was writing his own. The women in Storey's play particularly resemble some of Beckett's characters in a number of details, however: like Gogo in *Waiting for Godot*, Kathleen complains of her painfully ill-fitting shoes; like Winnie in *Happy Days*, Marjorie puts up a worn umbrella although there is no rain. Like many of Beckett's characters, too, they pass their time in idle theological speculation and pointlessly systematic nonreligious beliefs, considering at one point in their uneventful day whether the Second Coming will occur on one of their lucky days:

KATHLEEN. If he ever comes again I hope he comes on Whit Tuesday. For me that's the best time of the year.

MARJORIE. Why's that?

KATHLEEN. Dunno. Whit Tuesday's always been a lucky day for me. First party I ever went to was on a Whit Tuesday. First feller I ever went with. Can't be the date. Different every year.

MARJORIE. My lucky day's the last Friday in any month with an 'r' in it when the next month doesn't begin later than the following Monday.

KATHLEEN. How do you make that out?

MARJORIE. Dunno. I was telling the doctor that the other day.

(*H*, 38)

Later, they ponder the sacrament of marriage and the fact that Christ had no wife and family of his own (a theme that is also discussed at length in *Radcliffe*):

KATHLEEN. [Marriage is] Not natural ... One man. One woman. Who's He think He is?

(HARRY *looks round.*)

No ... Him. (*Points up.*)

121

HARRY. Oh, yes.

KATHLEEN. Made him a bachelor. Cor blimey: no wife for him.

HARRY. No.

KATHLEEN. Saved somebody the trouble.

HARRY. Yes.

KATHLEEN. Does it all by telepathy.

HARRY. Yes.

(*H*, 58)

Like the characters in *Endgame* and *Krapp's Last Tape*, Harry and Jack are particularly burdened by their awareness of time (another recurrent Beckettian theme):

HARRY. The past. It conjures up some images.

JACK. It does. You're right.

HARRY. You wonder how there was ever time for it all.

JACK. Time ... Oh ... Don't mention it.

(*H*, 8)

Furthermore, like all of Beckett's characters, the men realize the rarity—if not the impossibility—of genuine communication:

JACK. So rare, these days, to meet someone to whom one can actually talk.

HARRY. I know what you mean.

JACK. One works. One looks around. One meets people. But very little communication actually takes place.

HARRY. Very.

JACK. None at all in most cases!

HARRY. Oh, absolutely.

JACK. The agonies and frustrations. I can assure you. In the end one gives up in absolute despair.

HARRY. Oh, yes. (*Laughs, rising, looking off.*)

(*H*, 21)

Isolated from other individuals by the failure of communication, man is no less isolated from God—a fact that caused Jack to abandon a prospective career as a priest:

JACK. I could never ... resolve certain difficulties, myself.

HARRY. Yes.

JACK. The hows and wherefores I could understand. How we came to be, and His presence, lurking everywhere, you know. But as to the "why" ... I could never understand. Seemed a terrible waste of time to me.

HARRY. Oh, yes.

(*H*, 20)

Because by their own admission they seem to have neared (if not actually to have attained) the point of "absolute despair"—something that no character of Samuel Beckett's ever achieves—their situation is more bleak than any in the exiled Irishman's works, since for Harry and Jack there seems to be no hope at all. They lack even the faint and tenuous reassurance provided, for example, by the appearance of the child at the end of *Endgame* or the promise—always unkept, always reiterated, hardly credible—that Godot will arrive tomorrow.

Despite the numerous similarities between *Home* and various works by Samuel Beckett, there are also a number of other literary affinities that reinforce Storey's themes, though none, he insists, were sources or conscious influences at the time he wrote the play. Nevertheless, Harry and Jack are certainly as ineffectual, effete, and abulic as J. Alfred Prufrock, and Harry (who is consistently self-deprecatory as he reflects on his past) describes himself with the Shakespearean metaphor that Eliot's character made famous:

HARRY. * * * No great role for this actor, I'm afraid. A little stage, a tiny part.

KATHLEEN. You an actor, then?

HARRY. Well, I did, as a matter of fact, at one time ... actually, a little ...

KATHLEEN. Here, little again. You notice?

HARRY. Oh ... You're right.

KATHLEEN. What parts you play, then?

HARRY. Well, as a matter of fact ... not your Hamlets, of course, your Ophelias; more your little bystander who passes by the ...

KATHLEEN. Here. Little.

HARRY. Oh ... yes! (*Laughs.*)

(*H*, 54)

Clearly, Harry is not Prince Hamlet, nor was meant by Storey to be: he does not even *appear* to be mad, unlike the Prince of Denmark, and he certainly has not lost his sanity as dramatically and demonstrably as Ophelia. Instead, like Prufrock, he is a "little bystander" who has been overwhelmed by the ordinary circumstances of life that he has been unable—or has not dared—to affect; for this reason, ironically, he has been confined to a "mental home." Even his name suggests a Shakespearean irony, since he so conspicuously lacks the boldness and intemperance of the Bard's best-known Harry, Hotspur in *Henry IV, Part I*. Similarly, his companion Jack has neither the robust vitality nor the jollity of his Shakespearean namesake from the same play, Jack Falstaff.

But for Storey's Jack there is also an intriguing analogue in another masterwork of modern literature: like Humbert Humbert, the narrator of Nabokov's *Lolita*, Jack is sexually attracted to prepubescent girls, although (again like Prufrock) he has apparently never acted on these impulses, as Harry discloses to Kathleen:

KATHLEEN. Your friend come in for following little girls?

HARRY. What ...

KATHLEEN. Go on. You can tell me. Cross me heart and hope to die.

HARRY. Well ... that's ...

KATHLEEN. Well, then.

HARRY. I believe there were ... er ... certain proclivities, shall we say?

KATHLEEN. Proclivities? What's them?

HARRY. Nothing criminal, of course.

KATHLEEN. Oh, no ...

HARRY. No prosecution.

KATHLEEN. Oh, no ...

HARRY. Certain pressures, in the er ... Revealed themselves.

KATHLEEN. In public?

HARRY. No. No ... I ... Not what I meant.

(*H*, 56)

The essential point about all of these characters—Prufrock, Humbert Humbert, Harry and Jack—is that, for all their eccentricities, frailties, and failings, they *are or at least appear to be* completely ordinary, typical, "representative" men; they are not particularly noticeable and certainly not certifiably "mad" or in apparent need of institutional confinement. The same is true of Kathleen, Marjorie, and even Alfred—the ex-wrestler who (like Mathew in *Cromwell*) may seem occasionally minacious but is evidently not so malevolent that he should necessarily be confined, since presumably (like Glenny in *The Contractor*) he could function adequately with appropriate care and within his limitations in some capacity (as a professional wrestler, perhaps) in the world outside. Such literary parallels, whether consciously inserted in the play or not, reinforce Storey's contention (quoted by William Lanouette in the *National Observer*) that the characters are "ordinary people, really" who are not "afflicted in any way more than anybody else is afflicted."[3]

The wellspring of the affliction of all of the characters in *Home*—and, by extension, of all other "ordinary people, really"—is the breakdown of the modern family. Jack, who reveals that he was one of seven children and is the father of two—epitomizes the radical transformation of family life that has occurred during his lifetime:

JACK. Large families in those days.

HARRY. Oh, yes.

JACK. Family life.

HARRY. Oh, yes.

JACK. Society, well, without it, wouldn't be what it's like today.

HARRY. Oh, no.

JACK. Still.

HARRY. Ah, yes.

(*H*, 23)

There remain vestiges of the traditions and institutions that were founded on the solidarity of the large family, but the characters' modern nuclear families have been easily split, with each member seeking independence and autonomy, often denying traditional responsibilities thereby. Jack has, in effect, been abandoned by his children, and he reflects rather ruefully on his erstwhile parental "responsibility. At times you wonder if it's worth it" (*H*, 32), since he seldom if ever hears from his "boy married. Girl likewise. They seem to rush into things so early these days" (*H*, 32). Similarly, Marjorie has lost contact with her daughter, whose birth she associates with the loss of her teeth:

MARJORIE. [A Pakistani dentist] Took out all me teeth.

KATHLEEN. Those not your own, then?

MARJORIE. All went rotten when I had my little girl. There she is, waitress at the seaside.

KATHLEEN. And you stuck here ...

MARJORIE. Don't appreciate it.

KATHLEEN. They don't.

MARJORIE. Never.

(*H*, 37)

[3]William J. Lanouette, "Digging Away, Storey Unearths a Biting Drama," *National Observer* 23 November 1970: 20.

Yet while the existence of children provides little if any consolation, the childless marriage—Harry's situation—yields no more satisfaction. Despite his professed "great faith in the institution of marriage as such" (*H*, 22), Jack contends that marital failure—like that of all else in an entropic world—is inevitable:

> JACK. My friend, I'm afraid, is separated from his wife. As a consequence, I can assure you, of many hardships ...
>
> MARJORIE. Of course ...
>
> JACK. And I myself, though happily married in some respects, would not pretend that my situation is all it should be ...
>
> KATHLEEN. Ooooh!
>
> JACK. One endeavours ... but it is the nature of things, I believe, that, on the whole, one fails.
>
> (*H*, 40–41)

Similarly, he laments the fact that "Respect for the gentler sex * * * is a fast diminishing concept in the modern world" and waxes nostalgic for "the time when one stood for a lady as a matter of course" (*H*, 48). Moments later, as Marjorie and Kathleen persist in finding crude double-entendres in even his most innocuous remarks (and thus prove themselves to be far from ladylike and therefore unworthy of the respect that Jack yearns to give), he begins to cry—though it may seem to many to be, as John Gielgud remarked in an interview with Dick Cavett on PBS, "for no apparent reason."

Even the deprivations and hardships of the war years seem preferable to the postwar condition, since, paradoxically, even though the war necessarily separated men from their families, it also strengthened family ties. Accordingly, Jack evokes an ideal of family life in his reminiscence of those times (a theme that is also prominent in *In Celebration*):

> JACK. * * * One of the great things, of course, about the war was its feeling of camaraderie.
>
> HARRY. Friendship.
>
> JACK. You found that too? On the airfield where I was stationed it was really like one great big happy family. My word. The things one did for one another.
>
> HARRY. Oh, yes.
>
> JACK. The way one worked.
>
> HARRY. Soon passed.
>
> JACK. Oh, yes. It did. It did.
>
> HARRY. Ah, yes.

126

JACK. No sooner was the fighting over than back it came. Back-biting. Complaints. Getting what you can. I sometimes think if the war had been prolonged another thirty years we'd have all felt the benefit.

HARRY. Oh, yes.

JACK. One's children would have grown up far different. That's for sure.

(*H*, 32)

Jack's frequent tears are not shed only for his bleak personal plight, nor are they solely for the passing of an old order with its traditional values and customs, nor even for the disintegration of the family. He weeps for "the way of the world" in postwar Britain and elsewhere, throughout the desacralized societies of Western civilization.

Among the consequences of the disappearance of the family in *Home* is the absence of meaningful rituals in the characters' lives. The monotonous routines that occupy their empty days are mere habits, patterned behavior that is neither particularly purposeful nor in any way "significant," conveying no status or confirming no specific role. As Storey himself has acknowledged, for these characters the sole source of personal "reassurance" (a traditional function of ritual) is madness itself—the ultimate "haven in a heartless world" for those who can find no other "refuge" in a desacralized society: "The point about insanity in *Home* [is that] insanity gives you the same kind of reassurance as work. It unifies your particular condition in an asylum. It's easy to generalise your condition in madness, you can inhabit it and become one with other people. It provides a reassurance to life which it wouldn't otherwise possess. The longer you stay bonkers, the safer you are."[4] *Home* is thus an elaboration of Arnold Middleton's remark that "Insanity ... is the one refuge I've always felt I was able to afford" (*RAM*, 87), even if its price is consignment to—and confinement in—a "home" that has none of the attributes that the word connotes. Indeed, as Storey remarked in another interview, confinement itself offers a sort of reassurance, since "the fact that the people can't go, they have to stay there, even if it's only a wholly voluntary basis, provides a structure that otherwise their lives simply wouldn't possess."[5] Even holidays and their attendant rituals and festivities have become meaningless for these "ordinary people, really": Kathleen blandly remarks that Christmas " 'S'happy time," while Marjorie recalls it primarily as the occasion when she "started crying everywhere [she] went" and "Didn't stop till Boxing Day" (*H*, 30). Similarly, Jack and Harry agree that Christmas has been devalued:

[4]Peter Ansorge, "The Theatre of Life: David Storey in Conversation with Peter Ansorge," *Plays and Players* September 1973: 35.
[5]Quoted in Lanouette 20.

JACK. Season of good cheer.

HARRY. Less and less, of course, these days.

JACK. Oh, my dear man. The whole thing has been ruined. The moment money intrudes ... all feeling goes straight out the window.

HARRY. Oh, yes.

(*H*, 18)

Yet, despite the enervation caused by the monotony of habit and the meaninglessness of commercialized celebrations and rituals, the perennial human *need* for ritual remains unabated.

In *Home*, this need is most evident in the behavior of Alfred, who obsessively lifts the metal furniture, testing (and thus confirming anew) his strength if not his status, his stamina if not his significance. Storey's stage directions specify that "ALFRED lifts the table up and down *ceremoniously* above his head" when he self-consciously performs for an audience, and he "lowers the table slowly, *almost like a ritual*" when the observer has gone (*H*, 52; emphasis mine). Alone, he continues "to wrestle with it as if it too possessed a life of its own" (*H*, 52), demonstrating (to the audience) that the impulse prompting this action fulfills a personal— albeit idiosyncratic—need that is unaffected by the presence or absence of others. But Storey rightly insists that Alfred's patterned and (to him) purposeful behavior is "*almost like* a ritual," since it cannot confirm status or significance as even the most idiosyncratic "actual" rituals do. The fact that the person performing this close approximation of a ritual has been partially lobotomized clearly indicates the primacy of the need for rituals within the human personality (or "spirit"), remaining unabated even when other mental faculties have been destroyed.

Like all worthwhile "minimalist" drama, *Home* allows a number of metaphoric interpretations, its characters and their situation becoming a synecdoche that can be elaborated in various suggestive ways. Whether a play permits such multiple meanings has become a criterion for Storey's own evaluation of his writing, as he explained to John Russell Taylor: "It seems to me that if, on reading something through, I know completely what it is about, then it is dead. It is when I feel that I don't really know what it is about that it lives—it lives for me almost in the measure that it escapes and refuses definition. . . . *Home* . . . rather mystified, but it had taken on an independent life of its own."[6] In an interview with Ronald Hayman, Storey suggested one such interpretation, whereby Harry and Jack embody two distinct personality types: "I see Jack as the residue of the extrovert who tried to live a decent life and get on with

[6]John Russell Taylor, "British Dramatists: The New Arrivals, III—David Storey, Novelist into Dramatist," *Plays and Players* June 1970: 23.

people and get out in the world and have a place in society, and Harry as the residue of the poor old artist, [who is] totally immobilized by his incapacity to make any sense of it all and is quietly fading away in delusion and murmuring and grief and a sense of his own loss but [having] no way of expressing it."[7] That Storey refers to his principal characters as "residue" and cites an artistic "incapacity to make any sense of it all" once again suggests links between this play and the "theatre of the absurd" in general and the works of Samuel Beckett in particular, despite Storey's consistent denials. Their techniques are quite different, however, since Storey's "poetic naturalism" (developed here on a nearly bare stage with only minimal props—primarily a white metalwork table and chairs) is more readily accessible than Beckett's stark and symbolic landscapes or interiors.

In comparison with a typical Beckett work, *Home* expresses a gentler melancholy, and its characters are more sympathetically and compassionately portrayed; yet though Storey's work is both more elegaic and more accessible, readers and theatregoers alike may well find *Home* in some ways even more bleak than Beckett's works. Specifically, the ending of Storey's play lacks even the faintest hope or reassurance. When, during our conversation about the plays, I mentioned that *Home* seems to end in complete despair, Storey replied that

> my work tends to do that, really. I don't know why, but it all ends up rather the same. . . . You know, that's true! I don't think it's a merit of the work. I think it's a liability, really. I think in any work of art there should be *some* kind of affirmation. I mean, even in Shakespeare's tragedies there's an expansiveness. I don't feel as though *they*'re plays of despair, whereas these plays I feel *are* plays—and novels—of despair. At least I find them so.

As he does so often within his plays themselves, Storey evokes the grandeur and greatness of the more heroic past—of Shakespeare's plays no less than Arnold Middleton's knight's glories or Cromwell's vain attempt to unite spiritual and political action—as a standard against which the "liabilities" of contemporary life and art become more clear.

In discussing the elegaic tone of the play and the characters' weeping "for no apparent reason" as some (including John Gielgud) have contended that they do, Storey remarked that "there is within that play an inexplicable sadness which actually the text doesn't give you sufficient to explain or suggest about." In fact, however, the tears shed by Harry and Jack at the end of *Home* (like those of Tolstoy's Ivan Ilych) are the overwhelming and cumulative effect of a number of specifically identifiable problems, which extend far beyond the afflictions of their personal lives and the deprivations of their family life. In many ways, for

[7]Hayman 53.

example, Jack and Harry embody the faded glories and lost greatness of the specifically English past and the empire that has been dissolved within their lifetimes:

JACK. This little island.

HARRY. Shan't see its like.

JACK. Oh, no.

HARRY. The sun has set.

(*H*, 76)

Confident that their "ideals of life, liberty, freedom, could never have been the same—democracy—well, if we'd been living on the Continent, for example" (*H*, 17), they remain quintessentially English, even though (reiterating a favorite theme from *The Restoration of Arnold Middleton*), they recognize that there are now no heroic figures, no embodiments of spiritual greatness in the modern world. Yet surprisingly, whereas Arnold Middleton cited kingship and knighthood (i.e., military leadership akin to that discussed in *Cromwell*), Harry and Jack hearken back to *intellectual* leaders—Darwin, Newton, Milton, and Raleigh (*H*, 75–76)— to supply the standard by which inhabitants of the twentieth century (whatever their nationality) may be measured and found wanting.

Unable to understand the "why" of the ultimate spiritual reality, unable to articulate (save rare exceptions) the reality that they *can* (within limits) understand, unable to act with the conviction of past generations, and, indeed, unable to form any convictions on which to act, the characters of *Home* —like those in the final scene of Shaw's *Heartbreak House*—await rocket-borne annihilation "when[ever] the next catastrophe occurs" (*H*, 26). They know full well that they—and all other "ordinary people, really"—are powerless to prevent it. Until then, or until death by more natural causes—that is to say, whichever annihilation comes first—they can only weep, as the men do at the end of the play, surveying again the modern vista from their asylum "home":

HARRY. See the church.

(*They gaze off.*)

JACK. Shouldn't wonder He's disappointed. (*Looks up.*)

HARRY. Oh, yes.

JACK. Heart-break.

HARRY. Oh, yes.

JACK. Same mistake ... won't make it twice.

HARRY. Oh, no.

JACK. Once over. Never again.

(H, 78–79)

As the light slowly fades at the end of the second act of *Home*, Harry and Jack weep because of their helplessness, their loneliness, their isolation from their families, the remoteness of God, the near impossibility of meaningful communication, and the eventual failure of all human undertakings. In short, they weep because of the modern human condition; few literary works have ever summarized it so well.

As in *Home*, the audience's gradual realization of the nature of the "home" depicted onstage provides much of the dramatic interest in the first two of the three acts of *Sisters*—one of Storey's least-known works. After its initial production at the Royal Exchange Theatre in Manchester in September 1978, the play was not transferred to London, nor has it been commercially produced in the United States. Mistakenly identified as one of Storey's first works in some of its few reviews, *Sisters* in fact resembles a number of the plays from the middle period of his career and seems likely to have been written at some time after *Life Class* and *Mother's Day* , though he does not now recall a specific date. Although it depends on the same technique of gradual realization that is used in *Home*, *Sisters* is not a minimalist work; its set, like that of *In Celebration*, is a realistically detailed "living-room of a parlour-house: i.e., a [government-owned] council house that has both a downstairs sitting-room and a living-room" and is somewhat more of a "conventional middle-class house" than that of the elder Shaws in the other play (*S*, 59). The plot of *Sisters*, like that of *In Celebration*, involves a reunion of family members, though there is no generational conflict in this play, since the sisters meet after a seven-year separation during which both parents have died. Nevertheless, a number of Storey's familiar themes of family life—and the consequences of the modern lack of family stability—are reiterated in *Sisters*, even though the play adds relatively little that is new.

The play begins with the unexpectedly early arrival of Adrienne Stanforth, the long-lost sister (now in her early thirties), at the home of Carol Lomax and her husband Tom, a "very rough" ex-football player who has been married once before. Arriving by taxi, Adrienne is met by Mrs. Donaldson, the next-door neighbor (a character who closely resembles Mrs. Burnett in *In Celebration*), who tends house for the younger married couple and is in effect their surrogate mother; in fact, she prefers to be referred to as Mother, sometimes shortened to "More." When Carol returns, she greets her sister cordially, although sources of strain soon become apparent as the exposition of the family background proceeds. Adrienne's two-year-old divorce from a newly successful husband, her

131

failure to attend the funerals of her mother and father, and her unful-filled desires for success of her own are all briefly disclosed, and an underlying source of tension between them soon becomes apparent:

> CAROL. * * * [When Adrienne left home] I thought, "That *cow*. She's all I've got left. She's gone off to live this wonderful life." There I was, landed with Father, landed with Mother: both quite ill in their ways and *covered* with debts: Father with his ridiculous schemes for making money and Mother with her endless schemes for spending it.
>
> ADRIENNE. I left home, I suppose, to get away from it. I was eighteen at the time, Carol, and you were what? Twelve? I couldn't stand the delusions: I couldn't stand the mediocrity: I couldn't stand those provincial people with their primness and complacency and their sickening, stifling self-righteous-ness. I felt if I didn't get out I would never breathe.
>
> (*S*, 72)

Furthermore, a rather stereotypical difference soon emerges between the practical sister who remained at home and the imaginative "dreamer" who escaped its confines:

> CAROL. You were such a dreamer, Aid.
>
> ADRIENNE. I don't think so.
>
> CAROL. Oh, I don't mean in any passive sense. But those schemes: those wonderful fantasies. Do you remember lying in bed at night: how I'd come into yours when it got very cold and you used to cuddle me and tell me stories?
>
> ADRIENNE. I don't remember that at all.
>
> CAROL (*brightly*). You must remember. I could never forget a thing like that!
>
> ADRIENNE. I ... There are so many things I don't remember.
>
> CAROL. Don't want to remember.
>
> ADRIENNE. I was never very happy at home.
>
> (*S*, 70)

At the end of the first act, two additional women arrive—Joanna and Beryl, who are described as "intermittent paying guest[s]" (*S*, 83) and about whom Tom had earlier asked whether "anyone [had] booked in" (*S*, 78). Complaining that "last night was an absolute dead loss" (*S*, 85) and nibbling snacks that "Mother" has prepared, they plan to bathe before their evening begins—and the act closes with Beryl's declaration that "If you ask me that girl [Adrienne] has brought us trouble" (*S*, 86).

At the beginning of the second act, later the same evening, Adrienne enters to meet Terry, a twenty-three-year-old geography teacher who explains that he does not live in the house permanently, though various "people come in from time to time" (*S*, 88). Like Arnold Middleton, he holds forth at considerable length on his academic subject and its implications for modern life, and his reflections, like Allott's (though with less poetic compression), evoke a sense of abandonment in space and time:

> I like to get to the root of everything. There *is* a root to everything. For instance: the world came out of nothing—a fact like that, by calculation, can't be true. Nothing is as impossible to imagine as a new colour. Something has always been there: something always will be there. * * * When I have a personal problem * * * I think, "Ten thousand years ago this place wasn't even here: I wasn't here: this problem wasn't here. In another ten thousand years it's not unlikely it won't be here again. I won't be here. Whatever I was will be a handful of dust, a number of ill-assorted chemicals. In God knows how many aeons of time after that the earth itself won't even be here: what price our unhappiness—what price our problems then?" (*Laughs.*) An envelope of gas and debris slowly swirling around the sun. (*S*, 93–94)

Though its final image is similar to Allott's more evocative "dirge for a forgotten planet," Terry's reflection on the transitoriness of human existence is neither particularly original nor particularly profound. His reflections on religion, however, are somewhat more refined than those of Arnold Middleton; confiding to Adrienne that he has not "found [his] focus yet," he admits that he "thought he was" religious "for a time," but—like the characters in *Home*—he encountered certain difficulties:

> I'm never sure what religious means. If I could define it—like Christianity— I don't think I'd want to believe it at all. Christ made one or two crucial errors. I'd say he was part of an evolving consciousness: I think that's how modern psychology would describe it: not as a fixed point of reference, but as something evolving which, in many ways, we've already discarded. * * * In prayer one's talking to oneself. To those parts of oneself which are inaccessible in everyday life. But who would ascribe—who needs to ascribe—those obscure parts of oneself to God? I'm sure they're in *us* and have no extraterrestrial significance. (*S*, 93)

Promising Adrienne that "I may see you later" (*S*, 96), though he recognizes that she has not been "told * * * about this place" and is (by her own admission) confused by "this coming in and out: this living out of one another's pocket" (*S*, 94), Terry leaves to go upstairs as Joanna comes in after her bath. Though he introduces a number of Storey's familiar themes, his presence does little to advance the plot apart from adding to the mystery about the details of the house's actual domestic arrangements.

Shortly after Terry's departure, another male guest enters the room: Gordon Crawford, a policeman in his mid-forties, comes down from an upstairs room (where he has left his jacket) and tells Adrienne to get him a beer as he puts on his shoes and finishes dressing. After finding out some details of Adrienne's past (as she—quite improbably—tells this complete stranger about her divorce two years ago after four years of marriage and the miscarriage of a child), Crawford too learns that she does not know "what this house is" and "what's going on upstairs"— though he is rebuffed as he tries to put his arm around her. "They're all rough 'uns, in this house," he tells her, "Nice on top, but rough beneath. * * * In a place like this, sensitivity, tha knows, goes by the board" (*S*, 102). Nevertheless, they are planning a celebration—complete with decorated cake that "More" is said to be preparing "for a surprise. For a *homecoming*" (*S*, 104). Finally, Crawford discloses (in Adrienne's absence) the nature of the "house" that she is in:

> CRAWFORD. If she's living in a knocking-shop, I think somebody ought to tell her.
>
> CAROL. It's not a knocking-shop.
>
> CRAWFORD. It is in my book. And my book, I ought to tell you, is the law's.
>
> (*S*, 105)

Unlike the disclosure of the nature of the "home" in *Home*, however, this realization is neither particularly subtle nor especially emotionally affecting; nor does it require the audience to reassess the plights of the characters in terms of their own limitations and incapacitations, which *Home* so poignantly and gradually makes clear. Instead, the characters in *Sisters* proceed with a businesslike discussion of employment, scheduling, commissions, police rake-offs, and other various tricks of the trade, until Mrs. Donaldson enters with an iced cake decorated with four candles for the homecoming party. Amid taunts and slurs, before Adrienne comes down from her room, Crawford violently attacks Beryl, threatening to kill her as he is finally restrained by Terry and Carol. "We're held together, you see, like all the best social institutions, by our mutual dependency" (*S*, 113), Terry remarks, as Crawford and Carol's husband exchange threats of exposing each other's involvement in the business. Finally, Adrienne enters, elegantly dressed; delighted with the cake, she joins Carol in making a wish and, as the stage is darkened (lit only by the candles), they blow out the candles; when the lights are turned on again, they cut the cake together, as Adrienne summarizes one of Storey's most recurrent themes: "It's not often in life you have anything to celebrate: the prodigal's return: the family united: the discovery of friends ... the feeling that life after all has got a purpose" (*S*, 115). Unlike the celebratory rituals in Storey's other plays, the one in *Sisters* is partially depicted on stage; the party continues as Adrienne proposes a rather lengthy toast "to all we might have missed and have now retrieved ... to now," and she dances gracefully with Terry as the others "watch with surprise, admiration, and pleasure" (*S*, 116) as the second act of the play ends.

The third act occurs on the following morning and begins with the set in disarray as Mrs. Donaldson begins to clear away the mess. Discord among the characters matches the disarray, however, as Carol's husband quarrels with Terry over the latter's having to pay for food, room, and services of the night before. Shortly thereafter, Tom is confronted by Adrienne in an unexpectedly blunt conversation:

ADRIENNE. Does my sister sleep with men for money?

TOM. What do you think I am? A *pimp*?

ADRIENNE. I thought that's what you were. [*Direct, yet flinching*].

       *

TOM. I'm in business.

ADRIENNE. What business?

TOM. I hire pleasure out.

ADRIENNE. Do you hire my sister out?

TOM. ... Your sister helps to run this place. Your sister is a businesswoman.

ADRIENNE. I have a little money, you see.

TOM. What?

ADRIENNE. Not much. A little. In addition to which I have the prospect of a great deal more.

       *

TOM. This trip up here I can see has been no accident. What are you here for? To open a provincial branch?

ADRIENNE. You could call it that.

       (TOM *gazes at her; she gazes at him.*)

TOM. I'm onto your wavelength: you realize that.

ADRIENNE. I think we understand one another, if that's what you mean.

       *

ADRIENNE. You're very insecure.

TOM. Am I?

ADRIENNE. I think so. I wonder why it is.

TOM. I'm so insecure (*leaning over her*) I could put this in your face right now (*Bunches his fist before her.*)

       (*S*, 123–25)

135

Instead, however, he inflicts his violence on his wife during an offstage argument and confrontation, after which she enters the room, clearly having been abused; in his absence, Mrs. Donaldson reveals that Carol is nearly five months pregnant.

When the other characters have left to return to their jobs and homes and Carol and Adrienne are alone together, the play's final revelation occurs. Adrienne discloses that she has run away from a mental home, having allegedly been placed there by her husband, who is supposedly a famous actor (though this appears to be an alcohol-induced fantasy about a man to whom she actually has never been married and presumably does not even know). Hospitalized after taking an overdose of medicine, grief-stricken over the death of her child, finding herself abandoned by her husband (if any) and her friends, she escaped the mental home before the wards closed for the night. After the previous night's party, she continues, Tom came to her room instead of his wife's, and Carol goes out to confront him. In the interim, Crawford returns to attempt another liaison with Adrienne, who rebuffs him again; while he is there, an unmarked car pulls up outside the house, bringing medical personnel who, having located the address of her next of kin, have come to return Adrienne to the asylum. Despite her desperate pleas to remain with her sister and the others, she goes through the door voluntarily but screams as she is apprehended by the (unseen) attendants. "Well," Tom remarks in the ironic final line of the play, "Back to reality again, I reckon" (*S*, 148).

Inevitably, the final act of the play invites unfavorable comparisons with Tennessee Williams's *Streetcar Named Desire*. Furthermore, as David Mayer suggested in his review in *Plays and Players*,

> The play does provoke speculation about the literary and dramatic influences on this playwright. How much Storey draws on the shape and content of works he had seen or read and since erased from conscious memory is far from certain, but I cannot shake the feeling . . . that this play bears an uncomfortably close resemblance to Tennessee Williams' *A Streetcar Named Desire* transported and translated from New Orleans . . . to an anonymous semi on a bleak council estate somewhere in the North Midlands.[8]

Indeed, there are a remarkable number of parallels in the plots of the two plays: the reunited sisters are approximately the same age in both works; in each, a loutish husband brutalizes the neurotic sister after a birthday party (though the one in Storey's play is only birthday*like*); allegations of tragic marriages figure prominently in both works, as does prostitution; each features a character's retreat into the "safety" of mad-

---

[8]David Mayer, "*Sisters*," *Plays and Players* November 1978: 21.

ness (a theme that recurs in *Home, The Restoration of Arnold Middleton*, and *Life Class* as well); and finally, of course, each play culminates in the central character being forcibly returned to the asylum. Yet, in part because Williams's work has become so familiar since its premiere in 1948, the events in Storey's play (produced exactly thirty years later) seem unlikely to shock or even to surprise; furthermore, Storey's characters invariably suffer in comparison to their well-known counterparts in the earlier play.

Beyond the similarities to *A Streetcar Named Desire*, however, a second set of literary affinities is almost equally prominent in the first two acts of Storey's play: in many ways, the situations and characters of *Sisters* also resemble those of Harold Pinter's *Homecoming* (1964) and *Birthday Party* (1958), though Storey has repeatedly denied any knowledge of Pinter's works at the time he was writing his own. Adrienne's transformation—from a seemingly respectable middle-class woman into a prospective partner in a brothel—is essentially the same as that of Ruth in *The Homecoming*; furthermore, Adrienne's confrontation with Tom over his alleged insecurity is particularly reminiscent of Ruth's skillfully swift domination over Teddy, the pimp in Pinter's play. Mrs. Donaldson may well remind the reader or theatregoer of Meg from *The Birthday Party*, particularly when she brings the cake for the party and lights the candles in the darkened room—and that play, too, ends with the central character being forcibly taken away from his familiar surroundings. Because it provides another well-known precedent for the conclusion of Storey's play (twenty years before the latter was produced), this is another similarity that invariably undermines the effectiveness—and the shock value—of *Sisters*, however coincidental or unintentional such resemblances may be.

Despite its similarities to the works of Williams and Pinter, *Sisters* does also reiterate a number of familiar themes of Storey's own. "Families are an illusion, Carol," Adrienne insists in her final speech of the play, adding that "You have to destroy them to stay alive" (*S*, 147)—a sentiment that was also voiced by Howarth in *Flight into Camden* and recurs in his other novels as well. Terry and Tom, as a teacher and a former professional athlete, respectively, represent the mind/body duality that so often appears in Storey's works; Terry, noted for his "facility with words," is accused of thinking himself "so superior" (*S*, 119), though he denies the charge and says that he particularly admires Tom's dancing—which Tom attributes to his athletic talent, though "finally, incontrovertibly, I was screwed up by a woman," his first wife (*S*, 119). Terry's evocation of the area's lake in neolithic times, though eloquent enough in its way, remains an uncompelling image of loss through temporal change; it lacks both the poignancy and the particularity of its counterpart in *The Farm*, for example—Slattery's recollection of the fields of his youth. Thus, although *Sisters* reiterates a number of Storey's major themes, it does little to advance or enhance any of them and therefore remains the least-known and least-produced of Storey's published plays.

Whereas the central characters in *Home* are, by their own admission, inconspicuous and "little" men who have achieved no particular prominence in life, Sir Richard Kitchen—the central figure of *Early Days*, Storey's most recently produced play (1981)—has attained a certain eminence and even a degree of celebrity in the course of his political career. Yet, in his old age, as details of his achievements are blurred by memory and imagination, if not by delusion or willful distortion, Kitchen has much in common with Harry and Jack in Storey's earlier play—particularly as they were portrayed by Sir John Gielgud and Sir Ralph Richardson (for whom the role of Kitchen was specifically created). Though he lives with his family and has a hired companion (whom he claims to believe to be a German spy or a Russian agent wanting him to defect), and though he retains a perverse cantankerousness that his abulic counterparts in *Home* lack, he shares with them the inevitable frailties and shortcomings that accompany advancing age, against which his personal eminence—like any other human achievement—ultimately pales. Whatever his professional accomplishments, his public record, and his contributions to history, he is ultimately, *personally* no less one of the "ordinary people, really," than Harry, Jack, Marjorie, Kathleen, and Alfred in *Home*. As Stephen Wall noted in his review of *Early Days* for the *Times Literary Supplement*, "Storey's work has often been at its best when he has tried to irradiate the ordinary, and he hasn't allowed his hero's celebrity to tempt him into assuming that top people are different. The point is rather that the old, whoever they are, are too like us for comfort."[9] Accordingly, very few specific facts about Kitchen's past are revealed in the course of the play; they, like details about the lives of his counterparts in *Home*, must be inferred from oblique references that may or may not be true. Much of the essential information about his career is deferred until the final brief scene of the play; most political facts about him are simply left undisclosed—and are as irrelevant to the theme and tone of *Early Days* as the body counts from (and even the winning sides of) the various battles are in *Cromwell*.

Such details would be suitable for Kitchen's memoirs, however, which he claims his daughter is writing for him, although he "can't remember anything" (*ED*, 13) apart from disjointed incidents from his childhood. One of these is recounted at the very beginning of the play: "At the seaside. Travelling in a coach beneath a bridge. I see the bridge, which is

---

[9]Stephen Wall, "Kitchen Agonistes," *Times Literary Supplement* 2 May 1980: 495.

really a footwalk, so high above me—it seems I have passed beneath it ever since. * * * At some point earlier in the journey I have been left alone on a station platform; or, find that I am alone and those that had been with me are there no longer" (*ED*, 11). Loneliness, abandonment, and the image of *passage* are among the most prominent themes that recur throughout the play. Yet in *Early Days*, such recollections tend to be used imagistically—without elaboration or explanation—rather than metaphorically; in this way they resemble the "images" of a past life recalled by various characters in Beckett's works (Winnie in *Happy Days*, the narrator of *How It Is*, and others) or in Pinter's later "memory plays" (e.g., *Old Times*, *No Man's Land*). Repeatedly, disjointed reflections on entropy, apparent "madness" in the "home," and modern purposelessness come to Kitchen's mind, as when he recalls (to his hired companion) the first time that he viewed the sea:

> KITCHEN. The first time I saw it I thought the edge of the world had come. I thought the world went on for good. It went on for bad, and came to an end. The sea broke up against the bad * * * .
>
> BRISTOL. We all have to come to an end.
>
> KITCHEN. I wonder. I walk around the house and I think, "The people here are mad. They go on as if they know what they are doing." They don't. No one does. Yet they go from A to B as if that's precisely what they intended.
>
> BRISTOL. We all have a destiny to fulfill.
>
> KITCHEN. I wonder. (*Pause.*)
>
> (*ED*, 12–13)

Like the characters in *Home*, Kitchen has come to doubt whether there is a meaning or purpose in life—or any significance in any human events. His own political career—like the social achievements for which he has been knighted—can provide no consolation for him now. Though surrounded by members of his family and an attendant in their home, he faces the same temptation as Harry and Jack in *Home*: an overwhelming desolation, a capitulation to despair. Like them (and all other "ordinary people, really"), he ultimately must confront such meaninglessness alone.

The second scene of *Early Days* outlines the causes of the disappointments involved in Kitchen's political career, though few specific details are given. He recalls that once he "was almost the best, only a twenty-five-minute speech and a fifteen-second interview put an end to my career" (*ED*, 32), and he notes that "it's by opening my mouth too much that I lost the opportunity to become the leader of my party" (*ED*, 32). After his doctor leaves, having examined his patient, Kitchen's granddaughter arrives to tell him that she is soon to be married—an announcement that, as in Storey's other works, is joylessly received. Steven,

139

the fiancée, is another of the by-now-familiar "types" of Storey's plays—a poet who, though currently unemployed, intends to become a teacher. With a surprising vehemence that abruptly alters the tone of the scene from its earlier reminiscences of his granddaughter's childhood, Kitchen ardently opposes the marriage: "No artist in this world can afford to be married. Marriage is a commitment to life. Art is a commitment to self-aggrandizement" (*ED*, 36). His daughter should, he suggests, "Marry a man with a decent profession. Marry a mortician" (*ED*, 36). From the perspective of age and the disappointment of his unfulfilled political career, Kitchen foretells Steven's future in bleak and blunt terms:

> KITCHEN. * * * Beating and hardship will rid this young man of his poetical aspirations.
>
> STEVEN. It's a desolate world, Sir Richard. No art. No singing. No form of expression.
>
> KITCHEN. I did not construct this world. I was thrust into it, without warning, just like you. Having arrived, I didn't start painting pictures. I took a good look at what I saw. I didn't like it. I made a fuss. I got up and shouted. I became a liability. The world has very few. I became, in short, a pain in the arse. In the arse of the world I deployed my talents.
>
> (*ED*, 37)

Vindictively, Gloria repeats the accusation that he destroyed his wife, and she rebukes him as a *memento mori*:

> GLORIA. * * * Grandpa, we're not impressed. We do not approve of your party or its doctrine. The name of your party, old man, is Death.
>
> KITCHEN. Life! Life is what I've lived!
>
> GLORIA. Your achievements, Grandpa, are a pile of dust. The one person who loved you you callously destroyed, by doing the very things you accuse my father of, with your obscene calls and grotesque abuse and your promenading of your genitals in the village street. You used her, Grandpa, but you won't use us.
>
> (*ED*, 37–38)

Unlike the emotional confrontations in Storey's other plays, however, Gloria's outburst has a rhetorical shrillness unseen in Storey's writing since *Radcliffe*—the facile duality of capitalized abstractions (one character representing Life and the other Death, like the schema of Mind and Body in the early novel). Its belabored and blatant metaphor counteracts the author's customary technique of understatement. The scene concludes with Kitchen again alone (after additional brief conversations with Bristol and Gloria's mother), as he remarks that his existence in their home is "like living on an alien planet. I speak the language but no one listens. I make the signs but no one sees" (*ED*, 39-40).

The third scene of *Early Days* begins with characters sitting at a garden table upstage, though this one is of wood rather than metalwork (and thus unlike the one in *Home*). The family gathering—like its counterparts in *The Cherry Orchard* and *The Sea Gull*—is seemingly uneventful, as reminiscences and "small talk" are blended with occasional literary conversation. Steven reads one of his poems (entitled "Samson") to Gloria and her parents; his future mother-in-law offers polite though probably uncomprehending approval, but his fiancée disdains his reading aloud at all, which she terms his "spouting" (*ED*, 41). The modern-day Samson of Steven's poem is the devalued counterpart of his heroic namesake (as are Harry and Jack in *Home*); far from being a mighty man of action and slayer of Philistines (the avowed enemy of Storey's *other* teachers, Allott and Arnold Middleton), this Samson is newly shorn and therefore sapped of strength, reduced to just another of the "ordinary people, really," as he sees locks of his hair—intermingled with that of countless others in an egalitarian age—being hauled in a bin of debris from the barber's shop (which is itself a commercial, hence "philistine," enterprise). The modern Samson's question of "Where do our debris start?" (*ED*, 41) clearly echoes Arnold Middleton's desperate "... what are we now? Gropers in the debris of our ..." (*RAM*, 70). Bristol interrupts the parents' reminiscence about their college days after the war to announce that Kitchen is gone, probably having wandered off to the village. As the family members go off to search for him, the strains that his presence causes in the household become more apparent:

MATHILDA. He grasps at us. At times I feel he'll never let go.

BENSON. Oh, he'll let go. He'll have to. He'll not be here for ever. * * * We'll shove him in a strait-jacket if we catch him this time.

GLORIA. He's lived in one all his life: he's only now got out of it.

(*ED*, 43)

The lights dim upstage as the characters exit; downstage, Kitchen enters, lost and wondering whether it is "the village I've arrived at, or ... a place I knew as a child?" (*ED*, 44). When found by Steven, he claims he made an appointment with a thirty-five-year-old woman. After they exchange doggerel verses, Kitchen questions Steven's faith in the future and avers that "All the changes I've seen have been to the bad" and "The only relationship that counts is the one we hold with one another" (*ED*, 46)—a view that, like the final scene in *Cromwell*, seems to echo Arnold's "Dover Beach." Like his counterparts in *Home* and the father in *The Farm*, Kitchen has earlier observed the secularization that has occurred over the years,

141

though he seems more apathetic about it than most characters in Storey's plays; considering all systems of belief equally futile, he now finds a preference for none in particular:

KITCHEN. In my father's time they believed in God.

GLORIA. So what!

KITCHEN. Now all you believe in are ideals. As if anything has ever been changed by grasping at one faith instead of another.

(*ED*, 34)

Mathilda and the doctor next encounter Kitchen, who suggests that his daughter is romantically interested in the physician. Finally, Gloria comes in to return Kitchen to his home, and the scene ends as he repeats his dream of the childhood journey and the bridge, recalls his wife who "sacrificed her life" for him (*ED*, 48), and asks plaintively "Will you give me back the love I lost?" (*ED*, 49).

Although the final scene of the play is quite brief, occupying only three and one-half pages in the published script, it contains a number of crucial explanations that have been withheld earlier in the play. Gloria summarizes her father's career for Steven and reveals that her grandfather, unbeknownst to himself, has only a few months to live. Kitchen, who has been dozing at the garden table, wakens and summons Bristol to inquire about the servant's children, whom he had dreamed were dead. His daughter comes in to offer to move his chair into the shade and, in a reprise of one of the most poignant images in *Home*, she remarks that "the sun's going down," to which Kitchen replies, "It is" (*ED*, 51). Remarking that members of his family "come and go like ghosts" (*ED*, 51), Kitchen then begins a reverie that blends fragments of his past and present life with hallucinations of moving trees and a man who runs away after setting fires. Briefly coming to, he questions Bristol again, taking particular interest in the children:

KITCHEN. Are you ashamed of working for me?

BRISTOL. No, sir.

KITCHEN. What about the children?

BRISTOL. I doubt if they know who I work for, sir.

KITCHEN. Don't they know my name?

BRISTOL. No, sir.

KITCHEN. Do they know anything about me?

BRISTOL. No, sir.

KITCHEN. Do they know that I exist!

142

(*Pause.*)

BRISTOL. No, sir.

(*ED*, 52)

Having missed—or been deprived of—his opportunity to become a political leader whose name would perhaps live in history, Kitchen instead faces the unknown *as* an unknown, one of the "ordinary people, really"— exactly like his counterparts in *Home*.

Politically, Kitchen is clearly the antithesis of the Cromwellian figure: far from uniting political and moral actions in any decisive way, however catastrophic the consequences, his downfall occurred as a result of ill-chosen words rather than deeds, and his fate was summarily decided *for* him in a consensus of those whom Arnold Middleton characterized as "pygmies" or "lesser men" (*RAM*, 97), though they and their type dominate modern political life. As Gloria explains in the play's final scene,

> He joined the wrong party. At that time it believed in breeding. If he'd had a little he might have got on farther. He was the longest serving Minister of Health. Then he made a speech which was critical of his colleagues. He became a dark horse * * * an alternative leader * * * [but] when the time came to make his challenge he'd lost support. The pages of history closed on grandpa: he was given a knighthood and went into his act of being a cantankerous figurehead whom younger men looked up to and older men despised. Now he's the eldest: those who knew him are dead. (*ED*, 50)

Having arrived at the final "station" in his life's journey, he is—as his dream recounted earlier in the play suggests—"alone [,] and those that had been with me are there no longer" (*ED*, 11). Even his accomplishments as a Minister of Health—his political legacy—remain (like his name itself) largely unknown to the legatees. In the final moments of the play, as in the final days of his life, his mind returns to "what really matters": the childhood memory of the bridge and, more importantly, the woman he loved for so many years. The play ends as, in his reverie, he calls out her name.

Like the elderly Krapp in Beckett's *Krapp's Last Tape*, Kitchen finds that his earlier accomplishments are now less than memorable, however consuming they may have been at the time. Furthermore, in the same way that Kitchen reverts to a single experience of long ago and the woman he loved, Krapp recalls a moment of love in a boat:

> that memorable night in March, at the end of the jetty, in the howling wind, never to be forgotten, when suddenly I saw the whole thing. The vision, at last. This, I fancy, is what I have chiefly to record this evening, against the day when my work will be done and perhaps no place left in my memory, warm or cold, for the miracle that ... (*hesitates*) ... for the fire that set it alight.

143

What I suddenly saw then was this, that the belief I had been going on all my life, namely—(*Krapp switches off impatiently, winds tape forward*) * * * [10]

Each play renders its character's epiphany only obliquely, "the day when my work will be done" having come at last for the dying Kitchen (and, arguably, for Krapp too). Like Tolstoy's Ivan Ilych, each must revalue his life, recognizing at last—though too late, in many ways—the importance of a lost or neglected love and the vanity of the achievements that had been his preoccupations for so long.

Written in 1974, with the role of Kitchen conceived exclusively for Sir Ralph Richardson, *Early Days* was withheld from production at Storey's insistence, despite interest expressed by various theatre companies, including the Royal Court, New Haven's Long Wharf Theatre (which had produced the first American productions of *The Changing Room* and *The Contractor*), and Stratford Ontario's Shakespeare Festival. As Storey explained during our conversation,

> It was hanging around for six or seven years and at some stage I rewrote it, or rather, cut it down, and sent it to Ralph. . . . It went to Ralph on three separate occasions, and he declined to do it. Very nicely. . . . But it was written for him, and I couldn't see another actor making it work. . . . It ended up in the hands of Peter Hall at the National, where Ralph had a contractual obligation, I don't know for how long, that he would do two or three plays there. And Peter Hall said he would like him to do this. . . . Within a week Lindsay Anderson wrote from Los Angeles . . . in response to a letter from Ralph asking him were there any plays we could do together, and Lindsay wrote back suggesting *Early Days*, the same week that Peter Hall had. . . . Those two stimuli arrived within twenty-four hours, from what I can tell from what Ralph says. . . . And he thought, "Well, all right." . . . And so all those years eventually came to fruition in 1980–81.

In declining the offers of the play during the six-year interim between the initial offering and the eventual production at the National Theatre, Richardson's primary concern had been his physical stamina and the reliability of his own memory. As Storey remarked, "he got in touch with me and said his problem with the play wasn't the play, his problem was if he could remember it, and with committing it to memory and being onstage throughout. And really, he wanted to be persuaded that technically, you know, he could cope." Such concerns remained throughout the rehearsal period, as Garry O'Connor records in *Ralph Richardson: An Actor's Life*:

> Before the first out-of-town night, in Brighton, Storey found Ralph in the stalls looking "so old and tired, his wig all wrong." Imagining himself to be

[10]Samuel Beckett, *Krapp's Last Tape*, in *Krapp's Last Tape and Other Dramatic Pieces* (New York: Grove Press, 1960) 20–21.

entirely on his own, Richardson had sunk down in a stall seat, uttering in a tone of the deepest despair, "Oh, for a cup of hemlock!" He had then, realizing too late that Storey was still there, turned and looked aghast. But, Storey remembered, at that first night in Brighton, only an hour or two later, being amazed by Richardson's complete transformation . . . ; from being terrified out of his wits, pleasure irradiated his countenance . . . and the uncertainty he felt over remembering parts of the text became immaterial: he was in control of the dream.[11]

Such control, as many reviewers of the play noted, is in part the result of the fact that Kitchen's temperament is in many ways virtually the same as Richardson's own.

Accordingly, in creating Sir Richard Kitchen—the penultimate stage role of his career—Richardson gave what O'Connor has termed an "extraordinarily autobiographical performance."[12] Mercurial and cunning, independent and sly, with an eccentricity that may be feigned or real (or a combination of both) and an ability to exasperate that provides him an evident though furtive delight, Kitchen eludes the attempts of others to relegate him to a token existence by making him submit to their will or conform to their expectations; even in his old age, he remains, as his doctor remarks, "a bit of a rascal" (*ED*, 30). Rhetorically, too, Kitchen's habits are notably Richardson's own, as O'Connor points out: "in imitation, or exaggeration, of Richardson's own principle of counter-attack [in interviews as well as private conversations], Kitchen goes on the offensive, asking questions [and then] metamorphosing the answers into his own internal imagery."[13] As a result, Richardson's occasional lapses of memory and improvisations on Storey's already spare script (e.g., calling his son-in-law a "mollusc" or a "croissant" instead of a "fetish") made little difference, since the habits of Kitchen's mind were so like those of the actor portraying him. Furthermore, as O'Connor notes, "There are other elements in Richardson as a man and in Kitchen as a character which *Early Days* cunningly and successfully combines: the paranoia, the madness, the escape element, the desire to flee—we don't realize how odd he is, because he is 'so near to reality in his madness.' "[14] Seldom have character and actor been so ideally matched on the modern stage; in a play whose script is made deliberately spare to accommodate its actor's limitations of age and health, in a character whose past is sketched with only the most oblique details and whose present is poignantly and subtly revealed, in a performance that has fortunately been preserved for posterity on videotape, Ralph Richardson's portrayal of

[11]Garry O'Connor, *Ralph Richardson: An Actor's Life* (New York: Atheneum, 1982) 213.
[12]O'Connor 216.
[13]O'Connor 216.
[14]O'Connor 218.

145

Kitchen became an eloquent valediction, one of the most memorable performances of the latter portion of his long career.

With a running time of fifty-seven minutes (as opposed to seventy-five minutes for the stage version), the videotaped version of *Early Days* has been even further abridged, however. Apart from compression of the dialogue throughout the play and the removal of some repetitions and inessential remarks, most of the excisions have been made in the third scene. After he has wandered away from the family, Kitchen is found only by Bristol and Gloria before being returned home; the stage version's meeting with Stephen (during which the two exchange limericks) and his subsequent encounter with the doctor have been cut from the teleplay. In the second scene, Kitchen's remarks on the difference in generations— the exchange beginning with "In my father's time they believed in God" (*ED*, 34–35)—has also been deleted. A two-minute prologue has been added to the text in the televised version, in which Bristol and the members of Kitchen's family reminisce about him after his death—making the entire play into a flashback (the only one of Storey's plays to have such an altered time sequence).

When considered among Storey's other plays, whether in its longer or shorter version, *Early Days* occupies the same sort of position as *Krapp's Last Tape* among the plays of Samuel Beckett: each is a compressed, poignant, and threnodial portrayal of its central character's realizations of time, loss, and remembered love—though the potential sentimentality of each is undercut by the play's subtle irony and melancholy humor. Although both plays are considerably shorter than the full-length works for which their authors are better known, and although neither introduces particularly new themes among their respective authors' traditional concerns, each is a significant achievement in its own right and an important contribution to the tradition of "minimalist" theatre—a "plotless" but evocative play, a deftly drawn character study that presents, with surprisingly few lines and carefully selected significant details, an extraordinary and revealing portrait of its "ordinary" subject.

"Home is the place where, when you have to go there, / They have to take you in," wrote Robert Frost in "The Death of the Hired Man."[15] Yet, like Frost's hired man, Storey's characters in *Home* have no "home" and family in which to take refuge: "the place where, when you go there, they have to take you in" is, today, an asylum (in both senses of the word) that is administered and regimented by the state, where necessarily impersonal care is the entitlement of every citizen who can be bureaucratically certified to be "in need." Others, like young Arthur Slattery in *The Farm*, discover that even when there is a "home" and family to which

[15]Robert Frost, "The Death of the Hired Man," in *The Poetry of Robert Frost* (New York: Holt, Rinehart & Winston, 1969) 38.

one can return, "they" not only do *not* "have to take you in" but also may reject the prodigal outright. Not every homecoming is as futile as Arthur Slattery's, however, since the reunion in *In Celebration* successfully unites the Shaws during a few instances of ritualistic behavior, despite the hostilities and recriminations that break out throughout the day (and night). In *Mother's Day* not even the vestiges of such rituals remain, and the Johnson household degenerates into a sort of bedlam that is more anarchic than the literal asylum in *Home* where the perennial human need for ritual persists in approximated, surrogate forms. Storey's "family plays," when considered as a group, demonstrate again that the traditional sources of secular rituals—the home and family—have been devalued (much as their sacred counterparts have lost their meaning). The persistent, primal impulse for human beings to define their status and significance through patterned and purposeful behavior remains unabated, however. As a result, new and hitherto unrecognized forms of ritual must be found, and it is David Storey's most significant achievement as a dramatist to have presented two such "new" sources of ritual onstage, unadorned by plot or unrealistic contrivances, in *The Changing Room* and *The Contractor*.

CHAPTER 6

"Labor Ipse Voluptas Est":

The Changing Room and *The Contractor*

Fortunately, not all of the characters in Storey's plays share the bleak prospects and reconciliation to despair that the patients in *Home* epitomize, and the threnodial tone of that play—eloquent and affecting though it is—does not typify Storey's work. In fact, the characters in *Home* (like those in Beckett's works) embody the modern condition *in extremis*, their plight representing the ultimate consequences of certain social and spiritual tendencies (i.e., alienation, isolation, desacralization) that are widely acknowledged but seldom so starkly and effectively portrayed. Most of Storey's characters, however, display a remarkable resiliency that is conspicuously absent in *Home*: despite their social, psychological, and familial crises, the Shaws in *In Celebration* continue to cope with their various problems and return to their respective careers and obligations; Arnold Middleton achieves an incredibly sudden "restoration" that, however unconvincing it may seem, clearly denotes a renewal of his ability to cope, represented by his announced intention of returning to the classroom; Allott, though dismissed from his teaching position at the end of *Life Class*, ironically foresees "even greater" but unappreciated achievements in his future; and Proctor, the embattled hero of *Cromwell*, continues to pursue the distant, perhaps illusory, and certainly mysterious light that leads him onward as the play ends. A central climactic crisis is the pivotal event in the life of each of these characters, including those in *Home*; typically, it is an emotional breakdown that accompanies a long-suppressed familial confrontation and may coincide with some form of sexual aggression as well. Such an experience is inherently dramatic, offering even the classical "unity of action"—a central conflict or *agon*, a series of developing tensions, and a climactic confrontation. The latter may occur onstage (as in *The Farm* and *The Restoration of Arnold Middleton*) or offstage (as in *Life Class*, when Allott is confronted by his wife and, subsequently, dismissed from his job by the headmaster). Sometimes, as in *Home* the crisis has passed at some indeterminate time before the play begins; occasionally, like the anticipated clash between Andrew Shaw

148

and his mother (toward which *In Celebration* seems to build), the confrontation does not occur at all. Of course, the consequences of such conflicts—like the characters' means of responding to them—vary with the personalities of the characters themselves: most continue to cope in some way, although those in *Home* admit that they cannot do so and have instead resigned themselves to protective custody from the world by which they are overwhelmed.

The pattern of experience that makes all of these plays "dramatic" (conflict, complication, crisis, and resolution or resignation) also makes their characters' lives *atypical*, since most people's lives are not so structured; by extension, then, the experience that is thus presented may be considered unrepresentative, "artificially" contrived, and arguably even false. If the "problems within us" that Storey's plays consistently address are indeed pandemic, then their effects must be evident not only in the lives of those who confront some dramatic personal crisis but also among those whose lives are less sensational—or even wholly "ordinary." Such people are the subject of Storey's most innovative and most acclaimed plays, *The Changing Room* and *The Contractor*, in which no dramatic "plots," no core conflicts, and no climactic incidents are to be found. Instead, each play realistically depicts the ordinary events surrounding a common social situation: *The Changing Room* is a portrayal of the locker-room activities of a rugby team before, during, and after a match; *The Contractor* consists of the onstage construction of a tent prior to a wedding and, after the reception, the process of taking the tent back down. The apparent simplicity and plotlessness of the plays is deceptive, however, for each presents a series of intricately interrelated rituals (traditional and nontraditional, whether deliberately or unselfconsciously performed, secular or sacred) through which all of Storey's recurrent themes are reiterated. Furthermore, these unacknowledged and unrecognized rituals—these literally "invisible events" that comprise the play—have not been randomly selected for mere "slice-of-life" realism. Instead, when considered in terms of such works as Huizinga's *Homo Ludens* and Eliade's *Sacred and the Profane*, the central events of these two plays (i.e., the preparations for the rugby match and the construction of the tent) clearly recapitulate—and constitute the modern secular equivalents of—two of the oldest and most fundamental sacred rituals known to mankind.

The apparent and visible action of *The Changing Room* may be easily summarized. In the first act, the players on a professional rugby team enter their locker room, warm themselves at a coal fire, undress, don their pads and uniforms, and carry out the taping and binding that must precede the game; the act ends when, after some last-minute tactical advice from the trainer and a few words from the Club Chairman (i.e., the owner of the team), the players run onto the field. The second act begins before the first half of the game has ended, as the Chairman and the Club Secretary enter the locker room to warm themselves and chat with the team's janitor rather than watch the match; mid-way through the game, having tied the score, players return to the locker room, where one is given treatment for his injured hand and the others rest briefly and confer about strategy before returning to the field. Shortly thereafter, a player whose nose has been broken during the first scrum of the second half is carried into the locker room, where his wound is washed and dressed; a substitute takes his place on the field, gaining the first actual playing time of his professional career. The game continues as the second act ends. In the final act, the players bathe, dress, and congratulate themselves on their victory, noting in particular the auspicious beginning of their new teammate; after much coarse humor and horseplay in the bath, the players dress and leave as the play ends.

Surely, *The Changing Room* is among the least conventionally "dramatic" plays to have been presented on the modern stage: there is no major or sustained interpersonal conflict and no focal dilemma to form a central thematic action; the dialogue rarely rises above mundane banter and crude humor, and at the end of the play many theatregoers may feel that "nothing happened" during the entire play. Nevertheless, *The Changing Room* received considerable critical acclaim on both sides of the Atlantic and won the New York Drama Critics Circle Award for Best Play in 1971—not merely because it is a meticulously crafted "slice of life" but because, subtly but surely, through details of common experience, the essence of both the characters' lives and their society are tellingly—and poignantly—revealed. In *The Changing Room*, as surely as in any of Chekhov's plays, "subtext" is all. The true subject of the play is a crucial "invisible event"—a "change" of which clothing is merely an outward sign; it is a transformation in the lives of the players, occurring at the regular intervals of the scheduled matches but lasting no longer than their time together. Accomplished through rituals that are so familiar that they are unselfconsciously performed, this crucial but temporary "change" in their lives confers—and confirms—a significance that might well be absent from their lives otherwise.

The rugby match itself, the most obvious "event" in *The Changing Room*, remains unseen by the audience, since the game occurs "between the acts" and, of course, offstage. Like the anniversary dinner in *In Celebration* and the wedding in *The Contractor*, the game is little more than an official "occasion" for which the characters are assembled, a public event that prompts the actions depicted on the stage. Its effects—the mud stains, the injuries, the cuts and bruises—are apparent in the second and third acts of the play, but the reader or viewer learns surprisingly few details of the game being played. In fact, even the names of the teams are not disclosed; the team's sweatsuits are marked only with the word CITY, and the opponent is once referred to as "United." Yet, even though the audience is given few details (which are ultimately of little importance in the "real"—i.e., nonsports—world), it gains an intimate knowledge of the participants' lives. The majority of the team members come from the working class, although several are teachers at an unspecified university (i.e., members of the "professional" class). Despite occasional raillery about such differences—including the remark that one of the players is a "bloody college man ... [who is] going to go away disgusted with all you bloody working lads" (*TCR*, 70)—the differences among the players' backgrounds, educations, and interests are subsumed in the cooperative effort that teamwork requires. Such unity is, as Lionel Tiger remarks in *Men in Groups*, a consequence of the fact that "in team sports the group shares the risks involved. Team members will engage in conflict on behalf of their fellows—violence in team games is almost always inter- rather than intra-team. . . . They perform in terms of loyalty to their team as well as their own individual success."[1] Although class consciousness is overcome among the teammates, other social barriers remain intact: the owner of the team is always addressed as Sir Frederick, for example, despite his efforts at informality and his attempts at casual conversation with the players; at the other end of the social spectrum, the janitor works "anonymously, overlooked, almost as if, for the players, he wasn't there" (*TCR*, 83). From the peerage to the old-age pensioner, from the working classes and the "young professionals," the characters in Storey's changing room represent a cross-section of their society, brought together for purposes of sport in a way that they could seldom if ever be united in the "real" world outside the demarcated fields of play.

For every character in *The Changing Room*, the rugby match is a contractual rather than a "voluntary" obligation; to the players, the trainers, the team's owner, and even its janitor, the sport is a source of supplementary income—a commercial enterprise—rather than the source of enjoyment that "play" is traditionally held to be. The insidious influence of this commercial "professionalism" (which, as a modern invention, dates from the late nineteenth century) is evident throughout the play: the owner of the team does not watch its play, retiring to the locker room to warm himself and enjoy a drink and conversation instead; the victory celebration commingles the players' satisfaction at their achievement and their relief that, in miserable weather and despite physical pain, another of their contractual performances has been completed. As Christopher Lasch has observed, economic concerns taint the basic nature of sports as "Prudence and calculation, so prominent in everyday life but so in-

[1]Lionel Tiger, *Men in Groups* (New York: Random House, 1969) 121.

imical to the spirit of games, come to shape sports as they shape every-thing else"; as a result, he contends, "When sports can no longer be played with appropriate abandon, they lose the capacity to raise the spirits of players and spectators, to transport them to a higher realm."[2] Among players who can be sold or traded like commodities and retired by a decision of the owners, the whole concept of being a team is (as Lasch suggests) "drained of its capacity to call up local or regional loyalties" and therefore "reduces itself (like the rivalry among the corporations themselves) to a struggle for shares of the market. The professional athlete does not care whether his team wins or loses (since losers share in the pot), as long as it stays in business."[3] Although the athletes in Storey's work are "professional" in that they are paid for their partici-pation in the sport, it is *not* their primary occupation (or "profession"), and all hold "regular" jobs in the world "outside." They play intensely and unrestrainedly, but they are by no means obsessed with winning—a subject that they hardly mention among themselves; neither is there any concern about "representing" their particular locality. The owner of the team gives a typical pregame speech inciting them on to victory, but even he takes little actual interest in the game itself and leaves the stands before the first half ends. The players respect—but somewhat resent the intrusions of—the Club Chairman and his assistant, the Club Secretary, and they refuse to extend to these men the familiarity and camaraderie that exist among themselves. Even the team captain is ex-cluded from this team bond, since the owners have granted him special privileges—including a private bath—which seem to align him more closely with the employers than with the other "employees." Like workers aggrieved at the policies and practices of management, the players com-plain about the stinginess of the owners and want a "more hygienic" system of separate showers to replace the common bath. A distinction between the workers/players and the owners/management is thus clearly evident in *The Changing Room*, and it is the intrusion of economic issues—including charges of corporate ("Club") stinginess, low compensation, and unhygienic conditions—which has blurred the age-old distinction between "work" and "play."

Notwithstanding the fact that their "play" is actually contractual "work," the rugby players find that the sport provides a personal satisfaction that their "regular" jobs in the "outside world" may well lack. Again, Chris-topher Lasch has identified a social phenomenon that is central to Storey's play, in pointing out that with

[2]Christopher Lasch, "The Corruption of Sports," *New York Review of Books* 28 April 1977: 30.

[3]Christopher Lasch, letter/reply in "Corrupt Sports: An Exchange," *New York Review of Books* 29 September 1977: 40.

modern industry having reduced most jobs to a routine, games in our society take on added meaning. Men seek in play the difficulties and demands—both intellectual and physical—which they no longer find in work. . . . The rationalization of [religion, law, warfare, and productive labor] leaves little room for the spirit of arbitrary invention or the disposition to leave things to chance. Risk, daring, and uncertainty, important components of play, have little place in industry or in activities infiltrated by industrial methods, which are intended precisely to predict and control the future and to eliminate risk.[4]

The continuing encroachment of automation and the resulting reduction of the individual worker's importance (as well as that of his skill or craftsmanship) are specific concerns voiced by the Club Chairman: "I had a dream the other night ... I was telling Cliff afore the match ... I came up here to watch a match ... looked over at the tunnel ... know what I saw run out? (*Laughs.*) Bloody robots. (*Laughs again.*) And up in the bloody box were a couple of fellers, just like Danny, flicking bloody switches ... twisting knobs. (*Laughs.*) I laugh now. I wok [*sic*] up in a bloody sweat, I tell you" (*TCR*, 48–49). Like the elder Shaw in *In Celebration* and Slattery in *The Farm*, the team owner in *The Changing Room* recognizes the dehumanizing character of modern technology, and he realizes the value of personal responsibility and integrity of which much work is ever more deprived—and of which sport remains a refuge (or haven) in an increasingly mechanized (i.e., *literally* "heartless") world.

Regardless of the compensation that any of the characters receives, the "realm" of sport remains somehow separate from their lives "outside" and the jobs that they perform there. The essential reason for this is that, as Johan Huizinga remarked in *Homo Ludens*, "Play is not 'ordinary' or 'real' life. It is rather a stepping out of 'real' life into a temporary sphere of activity with a disposition all of its own."[5] Within this special and temporary "sphere," specific and binding rules are observed and administered by impartial officials, and a definite hierarchy—in which each person is expected to perform a specific role and duty that he knows well—prevails. In fact, as Huizinga points out, "inside the play-ground an absolute and peculiar order reigns. . . . Play . . . creates order, *is* order. Into an imperfect world and into the confusion of life it brings a temporary, a limited perfection."[6] Furthermore, for both the players and the spectators, the game may be seen as a ritualistic reenactment of an unending struggle between "us" (the team that one supports or is a member of) and "them" (whatever opponent it happens to be at the moment). These are the primary terms used to refer to the teams in

[4]Lasch, "Corruption of Sports" 24.
[5]Johan Huizinga, *Homo Ludens: A Study of the Play Element in Culture* (Boston: Beacon Press, 1950) 8.
[6]Huizinga 10.

Storey's play, and one of the basic appeals of sport may be its inherent Manichaeanism, making the game a contest between competing forces ("us" and "them") whose struggle is resolved with a certain finality at the end of the match, although—paradoxically—there are no *final* victories: even at world championships and tournament "finals" one hears "Wait until next year!" In sum, sports offer the participants the following attributes that they seldom if ever find in life: a functional and hierarchical "social" order; authoritative rules; impartial and uncorrupted officials, whose decisions are immediate and (with few exceptions) irreversible; "a temporary, a limited perfection"; personal autonomy and accountability; the opportunity to display specially developed skills; and an unambiguous resolution that yet allows the prospect of a different (and, to the loser, more appealing) outcome on another day. All of these attributes share one all-important characteristic: *certainty*—the quality that is most absent in the modern age of doubt, anxiety, alienation, and anomie.

An unselfconscious, "ordinary" process of "change" constitutes the central "invisible event" of *The Changing Room* and is most clearly depicted in the first act. As the players change their clothes, they set aside their various differences and the preoccupations of the outside world (which is both literally and metaphorically cold) and assume their responsibilities and interdependencies as members of a team. The literal "change" of clothing, to which the title of the play ostensibly refers, merely betokens the psychological (if not "spiritual") change that comprises the focal action of Storey's work. The nature and function of such a "change" were remarked on by Virginia Woolf in *Orlando* in 1928:

> Certain susceptibilities were asserting themselves, and others were diminishing. The change of clothes had, some philosophers will say, much to do with it. Vain trifles as they seem, clothes have, they say, more important offices than to keep us warm. They change our view of the world and the world's view of us. . . . Thus, there is much to support the view that it is clothes that wear us and not we them; we may make them take the mould of arm or breast, but they mould our hearts, our brains, our tongues to their liking.[7]

Nowhere has the validity of this observation been demonstrated more effectively than in the first act of *The Changing Room*. Specifically, the process of the "change" consists of three parts within the first act of the play. First, each of the players removes his "street clothes," which characterize (or at least reflect) his personal tastes, individuality, class, income, and occupation. Next, their unselfconscious nakedness (which startled many theatregoers in 1971) signifies a basic human equality (since they

[7]Virginia Woolf, *Orlando: A Biography* (1928; New York: Harcourt Brace Jovanovich, 1973) 187–88.

are literally divested of emblems of class and occupational differences) as well as a casual but nonsexual familiarity, tolerance, and acceptance. Finally, they don their uniforms, assuming their respective roles as participants in a collective effort that subsumes the individual efforts, interests, and allegiances of each. In effect, as the players put on their uniforms, they *become* uniform, casting off the differences among themselves in favor of identification with the group, wherein each has a clearly defined status, rank, and role (forward, scrum-half, wing three-quarter, etc.). The submergence of self into a larger social unit is, of course, a traditional function of ritual, and the means whereby this change is accomplished does in fact constitute a patterned, purposeful, and significant form of behavior, thereby fulfilling the criteria established for the definition of the term. Specifically, the recurrent three-part process of the "change" constitutes its pattern, and its purpose is merely the requisite preparation for the game; its significance, however, is to be found in the status and acceptance that each repetition of the procedure reinforces, intensifies, and resignifies. The resultant team bond has been forged over a long period of time—a form of intimacy that is extended only to those who have "proved themselves" in the game (and therefore excludes the owners and professional staff).

Whereas the first act of *The Changing Room* depicts the implicit renewal of the team bond through the ritual of the "change" (which is accompanied by the players' own diverse personal rituals and idiosyncratic habits), the second act demonstrates the strength of the bond that is thus formed and its ability to transcend the presence of any individual participant. The intensity of the teammates' brotherly regard is evoked with particular effectiveness in the players' concern for those who have been injured. Fenchurch, the wing three-quarter, receives treatment for his injured hand at mid-game but refuses to have it bandaged, since he "can't hold the ball with a bandage on" (*TCR*, 50); clearly, his effectiveness as a member of the team is more important to him than his personal pain. A more serious injury occurs shortly thereafter: Kendal, a twenty-nine-year-old forward, has his nose broken during the first scrum, and the trainer and one of the reserves carry him from the field into the locker room, where he must be held down in order to be examined and "doesn't know where he is" (*TCR*, 60) as a result of the pain. Like Fenchurch, he insists that he can and will return to the game, despite the fact that his "face is covered in blood" (*TCR*, 61) and he can see nothing but "bloody dots" (*TCR*, 64). Awaiting the car that will take him to the hospital, he admits that he will "have to get some glasses ... hardly see ..." (*TCR*, 67), confirming the young reserve's suspicion that Kendal did not (perhaps could not) see the boot that hit him in the face: "I don't think Ken wa' even looking," Moore (the reserve) says, noting that "his bloody head came down ... bloody boot came up ..." (*TCR*, 61). MacKendrick, the Club Secretary, offers an even simpler explanation for the accident, as he complains that Kendal is "too bloody old, you know. If I've said it once, I've said it ..." (*TCR*, 63). Even though Kendal is the second youngest of the five forwards (the eldest of whom, Walsh, is in his late thirties), it seems clear that his career has ended with this injury. Having "been round half the teams i' the bloody league" since he was fifteen (*TCR*, 64), Kendal can no longer play as well as he once did but needs the income from the sport to satisfy his wife and to provide occasional meager luxuries (an electric drill, a better overcoat) for himself. The end of Kendal's career also signifies the beginning of Moore's, however, and the reserve "quickly, jubilantly strips off his track suit" (*TCR*, 62) in order to begin his first professional match. Like any other entity for which ritual provides a fundamental continuity, the team transcends its individual participants, assimilating new members, confirming them when their worthiness has been proven, and replacing those whose association with the group—for whatever reason—no longer continues. An age-old metaphor for life itself, the game continues despite the exits and entrances of the individual players—which, in Storey's terms no less than in Shakespeare's, all men and women are.

The final act of *The Changing Room* demonstrates the temporality that constitutes the primary difference between the team bond that is confirmed through the players' ritualistic activities and the communions forged by earlier, more traditional forms of ritual. Structurally, the play's third act reverses the action of the first: gradually, the players prepare to resume their positions in the "outside" world, shedding both their uniforms and their roles as "team players," regaining the individuality and the differences (in class, etc.) that their "street clothes" represent. The athletes' pleasure in their victory and their pride in their individual achievements are evident in their exuberant talk and horseplay after the match, though these are allayed somewhat by various injuries and by relief at having completed the game in such miserable weather. One by one, the players leave the lockerroom, returning to their wives and girl friends, and reassuming their "outside" occupations and interests. Because their backgrounds and educations vary so greatly, it seems unlikely that there is much social contact among the men (or their families) beyond the interaction occurring in the locker room and on the field. Consequently, as the players leave the changing room, the bond that unites them dissolves.

Whereas traditional religious rituals confirmed a union and a significance lasting beyond the duration of the activity and sustaining the participants until their next involvement in the group, the wholly secular rituals of the changing room can perform no such function; this fact is merely an effect of living in a desacralized world. Yet, even though the effects of the rituals depicted in Storey's play are both fleeting and impermanent, the lives of the players would clearly be less satisfying without them. The experience of "belonging to" the team thus provides the players a temporary union forged through common purpose and shared endeavor—and confirmed through wholly secular rituals that are unselfconsciously but unfailingly performed. It is, in effect, modern society's primary secular example of what Paul Tillich in *The Courage to Be* called "the courage to be as a part"—a form of "self-affirmation . . . done in spite of the threat of non-being."[8] Among the athletes of the rugby team, no less than among the Communist cadres that Tillich cited as his examples, one finds

> the willingness to sacrifice any individual fulfillment to the self-affirmation of the group and to the goal of the movement. . . . Fate and death may hurt or destroy that part of oneself that is not identical with the collective in which one participates. But . . . the whole . . . transcends fate and death. It is eternal in the sense in which the collective is considered to be eternal. . . . Members of the collective . . . are infinitely concerned about the fulfillment of the group. And from this concern they derive their courage to be.[9]

Through their participation in the experience of team sports, with its rules and rituals, its unity of purpose and shared endeavor, the athletes achieve, albeit briefly, an instance of order and unity that their other activities—including work (whether in a factory or in a classroom)—cannot provide.

The transitoriness of the team association became particularly clear in Storey's own experience when, as a scholarship student at the Slade School of Art in London in 1953, he returned each weekend to his home in West Riding (in the industrial north of England) to play professional rugby at Leeds. As the author explained in an essay entitled "Journey through a Tunnel" in the *Listener* in 1963, his contractual obligation to the team brought him home each week

> not . . . to see my parents, nor out of a sense of duty, nor purely for economic reasons. I was, oddly enough, returning to that place which, at this moment of my life, I hated and dreaded the most, simply to play football . . . an extremely hard game, fierce and grinding. . . . It requires not so much tremendous physical strength as a very peculiar, innate stamina which has as much to do with a man's mental attitudes as it has with his actual physique.[10]

Not only was Storey's time thus sharply divided between his "public" life as a professional athlete in the north and his private life as an art student

---

[8]Paul Tillich, *The Courage to Be* (New Haven: Yale, 1952) 89.
[9]Tillich 100.
[10]David Storey, "Journey through a Tunnel," *Listener* August 1963: 159–60.

in London, but the separate "realms" of sport and of his career in the world "outside" were separated by a distance that could be traversed only by a four-hour journey by train. Accordingly, after "the aching ordeal of the match itself," there came "the shower, the bath, the hurry to the station, the feeling of relief and elation, and within twenty-four hours of leaving London, bruised, battered, totally exhausted, I would be on my way back home again,"[11] having left behind *both* the "realm" of sport and the "outside" world that his teammates inhabited as well. The dichotomy between athlete and artist, West Riding and London, north and south caused Storey "to be continually torn between the two extremes of [his] experience, the physical and the spiritual, with the demand to be effective in both."[12] The conflicts arising from these allegiances—"irreconcilable" and antithetical as Storey found them to be[13]—formed the structural and thematic bases of his early fiction, becoming most evident in the blatantly schematic and stereotypical third novel, *Radcliffe*, which was published in 1963. By 1971, however, when *The Changing Room* appeared, this simple schema had been abandoned—or at least modified to such an extent that the "spiritual" (based in ritual) could be found as an implicit heretofore unrecognized aspect of the "physical." During an interview with Martha Duffy, whose profile of him appeared in *Sports Illustrated*, Storey recollected an incident from his own career that strongly resembles the "invisible event" of *The Changing Room*:

> The pleasure to me is in the pitch of endeavor, sustaining it, going beyond it. In many ways I hated rugby, but it allowed people to do marvelous things. Often the real expression occurs at the point of physical and mental exhaustion. I recall one very hard game, played in pouring rain on a pitch that seemed to be 15 feet deep in mud. My relations with the team were at their worst. I should have hated every minute of that match, but suddenly something almost spiritual happened. The players were taken over by the identity that was the team. We were genuinely transported.[14]

Storey's description of the experience as "something *almost* spiritual" (emphasis mine) is a crucially precise phrase, suggesting his conscious awareness that a *truly* "spiritual" (i.e., religious) experience cannot by definition arise from a wholly secular activity and cannot occur in a desacralized world. Storey used a similarly precise but "qualified" phrase in his interview with Mel Gussow of the *New York Times*, disclosing that—surprisingly—the *direct* inspiration for *The Changing Room* occurred at the rehearsals for *The Contractor* and *not* as a result of reflections on his career as a professional rugby player:

[11]Storey, "Tunnel" 160.
[12]Storey, "Tunnel" 160.
[13]Storey, "Tunnel" 160.
[14]Martha Duffy, "An Ethic of Work and Play," *Sports Illustrated* 5 March 1973: 69.

"The play was very much prompted by watching the actors rehearse 'The Contractor' in England," Mr. Storey said. "I found it fascinating to watch 12 people who had really nothing in common apart from the fact that they were actors, being unified by work, by an activity which absorbed them completely for part of the day. When it was over, they broke up and went away. I felt there was a kind of religious feeling to this—people relinquishing their aspirations to be absorbed by a larger community."[15]

The phrase "a *kind of* religious feeling" is more ambiguous than it may at first appear: while it could mean "a variety or type of" religious experience, it seems more likely that the phrase was used in its more informal or vernacular sense (with "to"), denoting a *somewhat* or *rather* religious—i.e., "*almost* spiritual"—feeling rather than a genuine and authentic one.

The actors themselves, like the rugby players whom they portray, are "unified by work" in the play—which itself becomes an analogous "invisible event" as they assemble, play before an audience, and disband until the next scheduled performance. As Martha Duffy reported in *Sports Illustrated*, the actors contributed a number of idiosyncratic rituals in performance that are not indicated in the printed text of the play:

When [the director, Lindsay] Anderson told the cast to change, they darted into their uniforms and were set to go in five minutes. That left 40 minutes of the first act with all talk and no action. "The truth is," says Storey, "that it takes a real rugby player about 45 minutes to get ready. We taught them how to bandage each other, how to massage, how to fiddle with laces and do warmups, and then let each one select his own routine."[16]

Insofar as each *actor* established a patterned system of behavior to fill his time onstage, it became a habit; insofar as each *character* (or actual rugby player) maintains such patterned behavior as preparation for his role on the team (and/or to bring luck), it becomes a ritual. For even more verisimilitude, the cast members were actually taught to play rugby— and they quickly became not only an ensemble of actors but a team of players as well, as Duffy noted:

The [actors] went out to a field in Roehampton, under the tutelage of Bev Risman, an ex-Rugby Leaguer of international class. He taught them seven-to-a-side touch so they could make their second-act entrances . . . properly "winded and puffed." Risman recalls that the actors "were so keen that after a couple of minutes they were knocking hell out of each other." The playwright

[15]Mel Gussow, "To David Storey, a Play Is a 'Holiday,'" *New York Times* 20 April 1973: 14.
[16]Duffy 69. For additional anecdotal information on the auditions and rehearsals for the first London production of *The Changing Room*, see Philip Roberts, *The Royal Court Theatre: 1965–1972* (London: Routledge & Kegan Paul, 1986) 116–20.

himself went in, but not for long. Like his teammates of old, the actors wanted "to bury him under the ground." Observes Risman, "Actors have no sense of self-preservation."[17]

The fact that participants in a sport can be "genuinely transported"—a central theme of Storey's play—was thus demonstrated in the actors' own experience, as they quickly and willingly "were taken over by the identity that was the team"[18] and readily began "knocking hell out of each other" for the sake of the game (and, indirectly, for the sake of the play). Accordingly, the process of producing *The Changing Room* brought about an "invisible event" that is analogous to (but wholly distinct from) the one that occurs on the stage. From diverse backgrounds and with varied interests, the actors who were assembled for *The Changing Room* literally *became* a team in order to *portray* a team, forming a bond that lasted (presumably) as long as the play's run—and produced "ensemble acting" that was acclaimed with virtual unanimity by reviewers.

Storey's fascination with the actors' work also led him to write another play—still unproduced—on this subject. In an interview with John Higgins of the *London Times*, Storey described this play, called *Night*, as follows: "It is set on a bare stage and deals with the thoughts of a number of actors while they are in rehearsal. Their own problems are rather more interesting than the play they are about to perform—I got the idea while watching the preparation of one of my own in the theatre."[19] During my interview with him, Storey described the play's design and its production difficulties in detail:

> It was a rather curious play. It was about a group of actors who were obviously in a play, but you didn't hear the play they were in. What you heard were their comments about it. You could describe it in a rather facetious way as a play-within-a-play. It was a very good idea, but I couldn't really work it for some reason. I don't know why. It was in fact going to be done at the Royal Court. I think it also was to be at the [Edinburgh] Festival, and then I changed my mind about it and substituted *Mother's Day*. . . . The Edinburgh Festival turned down *Mother's Day* and then there was a scandal in the newspapers, an argument—a public debate as to why they had turned it down. The Edinburgh authorities had obviously turned it down because of its obscenities and didn't want to say so in case they were not seen as progressives, and so they just lied that it was turned down for financial reasons. But in fact they had already accepted *Night*, which I think had a slightly larger cast, and *Mother's Day* only had one set, the same as *Night*, so there obviously wasn't. . . . So that's the long history of *Night. Night* and *Day*.

[17]Duffy 69.
[18]Duffy 69.
[19]John Higgins, "David Storey: Night and Day," *Times* (London) 16 September 1976: 13.

Although the play remains unproduced—and Storey now characterizes it as "awful"—the details about *Night* confirm Storey's interest in the *process* of theatre itself and its ability to unite, if only for a brief time, disparate people through shared endeavor. It also corroborates—and compounds—the portrayal of the "invisible events" of *The Changing Room*, *The Contractor*, and a number of his other plays: simultaneously, the action of the play "simulates" ("enacts") one such "event" (i.e., the change, the construction of the tent, the art class) and provides the occasion for a separate, equally ritualistic "event" that—though it is undetectable by (or "invisible" to) the play's audience—constitutes the essence of theatre itself.

The same evolution from participation to "spectatorship" is clearly evident in the histories of both sport and theatre; yet, whereas the ritualistic origins of theatre have provided a mainstay of scholarship since the publication of Jane Harrison's *Ancient Art and Ritual* in 1918, the relationship between sport and ritual is a more recent subject of scholarship. Almost all sports events are inherently theatrical—conflicts (*agons*) that are "staged" in especially equipped arenas by "players" whose "performances" are assessed by knowledgeable but nonparticipating audiences. Yet, as Huizinga contended in *Homo Ludens*, so much of the ritual value of sports has been lost in modern times that "however important [the contest] may be for the players or spectators, it remains sterile [, and the] old play-factor has undergone almost complete atrophy" as a result of "the fatal shift towards over-seriousness" in sports "play."[20] Specifically, Huizinga deplored the Nazis' exploitation of sport for nationalistic and propagandistic purposes during the 1930s as "a part of the spectacle of a society rapidly goose-stepping its way into helotry."[21] In more recent years, sociologists have confirmed Huizinga's theory of the devaluation of sports (which the title of Allen Guttmann's *From Ritual to Record: The Nature of Modern Sports* effectively summarizes),[22] although the causes of the transformation are more often attributed to economic influences and "professionalism" rather than to political exploitation

[20]Huizinga 198,
[21]Huizinga 206.
[22]Allen Guttmann, *From Ritual to Record: The Nature of Modern Sports* (New York: Columbia University Press, 1978). For a history of a professional English "football club" and details about its corporate structure, see Charles Korr's *West Ham United: The Making of a Football Club* (Champaign: University of Illinois Press, 1987). Noteworthy sociological assessments of sport include Edwin H. Cady's *The Big Game: College Sports and American Life* (Knoxville: University of Tennessee Press, 1978) and Michael Novak's *The Joy of Sports* (New York: Basic Books, 1976). A useful overview of critical studies of sports in relation to both modern society and contemporary literature is Wiley Lee Umphlett's "The Literature of American Sport Culture: The Emergence of a Productive Field of Study and Research," *Proteus: A Journal of Ideas* 3.1 (Spring 1986): 28–33.

(charges of which occur with each quadrennial Olympiad).[23] Within the microcosm of *The Changing Room*, there remains a pervasive feeling that, despite working conditions and salaries that are far better than in earlier times, the game is not what it once was—and that the players of today are (in the phrase from *The Restoration of Arnold Middleton*) somehow "lesser men" than the literally legendary, seemingly heroic players of bygone days, whose hardships Mackendrick describes:

> God Christ ... If this place was like it was twenty years ago—and that's not *too* far back—you wouldn't find me here for bloody start ... As for fifty years ago. Primeval. * * * Washed i' bloody buckets then ... et dripping instead o' bloody meat ... urinated by an hedge ... God Christ, bloody houses were nobbut size o' this—seven kiddies, no bloody bath: no bed ... fa'ther [*sic*] out o' work as much as not.
>
> HARRY. There's many as living like that right now!
>
> MACKENDRICK. Aye. And there's a damn sight more as not.
>
> (*TCR*, 48)

The terms of Mackendrick's description heighten the distinction between contemporary athletes and those who lived in the primitive conditions of "primeval" (albeit surprisingly recent) times. Thornton, the Club Chairman, also complains of a loss of authenticity (i.e., a devaluation) that characterizes modern life, as he notes that there is "Nowt like a coal fire. Hardly get it anywhere now, you know ... Synthetic bloody fuel. Like these plastic bloody chickens. Get nowt that's bloody real no more" (*TCR*, 44). Yet, notwithstanding the devaluation of sport (and life) by professionalism and the less-than-heroic stature of modern man, the rugby match and related activities *do* manifestly provide something "real" in the players' lives. "The ancient connections between games, ritual, and public festivity," which Christopher Lasch described in an essay on "The Corruption of Sports," have been diminished but *not eradicated*, and Lasch noted that play retains "its capacity to dramatize reality and to offer a convincing representation of the community's values . . . rooted in shared traditions, to which [games] give objective expression."[24] Like the "sacred space" of traditional religions, the playground is, as Huizinga observed, "hallowed, within which special rules obtain. All are temporary worlds within the ordinary world, dedicated to the performance of an act apart."[25]

[23]See, for example, Alan Sillitoe's "Sport and Nationalism," *Mountains and Caverns: Selected Essays by Alan Sillitoe* (London: W. H. Allen, 1975) 84.

[24]Lasch, "Corruption" 30.

[25]Huizinga 10.

The fact that these terms are even *more* applicable to the activities of the locker room is fundamental to an understanding of *The Changing Room*: unlike the commercial public ceremony of the game itself, the "change" is *literally* "an act apart," occurring within a "temporary world within the ordinary world," a wholly secular sanctuary to which only those with proper "credentials" are allowed access, and in which the players' particular and binding but nontraditional rituals are unself-consciously performed.

The subject of *The Changing Room* is particularly appropriate for an English playwright since, as Huizinga remarked, "England became the cradle and focus of modern sporting life" which, in turn, reflected "the structure of English social life" and four particular national character-istics: 1) "local self-government [which] encouraged the spirit of asso-ciation and solidarity"; 2) "the absence of obligatory military training [which] favoured the occasion for, and the need of, physical exercise"; 3) "the peculiar form of education" that was offered in the public school system; 4) "the geography of the country and the nature of the terrain, on the whole flat and, in the ubiquitous commons, offering the most perfect playing-fields that could be desired."[26] Although the appeal of sport is universal and the activities of the locker room are themselves only slightly affected by nationality (e.g., in the observance of class dis-tinctions), Storey rightly insists on the particularly English qualities of both the game and its players. Indeed, in his interview with Victor Sage in 1976, the author seemed surprised at the acclaim that the play received in the United States earlier in the decade, and he remarked that when "in New York they put on *The Changing Room* ... all these people goggling at all these characters on stage talking broad Yorkshire ... couldn't un-derstand a word of it ... it's all *good*, though, they're sure of that."[27] Like all of Storey's other plays, notwithstanding the universality of their themes, *The Changing Room* is specifically and unmistakeably English, implicitly corroborating Jack's observation in *Home* that "the ideals of life, liberty, freedom, could never have been the same—democracy—if we'd been living on the Continent, for example" (*H,* 17).

The rugby match itself is little more than the official occasion or pretext for the significant action of the play, which is the temporary reaffirmation of what Huizinga termed "the feeling of being 'apart together' in an exceptional situation, of sharing something important, of mutually with-drawing from the rest of the world and rejecting the usual norms."[28] Despite his dour conclusion in the final chapter of *Homo Ludens* that the

[26]Huizinga 197.
[27]"David Storey in Conversation with Victor Sage," *New Review* October 1976: 65.
[28]Huizinga 12.

"ritual tie [having] now been completely severed[,] sport has become profane, 'unholy' in every way, [having] no organic connection whatever with the structure of society,"[29] Huizinga also maintained (in his first chapter) that certain vestigial formal elements of ritual and play survive today:

> The ritual act has all the formal and essential characteristics of play . . . , particularly in so far as it transports the participants to another world. . . . A closed space is marked out for [play], either materially or ideally, hedged off from the everyday surroundings. . . . Now the marking out of some sacred spot is also the primary characteristic of every sacred act. . . . *Formally speaking, there is no distinction whatever between marking out a space for a sacred purpose and marking it out for sheer play.* The turf, the tennis-court, the chess-court and pavement hopscotch cannot formally be distinguished from the temple or the magic circle [emphasis mine].[30]

Accordingly, the playing field is the profane world's counterpart for the "sacred space" of a theocentric culture. Yet, much more than the public arena, the lockerroom constitutes a secular "holy of holies"—a "closed space" entered only by those who are responsible for the performance of the public ritual that relies to a remarkable degree on "the feeling of being 'apart together'" that is fostered among themselves. As Christopher Lasch has observed, sports constitute the most efficacious modern means whereby both participants and observers may be (in Storey's phrase) "genuinely transported":

> Among the activities through which men seek release from everyday life, games offer in many ways the purest form of escape. Like sex, drugs, and drink, they obliterate awareness of everyday reality, not by dimming that awareness but by raising it to a new intensity. . . . Games enlist skill and intelligence, the utmost concentration of purpose, on behalf of utterly useless activities, which make no contribution to the struggle of man against nature, to the wealth or comfort of the community, or to its physical survival.[31]

Lasch has thus effectively summarized the attributes that link modern sports with traditional rituals—as well as those distinctions that separate them. The urge to heighten one's "awareness of everyday reality" (even while transcending it) is the "perennial need" from which both ritual and religion arise; the fact that games, sex, drugs, and drink are the primary means whereby this need is met in modern society demonstrates anew the "sterility" of the desacralized world and the paucity of its "counterparts" for meaningful traditional rituals. Unlike religious rites, these

[29]Huizinga 197–98.
[30]Huizinga 18–20.
[31]Lasch, "Corruption" 24.

contemporary activities are recognized by both participants and observers as "utterly useless activities," having no effect on the human condition (which, of course, traditional rituals were intended to influence). Nevertheless, there remains a vital significance of sports as the "purest form" of activity whereby such "escape" (i.e., transcendence) can now be achieved by the millions of spectators in modern society; for those who participate in sports, the "escape" is even more meaningful, and the interpersonal bonds forged thereby are more intense—albeit impermanent, as *The Changing Room* makes clear.

More than any of Storey's other plays, *The Contractor* encapsulates all of the author's major themes. Like *The Farm* and *Mother's Day*, *The Contractor* is a "family play" in which three generations of Ewbanks are brought together. As in *In Celebration*, the occasion of the family gathering is a traditional ritual—the celebration of a marriage. Like the Shaws' dinner in *In Celebration* and the rugby match in *The Changing Room*, this wedding—the central "event" of the play—remains unseen by the audience, taking place "between the acts" of this ostensibly plotless drama. Its central "onstage" action is the construction of a tent for the wedding and its disassembly on the day after the ceremony. As in *The Changing Room*, the nature of the relationships among the workmen comprises much of the subject matter and provides the sole conflict of the play, although in *The Contractor* the bond forged through work is juxtaposed against the familial ties that bring together the Ewbanks. There is also a thematic continuity between the two plays, since each demonstrates the significance of "invisible events" that are more efficacious than traditional rituals in fulfilling the "perennial human need" for patterned, purposeful, and status-defining activities. Surprisingly, when considered in terms of Mircea Eliade's *The Sacred and the Profane*, the central action of *The Contractor* becomes virtually identical with that of *The Changing Room*: each play portrays the demarcation of a secular counterpart for the "sacred space" of more spiritually oriented societies—an accommodation of the recurrent need for meaningful ritual and the devaluation of its traditional forms in the modern world.

The construction of the tent occurs during the first act of *The Contractor* as the Ewbank family prepares for the wedding festivities. Throughout the play, Storey's stage directions are necessarily quite detailed on the method of assembling the tent, and his initial description of the setting is typically explicit:

> The stage is set with three tent poles for a marquee, twenty or thirty foot high, down the centre of the stage at right angles to the audience. The poles should be solid and permanently fixed, the ropes supporting them, from the top, running off into the wings. Each pole is equipped with the necessary

pulley blocks and ropes, the latter fastened off near the base as the play begins. Two ridge poles, to be used for the muslin, are set between the poles. (*TC*, 9)

The workmen (including two self-describedly "bone-idle" Irishmen whose banter resembles that of their counterparts in *Cromwell*) receive their instructions from Ewbank, who owns the tenting company and is especially concerned about the condition of his lawn and the impression to be made on the guests at his daughter's wedding. "Get it up. Get it finished. And get away" (*TC*, 13), he tells Kay, the foreman. Another of the workers, Glendenning, is described as "in his early twenties, a good-natured, stammering half-wit" like Mathew in *Cromwell*; he is, Storey notes, "something, altogether, of a caricature of a workman" (*TC*, 18), who is teased unremittingly by the Irishmen (and, less often, by the others) whose company—and attention—he enjoys. In his stage directions, the playwright specifies that, as the act proceeds, "gradually, in spite of their chatter, the pace of work [begins] to assert itself" (*TC*, 23); the canvas is unfolded, laced, tied in place, secured with guy wires and quarter poles. When the outer canvas tent is complete and the parquet floor has been laid, the workmen depart for lunch, and the act ends.

When the second act begins, the colored muslin lining for the tent is being installed, and the various "finishing touches" are completed: metal tables and chairs are set in place, flower arrangements are carefully arrayed, and the floor is polished by hand. The effect of this process has been well summarized by Katharine Worth in *Revolutions in Modern English Drama*:

> Out of the rough old jumble of the stage scene—the noisy, confused effect of men at work, the fights, the swearing, the broad jokes, the simple animal behaviour (Ewbank, the contractor, has to warn the foreman against letting the men relieve themselves on the lawn in full view of the house in their usual, uninhibited way) out of all this comes the lovely, delicate thing, the marquee, with its white ironwork tables, its pots of flowers, its air of elegance and festivity. . . . It's a place where moments of tranquility and communion are achieved by people who find such moments hard to come by.[32]

The Irishmen's joking banter continues, although it gradually takes on more potentially hurtful overtones: first, they disclose that their foreman served time in prison for a crime that he will not reveal, despite their insinuations; shortly thereafter, Glendenning (who was earlier sent to fetch a glass hammer and rubber nails) is reduced to tears by their exaggerated reaction to his not having shared a bun that he was given by Mrs. Ewbank; eventually, they make light of Ewbank's drinking. Fi-

[32]Katharine Worth, *Revolutions in Modern English Drama* (London: Bell & Sons, 1973) 28.

166

nally, however, the tent is completed and the ladders removed; the workmen depart, and Ewbank looks approvingly at the completed marquee, realizing that "It'll not happen again, you know. . . . Too bloody old to start again" (*TC*, 80–81). Soon all three generations of Ewbanks gather beneath the tent "to have a look at it"; tentatively, in the silence, the prospective bride and groom dance, followed by Ewbank's son and his mother, and then finally by the contractor and his wife. After the other members of the family depart, Ewbank and his wife are left alone together for a moment of reflection on the imminent change in their lives. They too then return to the house, and the act ends as "slowly the light fades" on the carefully arranged and decorated tent.

The final act of the play opens in stark contrast to the beauty and "ordered perfection" of the tent at the close of the second act. By the morning after the wedding, Storey notes,

> The tent has suffered a great deal. Part of the muslin drapery hangs loosely down. Similarly, parts of the lining round the walls hang down in loose folds, unhooked, or on the floor. Part of the dance floor itself has been removed, other parts uprooted and left in loose slabs. Bottles lie here and there on the floor, along with discarded napkins, streamers, table-cloths, paper-wrappings. Most of the flowers have gone and the few that remain have been dragged out of position, ready to be disposed of.
>
> (*TC*, 87)

The workmen arrive to disassemble the tent—although, as one of them remarks, "There's not a lot left here for us to do" (*TC*, 87) except clear away the debris. The Irishmen's japes lead to much more acrimony than in the previous acts: they reveal that the wife of one of their co-workers (Bennett) has left him for another man (*TC*, 92), and they continue to goad the foreman about his prison term. Soon a confrontation occurs, as Bennett threatens to kill the Irishmen with the shacklen end of one of the ropes, when the foreman intervenes:

KAY. It looks to me, Fitzpatrick, that you've come here—this morning like any other—to cause trouble wherever you can ...

FITZPATRICK (*looking at* BENNETT). If a man puts his fist in my face I'll be damned if he doesn't get one back. Wherever that man might come from.

BENNETT. And you think that's something to admire, Fitzpatrick?

FITZPATRICK. No. No. It's not admiration at all I'm after.

(MARSHALL *laughs*.)

KAY. I think you better get home, Fitzpatrick.

FITZPATRICK. What?

KAY. I think you better get off. Come into the office at the end of the week

167

and you'll get whatever you're owed.

(TC, 102)

Just as Fitzpatrick leaves, Ewbank enters to complain about the lack of work being done; in response to the employer's direct question about why he is leaving, Fitzpatrick answers that he has been fired, to which Ewbank's response is "Don't be so bloody silly. Get on with this bloody walling ..." (*TC*, 103), and he notes that "There's been nobody sacked from this firm since the day it first began" (*TC*, 104). Within minutes, reassured and emboldened, the Irishmen resume their banter about the foreman's prison sentence, until Ewbank unwittingly reveals what they have wanted to know:

> FITZPATRICK. I say, Kay here isn't one to make a fuss.
>
> EWBANK. By God, bloody embezzlement. That'd make 'em shift, Kay. Four lasses.
>
> MARSHALL. Embezzlement?
>
> EWBANK. By God. There's nowt for him to embezzle here. * * *
>
> FITZPATRICK. Embezzlement. Now there's a wonder.
>
> MARSHALL. And all the time now ...
>
> FITZPATRICK. One of us.
>
> MARSHALL. Hiding his light, beneath a bushel.
>
> FITZPATRICK. Along, that is, with the cash from someone else's tub.
>
> (MARSHALL *and* FITZPATRICK *laugh.*)

(TC, 105–6)

Ewbank's father wanders in, continuing to tell the workmen of the rope that he made by hand and the working conditions of his time; shortly thereafter, Ewbank's son comes by to take his leave, and the father remarks that he "Comes up here, you know, for the bloody booze ... nowt else ..." (*TC*, 110). Nevertheless, the two seem reconciled to their differences, though each remains unable to accept the other's values:

> EWBANK. Off then, are you?
>
> PAUL. That's right.
>
> EWBANK. Aye ... (*Gazes at him.*) Back up, I suppose, when you need some money.
>
> PAUL. Manage by meself.
>
> EWBANK. Aye ... Still to see it.
>
> PAUL. Alus a first time.
>
> EWBANK. Aye ... can just imagine.

168

PAUL. Well, then ...

(*Pause, gazing over at one another.*)

(*TC*, 110)

The last poles and remaining pieces are removed, and the canvas is taken down, folded, and carried out. The foreman and Bennett resign themselves to the Irishmen's humor and, noting that "you have to laugh" (*TC*, 112), begin to tease them in return. When the tent has been taken down, Ewbank brings the workers a bottle and some pieces of wedding cake. After toasts to Ewbank's health and to "the happy couple" (*TC*, 119), the workmen leave. Joined by his wife, the contractor pauses for a moment of reflection, wondering "What's to become of us, you reckon?" (*TC*, 122) before leaving to bid his own parents farewell. The play ends as it began, with the stage "empty: bare poles, the ropes fastened off" (*TC*, 122), and the light slowly fades.

As in *The Changing Room*, two distinct "invisible events" provide the substance and structure of the play. The first, the wedding itself, is a traditional ritual—a ceremony that, like the rugby match, is observed by a number of spectators but (because it takes place between the acts) remains unseen by the audience in the theatre. The second, the construction and disassembly of the tent, is an "invisible event" in Storey's particular sense of the term: like the "change" that the rugby players undergo in the locker room, it is an occasion whereon a group of men with diverse interests and backgrounds are united in a common endeavor of manual labor. Yet, whereas in *The Changing Room* both "events" are performed by the same group of people, in *The Contractor* the groups are (except for occasional contact) completely separate: only Ewbank himself, in his roles as employer and head of the family, is an integral member of both groups, providing continuity for the play. Although strained relationships are evident in both groups, there is a qualitative difference between the bonds that unite them: both the family and the workmen are united only temporarily for a common purpose, but the former remains fundamentally disaffected, unable to achieve more than a temporary and tenuous unity before going again their separate ways. The workmen, despite their differences and the lack of familial ties, achieve an acceptance of one another and a reconciliation that seems more permanent (perhaps because they must meet and cooperate on an almost daily basis) than the strained yet loving tolerance that prevails in the family.

In some ways, therefore, the "invisible event" taking place onstage is more effectually ritualistic than the wedding itself, since the erection of the tent is necessarily a series of patterned and purposeful acts to be completed in a given order by the active participation (and exertion) of

169

all involved. In much the same way that the positions on the rugby team give the athletes in *The Changing Room* a clearly designated and closely defined role for each to perform, the tasks of the construction crew provide both a hierarchy in which each man knows his rank and a set of actions that becomes each man's personal responsibility in contributing to the collective success of the group. Through the ritual of tent-raising, the workmen thus find a vital quality that the Ewbank family lacks: a sense of coherence, hierarchy, and unity, forged through common purpose and shared experience—the same factors that contribute to the team bond and team "spirit" of the rugby players in *The Changing Room*. The efficacy of this nontraditional ritual is implicitly contrasted with the customary wedding rite—an increasingly devalued ritual (as contemporary divorce statistics reveal), its religious/spiritual significance having been diminished in a society that devalues such beliefs and thus regards its vows as less binding and less sacred than ever before. Significantly, the *secular* aspects of the wedding festivities—especially the reception—preoccupy almost all of the Ewbanks' attentions; the *sacred* ceremony and the exchange of vows are never mentioned in the play.

The characters in *The Contractor*, like those in *The Changing Room*, constitute a microcosm of English society. The prospective groom is, as Ewbank notes, "a bloody aristocrat * * * refined" (*TC*, 38), although he is also a doctor—a working member of the "professional classes" that Ewbank's daughter, a nurse, has also joined. Her father, however, remains solidly middle-class—a prosperous businessman whose success has been built on a trade he learned in part from his father. The contractor is clearly much more comfortable among the workmen than among those who are more educated and "refined," and he is not entirely "suited" by the coat and tie that he now wears, as Storey specifies in the initial description of Ewbank: "He's a solid, well-built man, broad rather than tall, stocky. He's wearing a suit, which is plain, workmanlike and chunky; someone probably who doesn't take easily to wearing clothes, reflecting, perhaps, the feeling of a man who has never found his proper station in life" (*TC*, 9). Ill at ease among the upper and professional classes, Ewbank insists that, like his father, he is "a bloody artisan * * * Not a worker" (*TC*, 39); nevertheless, his work is essentially managerial and proprietary, and he is not directly involved in the sort of manual trade in which his father, a ropemaker, earned his living. Ewbank's role as an employer confirms the fact that he seemingly cannot fully accept: that he is neither workman nor artisan but a member of the bourgeoisie. This class distinction is quite apparent to the workmen, however, as the Irishmen remark early in the play:

BENNETT. A house like that, and you don't need to do any work ...

MARSHALL. Built up from what ... ?

FITZPATRICK. The money he never paid us.

BENNETT. And a damn sight more besides.

FITZPATRICK (*gestures*).
   The windows bright with our sweat
   The concrete moistened by our sorrows.

MARSHALL. Did you get that out of the paper?

FITZPATRICK. I did.

(*TC*, 17)

Despite their occasional raillery over their work and wage, the Irishmen and the others have neither illusions nor regrets about their status as members of the working class, and they manifest none of Ewbank's discomfiture over their respective "stations in life." Asserting a self-confidence and solidarity that all of the members of the Ewbank family lack, the Irishmen take pride in both their class and their nationality:

FITZPATRICK. * * * I'm like the rest of them.

MARSHALL. An honest working-man.

FITZPATRICK. That's right.

MARSHALL. Born and bred in Ireland!

FITZPATRICK. Like every one before me.

(*TC*, 47)

Similarly, Bennett claims that he is "good old English stock" (*TC*, 47) and concurs—laughingly—with Marshall's vaunt, "Empire-builders! That's us!" (*TC*, 48). They are not, however, entirely representative of the modern British working class, since they are manual laborers, members of no union, and practitioners of no skilled trade. In fact, as Ewbank himself acknowledges, his workers are the least "qualified" in the labor pool: "Three years. That's about as long as anybody [remains in a job] in this place. They don't stay long. I employ anybody here, you know. Anybody who'll work. Miners who've coughed their lungs up, fitters who've lost their fingers, madmen who've run away from home. (*Laughs.*) * * * I've the biggest turnover of manual labor in this town. I take on all those that nobody else'll employ" (*TC*, 38). Accordingly, the construction crew contains a former prisoner, a "good-natured half-wit," and "bone-idle" transients who, despite their differences among themselves, undertake a common endeavor and find therein both success and a self-evident satisfaction.

The three generations of the Ewbank family provide a paradigm for the phases of postindustrial British society. The contractor's father, whom

171

Storey describes as "in his late sixties" and "gnarled," is "an old artisan" (*TC*, 25) who made rope by hand and now tirelessly recounts the hardships of workers in his youth. Carrying a piece of rope around with him to show anyone who will listen, Old Ewbank embodies a craftsmanship—and a pride of workmanship—that is clearly outmoded today:

OLD EWBANK. * * * Here. Now that's a bit of the rope I made.

MARSHALL. Oh. That's ... (*Polishing.*)

OLD EWBANK. All by hand. Up and down a rope walk. You wind it at one end and come up along it with a shuttle. Like this. You can walk up to twenty or thirty miles a day.

MARSHALL. That's a fine bit of rope.

OLD EWBANK. They don't make them like that no more. Machines. A handmade rope is a bit of the past. (*Gestures up blindly.*) All these: machines.

MARSHALL. Still, they do their job.

(*TC*, 69)

Contending that modern workers "haven't the strength to stand up. A bit of an ache and they're dashing for a pill and a sup from a bottle. They haven't the appetite, you know, for work" (*TC*, 107), the old man recalls having worked "Eighteen[,] Sometimes twenty hours a day" and alleges that "When I married my wife I never used to see her but one day in four" (*TC*, 108). Old Ewbank also explains that he "Started making tents in [his] old age [and] passed it on" to his son (*TC*, 45), who built a successful business from it. In so doing, of course, though Ewbank ordered and set specifications for such materials as ropes and canvas, he was no longer involved personally in their manufacture. Inevitably, as the contractor gained managerial skills and became more conscious of net costs and profit margins, less expensive materials—machine-made and mass-produced—were used. For the special occasion of his daughter's wedding, however, Ewbank has obtained a particularly high-quality canvas, as he tells his foreman:

EWBANK. * * * That's a nice bit of canvas, Kay.

KAY. It is. (*Nods, looking up at it.*)

EWBANK. They don't make them like that no more. (*Gestures at tent.*) 'Least, not if I can help it. (*Laughs at his own humour.*) It'd be too damn expensive.

KAY. Aye. It would.

(*TC*, 35)

Cost calculation and other such economic considerations are alien to Ewbank's son, however, and to his sister and her fiancé. Having grown up accustomed to the benefits and privileges (particularly in education) that his father's money provided, Paul is "feckless" and "a little unco-ordinated," a young man whose "initial attitude, deliberately implanted, is that of a loafer" and whose "manner is a conscious foil to his father's briskness" (*TC*, 13). Unlike the betrothed couple, Paul has not applied his education toward a profession or any other specific goal; instead, he travels, studies, and continues to spend his father's money. The Irishmen summarize the son's character early in the first act:

FITZPATRICK. A university man if I ever saw one. * * *

BENNETT. Who's that, Fitzie?

FITZPATRICK. The son.

MARSHALL. The mark of an educated man.

FITZPATRICK. Unlike his bloody old man.

> (*They laugh.* * * *)

An intellectual. (*Taps the side of his head knowingly.*) You can tell it at a glance.

MARSHALL. Never done a day's work in his life. (*They laugh.*)

> (*TC*, 17)

Surprisingly, Ewbank's son himself agrees with Marshall's assessment, and, when asked by Glendenning what he does for a living, Paul's reply is disarmingly forthright:

PAUL. Well, I'm a sort of a ... No, no. I'm a kind of ... I don't do anything at all as a matter of fact.

GLENDENNING. Oh, aye!

PAUL. You fancy a bit of that, do you?

GLENDENNING. Aye. (*Laughs.*)

PAUL. Ah, well, Glenny. Each one to his trade.

GLENDENNING. I ... I ... I ... I ... I'd like to give it a g ... g ... g ... go, though! (*Laughs*).

PAUL. Aye, well. That's a privilege few of us can afford, Glenny.

> (*TC*, 41–42)

Old Ewbank takes particular pride in his grandson's education and notes that, although Paul has "Not got his father's skill" and in fact "couldn't thread a needle" (*TC*, 46), he is receiving "the best education money can buy * * * Oxford. Cambridge. University College. All the rest. Ask him about anything and he'll come up with an answer" (*TC*, 45). Clearly, each succeeding generation of Ewbanks has risen in class and enjoyed the opportunities and privileges accompanying a standard of living that its

173

predecessor could hardly have imagined; yet, each has also lost the sense of identity, purpose, and security that sustained his father despite the hardships that he endured.

The events surrounding the wedding seem particularly joyless, even though it is apparent throughout the play that the celebration is lavish, the expenditure enormous, and the quantities of champagne impressive. Ewbank talks of the wedding exclusively in terms of economics and seems reluctant—especially at first—to discuss it with the men otherwise:

EWBANK. I'll never do it again. Never. Never have to.

KAY. No. Well. It's worth making a splash.

EWBANK. Splash? By God, this is a bloody thunderclap! It's not just the tent I'm paying for. God, Christ. I wish it was. No. No. * * * Three or four hundred people here. Bloody string orchestra. Waiters. Chef. I could buy four marquees with what I've laid out here.

(*TC*, 35–36)

In much the same way that the intrusion of financial considerations adulterated the joy of sport in *The Changing Room*, the persistence of economic concerns makes the wedding seem a matter of tawdry extravagance and bourgeois opulence—a philistine festival—rather than a celebration of holy wedlock. Reminded by her brother that "We don't get married every day," the bride responds with a curt "Let's all thank God for that" (*TC*, 39), which is, ironically, her sole reference to God and a declaration of gratitude that is almost as supercilious as that given her father later in the evening:

CLAIRE. It's lovely. (*Slides across the floor in a vague dance.*) Super. (To MAURICE.) What do you think?

MAURICE (*standing in the centre, gazing up*). Lovely.

MRS EWBANK (*to both*). Well ... I'm glad you like it.

CLAIRE. Course we do. Why not?

MRS EWBANK. Tell your dad. Not me.

CLAIRE. "Thanks, old man," she said.

EWBANK. Aye.

(*TC*, 82)

Presumably, a number of the guests fit the description that Ewbank gives of his son as having come "for the bloody booze ... nowt else" (*TC*, 110). The fact that the contractor makes such an allegation about his son *in the presence of the workmen* illustrates the tenuousness of the family unity that a wedding—more than any other traditional ritual, perhaps—should

174

foster. Although the three generations are assembled for the occasion, each remains fundamentally disaffected from the others: the grandparents would withdraw from the present into memories of an allegedly better and (for them, certainly) happier time; the contractor finds these parents to be a burden and his children to be almost strangers; and it is Paul—alienated, rudderless, and uncommitted—who (rather than the bride and groom) represents the younger generation. Yet, the Irishmen suggest that his situation is not as bleak as the father believes it to be:

EWBANK. [Paul is] Off on his bloody travels.

MARSHALL. Travels?

FITZPATRICK. Abroad, is that?

EWBANK. I wouldn't know if you told me ... He's never in one place two minutes running.

FITZPATRICK. Ah, travelling. A great broadener of the mind.

EWBANK. A great emptier of the pocket if you ask me, more likely. * * *

FITZPATRICK. Don't worry. One day he'll settle down.

EWBANK. Will he? That's your opinion, Fitzpatrick?

FITZPATRICK. Modern times, Mr Ewbank. The up and coming generation.

EWBANK. Aye, well. They can up and come all right ...

(*TC*, 106)

Shortly thereafter, the contractor expresses a resigned acceptance of the modern "way of the world" that remains incomprehensible to him:

EWBANK. * * * I've lived all this time—and I know nowt about anything. Least ways, I've settled that. I've come to that conclusion. (*He laughs. Shakes his head.*) A bloody wanderer.

KAY (*watches him. Then:*) Your lad?

EWBANK. I've no idea at all. None. Do you know? ... Where he's off to. I don't think he has himself. His mother sits at home ... (*Shakes his head.*) The modern world, Kay. It's left you and me behind.

KAY. Aye. Well. It can't be helped.

(*TC*, 117)

Occasioned by a celebration of a (supposedly) joyous union in marriage, the family reunion dissolves in sorrow and mutual incomprehension. Mrs. Ewbank has "wept bloody buckets" at Paul's departure, his father says, adding "I don't know why. He'll be back again tomorrow" (*TC*, 116). Told that his father has once again mislaid the piece of rope that he carries like a talisman, Ewbank offers a pragmatic but callous solution: "I'll cut him off a bit. He'll never know the difference" (*TC*, 121). Clearly,

175

insofar as one of the functions of ritual is to unite those who lead disparate lives, the wedding celebration fails; family unity lasts little longer than the tent itself—and is most evident as, momentarily, they dance silently beneath it on the eve of the ceremony.

The physical construction of the tent, however, *requires* much more unified effort and cooperation than the Ewbank family ever achieves. The workmen too have their disagreements (which, in fact, almost lead to a violent confrontation), but—unlike the family's—theirs remain strictly internecine; at no time do the workers disparage one another *in the presence of outsiders* (i.e., nonmembers of the group). Like the rugby players in *The Changing Room*, the workmen in *The Contractor* feel an implicit bond among themselves—a sense of coherence, hierarchy, and unity forged through common purpose and shared endeavor. Intuitively, they abide by a separate set of "rules" of conduct when the group is inviolate ("alone together"), and they revert to a more formal code of behavior in the company of their employer and members of the family. The forms of address used by the workmen denote a certain mutual acceptance, for (as among the rugby players) the use of nicknames—Glenny, Marshy, Fitzie—implies a familiarity that is withdrawn when disagreements arise and "formal" names are used. Typically, as in *The Changing Room*, nicknames are used only among those who are "on the same level" in the hierarchy; neither the foreman nor their employer is called by a nickname (though neither's name can readily be given a diminutive ending), and they seldom address their subordinates with such terms; the sole exception occurs at the end of the play when Ewbank distributes cake and champagne to the men, having secretly saved an extra piece of cake for "Glenny," in whose case the diminutive name reinforces both his own childlikeness and Ewbank's paternalistic concern. Like the coarse raillery that occurs among the teammates in the locker room, the forms of address that the men use betoken an acceptance and tolerance that the Ewbank family does not sustain; they, predictably, refer to each other only by formal names, which imply no particular endearment and suggest a lack of intimacy. In their cooperation, their mutual acceptance, and their forms of address, the workmen are "familiar" in both the denotative ("of established friendship") and etymological (Middle English, "familial," from the Latin *familia*) meanings of the word. Ironically, the Ewbanks— like the Shaws, the Slatterys, and the Middletons—are a family whose members are seldom "familiar" (informal, at ease with one another) and only strainedly "familial" (united by bonds of kinship); the Johnsons of *Mother's Day* are (or seem to be) overly "familiar"—even incestuously so— but equally "un-familial." Through the necessity of cooperative effort and shared labor (neither of which is required of the modern family, unlike its counterparts in earlier and "harder" times), the workmen find a purpose and unity that the Ewbanks cannot achieve. Accordingly, *The Contractor*—like *The Changing Room*—is a thorough elaboration of Allott's maxim in *Life Class*: *Labor Ipse Voluptas Est.*

The labor performed in *The Contractor* is not "mere" work, however, since—like the work of play in *The Changing Room*—it retains vestiges of a significance of which the characters themselves are not consciously aware. In contrast to the surrogate religions sought by Allott in modern art and by Arnold Middleton in preserving the residua of a heroic past, the construction of the tent in *The Contractor* recapitulates an authentic, primordial religious experience—a means whereby, through one of the oldest distinctively human activities, early man defined his relationship with the world and the forces that control it. Against the storms and strife of the natural world, the man-made shelter asserts human control and *order*. Like the locker-room setting of *The Changing Room*, therefore, the site of the tent constructed in the course of *The Contractor* constitutes a wholly secular counterpart of the archaic "sacred space," and the events that take place there provide a similarly vital significance in many of the characters' lives.

Whereas in *The Changing Room* the setting remained constant as the characters "changed" (in both senses of the word), in *The Contractor* it is the transformation of the setting that comprises the action of the play. The temporariness of each change is unmistakable—an implicit indication of the impermanence of all forms of transcendence in a desacralized world. Although the wedding presumably takes place in a church, the literal "sacred space" in which vows are to be exchanged remains unspecified, and neither the bride nor the groom nor any member of the family expresses any concern about it—or any other religious aspect of the activity. Since, instead, the secular festivities of the reception preoccupy them all, it is appropriate that this temporarily demarcated, profane counterpart of the "sacred space"—rather than the site of the devalued traditional ritual—is the focus of the play.

More than any of Storey's other plays, *The Contractor* presents a central symbol that accommodates a variety of diverse interpretations, as Storey acknowledged in his conversation with Victor Sage:

> I find *The Contractor* one of the most satisfying things I've written. Each time I see it in a different light. In this revival I see it more and more as being about—or somehow related to—the decline and fading away of a capitalist society. Or I have seen it as a metaphor for artistic creation: all the labour of putting up this tent, and when it's there, what good is it? What is it there for? And I get letters from people who ask me does it mean this, and does it mean that, and I often see some justice in their suggestions. And still the play is not

confined to any one of these definitions; it contains the possibility of them, but it still continues to make sense—and complete sense—as the story of these men who put up this tent, and that's that.[33]

In fact, for reasons that Eliade has explained in *The Sacred and the Profane*, the construction of a tent is a paradigmatic human event—"the archetype of every creative human gesture"[34] from the creation of capital to the creation of art. Although the workmen are not consciously aware of the significance of their seemingly mundane, workaday activity, the construction of the tent recapitulates an authentic, primordial religious experience; at one point, Fitzpatrick even mockingly attempts to use this wholly secular "sacred space" of the tent as a confessional (another sacrosanct place) for Kay, asking him "Between these four walls—or three and a half to be exact—what manner of crime was it you committed? Were you driven to it by the pressures of the world; or is it simply that you're a rotten *sod*?" (*TC*, 65). "Something of the religious conception of the world still persists in the behavior of profane man," Eliade maintains, "although he is not always conscious of this immemorial heritage."[35] Specifically, he insists, the construction of the tent is a paradigmatic act of creation that "is always a consecration [, since] to organize a space is to repeat the paradigmatic work of the gods" in creating the world.[36] Furthermore, Eliade argues, "in all traditional cultures, the habitation possesses a sacred aspect by the simple fact that it reflects the world. . . . In other words, *cosmic symbolism is found in the very structure of the habitation*. The house is an *imago mundi*. The sky is conceived as a vast tent supported by a central pillar; the tent pole or the central post of the house is assimilated to the Pillars of the World and is so named" (emphasis his).[37] The habitation—the world—thus created in *The Contractor* is deliberately impermanent; the traditional rituals associated with it have been devalued in the modern world. Nevertheless, Eliade argues, "every construction or fabrication has the cosmogony as paradigmatic model [, and the] creation of the world becomes the archetype of every creative human gesture, whatever its plane of reference may be."[38]

Implicitly, therefore, the construction of the tent constitutes an affirmation of order against the storms and perils of the natural world. The instance for which the Ewbanks' tent lasts is, in effect, a respite from the chaos of their lives, an occasion during which the family maintains the

[33]Quoted in John Russell Taylor, "British Dramatists: The New Arrivals, III—David Storey: Novelist into Dramatist," *Plays and Players* June 1970: 23.

[34]Mircea Eliade, *The Sacred and the Profane: The Nature of Religion*, trans. Willard R. Trask (New York: Harper & Row, 1959) 45.

[35]Eliade 50.

[36]Eliade 32.

[37]Eliade 53.

[38]Eliade 45.

(devalued) order required by the traditional rituals and ceremonies associated with the wedding. Yet, because the traditional values thus reaffirmed no longer command the reverence and allegiance that they once were accorded, the order that is thus created remains as temporary—if not as perfunctory—as the tent itself. Its destruction, accordingly, "is equivalent to a retrogression to chaos," as Eliade suggests, since it represents "the abolition of an order, a cosmos, an organic structure, and reimmersion in the state of fluidity or formlessness—in short, of chaos."[39] For the Ewbank family and the workmen alike, the third act of the play embodies this return to chaos and the disharmony of their personal lives. The family members go their separate ways in renewed mutual incomprehension, drifting back into the fluidity and formlessness of everyday life in the modern world. The workmen's disputes escalate as the tent is disassembled, though their disagreements were necessarily suppressed during the essential cooperation of building it. The demolition requires much less orderly and methodical procedures, and violence—chaos—is threatened when the cooperative, collaborative effort is no longer required. The interval for which the tent lasted was, in effect, a respite from the chaos of life, an occasion on which the (devalued) order required by traditional rituals and ceremonies was temporarily maintained. A more significant order—albeit no less temporary and equally subject to strain—is renewed daily among the workmen in the nontraditional rituals of their work.

Like *Home*, *The Contractor* concludes with a prevailing tone of melancholy. Although marriage is the age-old rite of renewal (and the traditional resolution of comedy), such affirmation is noticeably absent in Storey's play. Instead, when the debris is cleared away, Ewbank and his wife are left to share their newly desolate prospect alone. As in *Home*, however, the source of this melancholy subsumes such personal considerations and is in fact an inevitable consequence of desacralized life, since, as Eliade has shown,

> The perspective changes when the sense of *the religiousness of the cosmos becomes lost*. This is what occurs when, in certain more highly evolved societies, the intellectual elites progressively detach themselves from the patterns of traditional religion. . . . The religious meaning of the repetition of paradigmatic gestures is forgotten. But *repetition emptied of its religious content necessarily leads to a pessimistic vision of existence*. When it is no longer a vehicle for reintegrating a primordial situation, and hence for recovery of the mysterious presence of the gods, that is, *when it is desacralized*, cyclic time becomes terrifying; it is seen as a circle forever turning on itself, repeating itself to infinity.[40] (Emphasis his)

[39]Eliade 49–50.
[40]Eliade 107.

179

Unlike *Home*, however, *The Contractor* does not end in despair, since its final scene suggests a consolation that is not present at the close of the later play:

EWBANK. I don't know ... What's to become of us, you reckon? (MRS EWBANK *looks at him, smiles, then shakes her head.*) Never do this again, you know.

MRS EWBANK. No ... (*She smiles.*)

EWBANK. Me heart wouldn't stand it.

MRS EWBANK. No ... (*She laughs.*)

OLD MRS E (*off*). Frank ... !

EWBANK. Aye, well. (*Half-laughs.*) That's summat.

(*They turn slowly, arm in arm.*)

OLD MRS E (*off*). Frank ... !

EWBANK. S'all right. We're coming. (*To* MRS EWBANK) Well, then. We better go.

(*They go.
The stage stands empty: bare poles, the ropes fastened off. The light fades slowly.*)

(*TC*, 122)

The fact that Ewbank and his wife leave the stage "arm in arm" suggests a consolation that the contractor's "S'all right" affirms; his wife's tacit and sympathetic understanding denotes a loving solidarity with which to face the uncertainties of the future and impending old age. The Ewbanks will at least be "alone together" and, as he himself remarks, "That's summat." In a world devoid of "spiritual" values and without the certainty of secular traditions and mores which earlier generations accepted unquestioningly, being "alone together"—whether in work or in a family—is the most that can be hoped for. That "summat" is indeed all.

Epilogue

By the time of our conversation in 1983, David Storey had become convinced that, for a variety of reasons, most of which are beyond his control, his career as a playwright had come to an end. Toward the close of our conversation, I asked him whether—after the success of *Early Days* at the National Theatre—more plays would be forthcoming there or back at the Royal Court. "I think the plays are a dead duck now, as far as I'm concerned," he replied, adding that "I don't think I could get another play on—certainly not over here." Citing changes at the Royal Court, he remarked that "It's been taken over by young, left-wing radicals who see me as a sort of working-class turncoat, and politically my work isn't acceptable. They've never asked me to contribute since they've taken over, and I don't think they would be inclined to."

"Has the 'golden age' of the Royal Court ended, then?" I asked.

"Well, *you* could make that comment," he replied, laughing. "It has ended for me. I don't know about for anyone else. It's become very parochial and sort of preoccupied with politicizing drama. I find that a form of philistinism. I think the 'theatre of ideas,' which is basically what they have—polemical theatre, political theatre—is, as far as I'm concerned, philistine. I can't really see it acted, and anything I write is quite the reverse of it." Yet, even if there *were* such a desire on the part of the theatre's management, recent cuts in the Royal Court's subsidies from the Arts Council have been so severe that, as Rob Ritchie observed in his essay on "The Royal Court and New Writing" in *Drama*, a cast of ten in a play being staged there is now "exceptional. If the theatre wanted to revive . . . *The Changing Room*, they would have to persuade the author to switch the action to when the players had gone home."[1] Nevertheless, Storey insists that the stage at the Royal Court is "the only space I relate to creatively. . . . All the plays were written with that theatre in mind— inspired by it, [ever since] seeing *Arnold Middleton* there. . . . When I go away from there, I can't really . . . *Early Days* was written for that theatre, absolutely. . . . That was the stage I had in mind," even though it was later produced at the National Theatre.

[1] Rob Ritchie, "Not Quite A Revolution: The Royal Court and New Writing," *Drama: The Quarterly Theatre Review* 155 (1st quarter 1985) 24.

Epilogue

In contrast to the Royal Court, with its small stage, its limited seating capacity, and its continually imperiled financial support, the modern, subsidized, spacious National Theatre complex is, for Storey, "complete anathema." It is not, he explains, "a writer's theatre at all; it's really an impresario's idea—a computer's idea—of a theatre. I can't do creative work as a writer there. It's only for revivals and doing middle-class, middlebrow drama—Peter Shaffer and [Alan] Ayckbourn.... It's a kind of middlebrow theatre that thrives there . . . but I don't think there's any real writing going on. . . . Unlike the Royal Court, it has a big middlebrow audience who come for anything at all. There's only one play in the entire history of the new National that's ever been taken off, and that was a new play, which was a mistake, but every other play has been, *is* a success—I mean, 70, 80, 90 percent capacity, which is extraordinary. And it caters to that kind of audience. It's impossible for a writer; it's an institution. A writer can't really write for an institution, unless he's an institution-type writer, like Shakespeare, or one who'll write for a given audience, which I won't or can't. It's finished, as far as I'm concerned; I couldn't write creatively in that atmosphere. I'd write plays which are a liability; they'd only take them off, if by mistake they put one on."

Toward the "fringe" theatres—the only other apparent alternative for getting his plays produced—Storey expressed an equal disdain: "There's no other theatre that exists for a writer, unless you go to the fringe theatres. But that's very parochial again. Its dynamic is amateurish. It's basically a subsidized form. If you took the subsidy away, its artistic life wouldn't be sufficiently vigorous to run a theatre at all. So there we are: End of your book."

Such a view of the theatre is embodied, to an extent, in Storey's little-known recent play, *Phoenix*, which was first produced by the amateur group Ealing Questors in 1985 and was subsequently staged by Century Theatre in Huddersfield and Rotterham; to date, it has not been published and is, Storey advises, still subject to revisions. Though the text is currently unavailable, the general nature of the play can be construed from the few reviews that the regional productions received.[2] The play is set in a subsidised theatre that is located in the Northern provinces and scheduled for demolition; its central character, Alan Ashcroft, is the artistic director of the theatre whose government subsidy has been cut off. A former boxer and the son of a collier, Ashcroft had returned to his hometown seven years earlier to bring art to an audience that does

[2]The reviews cited herein are Philip Andrews in the *Stage and Television Today* 2 May 1985: 11; Eric Shorter in the *Daily Telegraph* 13 March 1985; and Robin Thornber in the *Guardian* 13 March 1985. The reviews by Shorter and Thornber are reprinted in the *London Theatre Record* for 27 February–12 March 1985: 230.

not understand—or care about—it, despite fine reviews that it has received. Like Allott, Arnold Middleton, and many of Storey's other protagonists, Ashcroft finds himself beset by personal and familial problems that compound the impending crisis that threatens to end his professional career; his personal and professional lives are disintegrating at the same time. According to Robin Thornber in the *Guardian*,

> His wife left him to have an abortion and is now in a mental hospital. His mistress was "discovered" in one of his shows and is now a cinema star in London. The farmhouse where he threw scandalously memorable parties has been repossessed by the building society and he's been sleeping on the stage.
>
> Wielding a whisky bottle, he seems to feel threatened by his resident writer, of the leftish trend that hands out rifles to the audience. He faces a gaol sentence for assaulting his wife's psychiatrist, and there's the matter of his mistress's missing dog.

Having resolved to fight the demolition of the theatre until the bitter end, Ashcroft is as resolutely opposed to the philistines as Arnold Middleton was (in the play that was originally titled *To Die with the Philistines*). As the play proceeds, the director is visited by—and confronts anew— the various people who have shaped his domestic life and the current professional crisis. His former mistress's success is contrasted with his own conspicuous failure, and the leftist writer obviously embodies the style of agitprop drama that, whether at the Royal Court or elsewhere, Storey particularly deplores.

Nevertheless, according to the review by Philip Andrews, at the end of the play, "Storey's . . . stark view of life . . . is leavened by a final optimism, for when we last see Ashcroft he is reconciled with his wife and leaves his doomed theatre, perhaps to rise to a better life out of its ashes"—much as Arnold Middleton seems ready to do at the end of his own "restoration." At the very end of the play, however, as the literal demolition of Ashcroft's theatre begins, "masonry crashes down from the roof and the entire building (the auditorium as well as the stage) shakes to its foundations." However reassuring Ashcroft's personal reconciliations seem to be, and whatever the implications of the title about a personal "return from the ashes," the final scene's literally crashing impact seems to offer an unambiguous symbol of Storey's view of the present state of the theatre.

Whatever the course of Storey's future development as a writer, and whatever the critical judgments about his fiction may be, his achievement in the theatre should place him securely among the foremost playwrights of his time. If, as he has insisted, his career as a playwright has ended, and the plays produced between 1966 and 1985 therefore comprise his complete oeuvre for the theatre, they are remarkable not only for the diversity of their forms but for their thematic continuity. Beyond the apparent refinements of dramatic technique that separate *The Restoration of Arnold Middleton* from *Life Class*, for example, there is among Storey's plays a unique and consistent redefinition of the theatrical "event" itself— a redefinition that, though akin to Chekhov's ambitions for a new form of theatre, seems likely to be Storey's most permanent contribution to the development of contemporary drama.

Certainly, no playwright has taken more seriously William Gaskill's initial conception of the Royal Court as a "writer's theatre" when he founded the English Stage Company there in 1956, with a consequent commitment to a diversity of unique talents and the full range of individual authorial voices. Finding that outlet for his creative work no longer available to him, unwilling or unable to be the "institutional writer" that he feels the National Theatre requires, Storey has returned to writing novels—long his preference as the result of his "sentimental attachment" to the form, though he finds the writing much more difficult and is often dissatisfied with the results. Thus even the critically acclaimed *A Prodigal Child* is, to Storey, "a very unsatisfactory novel. . . . When I got halfway through, I couldn't go on with it, so I just chopped it off and put an end on it. . . . I spent about five years trying to get it all into shape, and it just refused to come into shape. I thought the best thing was to cut my losses and jacket it. I knew if I didn't publish it, however bad or however fragmentary it was, I'd just go on tinkering with it. . . . I don't like it as a novel. I see its limitations, what it could have been or should have been." At various times, Storey has indicated similar reservations about *Radcliffe*, *Pasmore*, and *A Temporary Life*, and it was his frustration with the abandoned novel from which *Pasmore* was taken that led him to write for the theatre at all. Yet, with the sole exceptions of *Cromwell*, the abandoned work called *Night*, and the unpublished *Phoenix*, he has expressed no such dissatisfaction about his plays.

When, in an empty space, a human event takes place and is observed, it is by definition an act of theatre, as Peter Brook has shown in *The Empty Space*.[3] Whether it occurs on a stage, in a park, on a street, in a living room or lockerroom, or on a section of lawn, the event becomes inherently theatrical as the object of an "act of attention." Whether or not there is a script, whether on not the action has been rehearsed, whether or not the participants are self-consciously playing roles, whether the observer is seated in a theatre or merely "people-watching" in a public place, whether he observes silently or watches the reactions of someone with whom he is involved, "acts of theatre" are ceaseless and innumerable in everyday life. The fact that "all the world's a stage and

[3]Peter Brook, *The Empty Space* (New York: Avon Books, 1969) 9.

all the men and women merely players" is hardly new, of course; yet, although the theatre itself is no longer the *imago mundi* that it was in Shakespeare's time, in the twentieth century "theatricality" and reality have become inextricably mixed. The unique insight of David Storey has been that, without elaboration or contrivances of plot, such seemingly "untheatrical" events as the construction of a tent, the activities of a lockerroom, or the conversations of patients in a "home" could be made into powerfully effective theatre.

"In real life," Chekhov once observed, "people don't spend every minute shooting each other, hanging themselves and making confessions of love. They don't spend all their time saying clever things. They're more occupied with eating, drinking, flirting, and talking stupidities—and these are the things that ought to be shown on the stage. A play should be written in which people arrive, go away, have dinner, talk about the weather, and play cards. Life must be exactly as it is, and people as they are—not on stilts. . . . Let everything on the stage be just as complicated, and at the same time just as simple as it is in life. People eat their dinner, just eat their dinner, and all the time their happiness is being established or their lives are being broken up."[4] The fact that dramatic potential exists within such seemingly undramatic occasions was the Russian playwright's most innovative insight, although his own plays—which detractors also consider "plotless"—do not dispense entirely with traditionally "theatrical" incidents and *agons*: an attempted shooting provides the climax of *Uncle Vanya*, a suicide is disclosed at the end of *The Sea Gull*, and the conflict between representatives of the old and new social orders pervades the action of *The Cherry Orchard*. Although there are a few such episodes in some of Storey's plays (e.g., the simulated rape in *Life Class* and the breakdown and recovery in *The Restoration of Arnold Middleton*), his most innovative and significant works—*Home*, *The Contractor*, and *The Changing Room*—do not include such sensational events or "extraordinary" conflicts. By focusing the attention of theatregoers on such seemingly mundane events of ordinary life, without the distractions provided by the (by definition "extraordinary") occurrences that constitute a "dramatic" plot, David Storey subtly reveals the significance of the otherwise "invisible" events of ordinary life. To have presented these events with poignancy, humor, and an understated eloquence has been his most important—and most remarkable—achievement as a playwright.

Storey's plays thus fulfill the potential for a drama of truly "ordinary" life that Chekhov envisioned over three generations ago. At the conclusion of *Three Sisters*, Chekhov's most static and "plotless" play, Irina speaks of a number of themes that Storey would later make his own: "A time

---

[4]Quoted in Ronald Hingley, *Chekhov: A Biographical and Critical Study* (London: Allen & Unwin, 1950) 233.

will come when everyone will know what all this is for, why there is all this suffering, and there will be no mysteries; but meanwhile, we must live ... we must work, only work! Tomorrow I shall go alone, and I shall teach in the school, and give my whole life to those who need it. Now it is autumn, soon winter will come and cover everything with snow, and I shall go on working, working ..."[5] Typically, Storey's characters are (as *Home* makes clear) no nearer knowing "what all this is for" than Chekhov's; the spiritual sense of purpose, the religious sense of "mystery," and the faith-based validation of suffering have been depreciated—and deprecated—in an increasingly secular world. Nevertheless, with the exception of those in *Home*, Storey's characters—like Irina—resolve to "work, only work," and several of them (Arnold Middleton, Steven Shaw, Wendy Slattery) return to teach in the school. Yet whatever the nature of their jobs—building tents, playing rugby, teaching school, tending a farm, mining coal—it is the necessity of such work (preferably involving actual physical labor, even if in the work of play) that provides continuity and coherence in their lives, preventing the capitulation to despair that occurs in *Home*. Work—the curse of Adam, the counsel of John the Baptist, the consolation of Martin at the end of *Candide,* and the exhortation of Thomas Carlyle—became, in the 1970s, the unique theme and theatrical subject of David Storey, the source of nontraditional rituals through which life in a desacralized world can be more readily sustained.

[5]Anton Chekhov, *The Three Sisters*, trans. Ann Dunnigan, in *Chekhov: The Major Plays* (New York: Signet-New American Library, 1964) 312.

186

Bibliography   Index

Bibliography

The Works of David Storey

Plays and novels are listed chronologically.

Individual Plays

The Restoration of Arnold Middleton. London: Jonathan Cape, 1967.
———. In *Plays of the Year* [1967]. Vol. 35. Ed. J. C. Trewin. London: Elek Books, 1968.
———. In *New English Dramatists* 14. Harmondsworth: Penguin, 1970.
In Celebration. London: Jonathan Cape, 1969.
———. New York: Grove Press, 1969.
———. In *Plays and Players* June 1969: 35–55.
———. In *Plays of the Year* [1969]. Vol. 38. Ed. J. C. Trewin. London: Elek Books, 1970.
———. Harmondsworth: Penguin, 1971.
———. With intro. by Ronald Hayman. London: Heinemann, 1973.
The Contractor. London: Jonathan Cape, 1970.
———. In *Plays and Players* December 1969: 63–86.
———. New York: Random House, 1970.
———. Harmondsworth: Penguin, 1971.
Home. London: Jonathan Cape, 1970.
———. In *Plays and Players* August 1970: 61–77.
———. New York: Random House, 1971.
———. In *Plays of the Year* [1971]. Vol. 41. Ed. J. C. Trewin. London: Elek Books, 1972.
The Changing Room. London: Jonathan Cape, 1972.
———. New York: Random House, 1973.
———. Harmondsworth: Penguin, 1973.
———. With intro. by E. R. Wood. London: Heinemann, 1977.
Cromwell. London: Jonathan Cape, 1973.
The Farm. London: Jonathan Cape, 1973.
Life Class. London: Jonathan Cape, 1975.
Mother's Day. In *Early Days/Sisters/Life Class*. Harmondsworth: Penguin, 1980.
Sisters. In *Early Days/Sisters/Life Class*. Harmondsworth: Penguin, 1980.

Bibliography

Collected Plays

The Changing Room, Home, and The Contractor: Three Plays by David Storey. New York: Bard-Avon, 1975.
In Celebration and The Contractor. Harmondsworth: Penguin, 1977.
Home, The Changing Room, and Mother's Day. Harmondsworth: Penguin, 1978.
Early Days/Sisters/Life Class. Harmondsworth: Penguin, 1980.
In Celebration, The Contractor, The Restoration of Arnold Middleton, and The Farm. Harmondsworth: Penguin, 1982.

Novels

This Sporting Life. New York: Macmillan, 1960.
————. London: Longman, 1960.
————. New York: Avon, 1975.
————. Harmondsworth: Penguin, 1976.
————. Intro. by the author and commentary and notes by Geoffrey Halson. London: Longman, 1978.
Flight into Camden. London: Longman, 1960.
————. New York: Macmillan, 1961.
————. Harmondsworth: Penguin, 1978.
Radcliffe. London: Longman, 1963.
————. New York: Coward-McCann, 1963.
————. New York: Avon, 1965.
————. Harmondsworth: Penguin, 1977.
Pasmore. London: Longman, 1972.
————. New York: E. P. Dutton, 1972.
————. New York: Avon, 1975.
————. Harmondsworth: Penguin, 1976.
A Temporary Life. London: Allen Lane, 1973.
————. New York: E. P. Dutton, 1974.
————. New York: Avon, 1975.
————. Harmondsworth: Penguin, 1978.
Saville. London: Jonathan Cape, 1976.
————. New York: Harper & Row, 1976.
————. Harmondsworth: Penguin, 1978.
————. New York: Avon, 1978.
A Prodigal Child. London: Jonathan Cape, 1982.
————. Harmondsworth: Penguin, 1984.
Present Times. London: Jonathan Cape, 1984.

Children's Literature

Edward. Illus. Donald Parker. London: Allen Lane, 1973.

Film and Television Adaptations

Early Days. 1981.
Home. 1973.
In Celebration. 1974.
This Sporting Life. 1963.

Teleplay

"Grace," from the short story by James Joyce. 1974.

Documentaries Directed

"Death of My Mother" (on D. H. Lawrence), 1963.
"Portrait of Margaret Evans," 1963.

Articles, Essays, and Reviews

"Cells." *New Statesman* 19 April 1963: 612.
"Journey through a Tunnel." *Listener* 1 August 1963: 159–61.
Letter. *Times* (London), 15 February 1974, 15.
"Marxism as a Form of Nostalgia." *New Society* 15 July 1975: 23.
"Ned Kelly on Film." *Manchester Guardian* 7 February 1963: 7.
"Nolan's Ark." *New Statesman* 31 May 1963: 840–41.
"On Lindsay Anderson." *Cinebill: The American Film Theatre—The Second Season*.
     New York: AFT Distributing Corp., 1975.
"Passionate Polemics." *New Society* 28 January 1967: 137–38.
"Robert Colquhoun." *New Statesman* 12 October 1962: 500–501.
"What Really Matters." *Twentieth Century* 172 (Autumn 1963): 96–97.
"Working with Lindsay." *At the Royal Court: 25 Years of the English Stage Company*.
     Ed. Richard Findlater. New York: Grove Press, 1981. 110–15.

Poetry

"Grandfather." In the program accompanying the Royal Court's production of
     The Contractor. London: G. J. Parris, 1969 [6].
"Miners." In *Playbill* for *The Restoration of Arnold Middleton*, Criterion Theatre,
     1967 (London: Playbill, Ltd., 1967): 14.
Revolutionary Times. Unpublished book.

Interviews and Articles Based on Interviews

Ansorge, Peter. "The Theatre of Life: David Storey in Interview." *Plays and
     Players* September 1973: 32–36.

Bibliography

Billington, Michael. "Making Life Work on Two Levels." *Times* (London) 4 April 1970: 21. /

Flatley, Guy. "'I Never Saw a Pinter Play.'" *New York Times* 29 November 1970, sec. 2: 1, 5.

Gussow, Mel. "To David Storey, a Play Is a 'Holiday.'" *New York Times* 20 April 1973: 14.

Hayman, Ronald. "Conversation with David Storey." *Drama* 99 (Winter 1970): 47–53. Rpt. in Ronald Hayman, *Playback*. New York: Horizon, 1974. 7–20.

Hennessy, Brendan. "David Storey Interviewed by Brendan Hennessy." *Transatlantic Review* 33–34 (1969): 5–11.

Loney, Glenn. "Shop Talk with a British Playwright: David Storey Discusses *Home* and Other Scripts." *Dramatists Guild Quarterly* 8 (Spring 1971): 27–30.

Sage, Victor. "David Storey in Conversation." *New Review* October 1976: 63–65.

"Speaking of Writing, II: David Storey." *Times* (London), 28 November 1963: 15.

Willett, John, et al. "Thoughts on Contemporary Theatre." *New Theatre Magazine* 7.2 (1967): 6–13.

Secondary Sources

Bibliography and Checklist

Carpenter, Charles A. "Bond, Shaffer, Stoppard, Storey: An International Checklist of Commentary." *Modern Drama* 24 (1981): 546–56.

King, Kimball. *Twenty Modern British Playwrights: A Bibliography, 1956–1976*. New York: Garland, 1977. 231–39.

Dissertations

Bedell, Jeanne Fenrick. "Towards Jerusalem: The Changing Portrayal of the Working Class in Modern English Drama, 1900–1970." Southern Illinois University, 1975.

Clark, Susan Mauk. "David Storey: The Emerging Artist." Purdue, 1976.

Froeb, Jeanne Riney. "The Fiction of David Storey, John Fowles, and Iris Murdoch." University of Tulsa, 1977.

Harris, Judith Dotson. "An Unholy Encounter: The Early Works of David Storey." Ohio State University, 1974.

Hutchings, John William, Jr. "The Significance of Ritual in the Plays of David Storey." University of Kentucky, 1981.

Lockwood, Bernard. "Four Contemporary British Working-Class Novelists: A Thematic and Critical Approach to the Fiction of Raymond Williams, John Braine, David Storey, and Alan Sillitoe." University of Wisconsin, 1967.

Nolan, Ernest Isaiah, III. "Beyond Realism: A Study of Time and Place in the Plays of David Storey." Notre Dame, 1975.

Reinelt, Janelle G. "The Novels and Plays of David Storey: New Solutions in Form and Technique." Stanford, 1978.

Weaver, Laura H. "Journey through a Tunnel: The Divided Self in the Novels and Plays of David Storey." University of Kansas, 1977.

Articles in Reference Books

Gindin, James. "David Storey." *British Dramatists Since World War II, Part II: M-Z*. Vol. 13 of *Dictionary of Literary Biography*. Detroit: Gale Research Co., 1982. 501–13.

Heiney, Donald, and Lenthiel H. Downs. "David Storey." *Contemporary British Literature*. Vol. 2 of *Essentials of Contemporary Literature of the Western World*. Woodbury, N.Y.: Barron's, 1974. 208–14.

Nightingale, Benedict. "David Storey." *Contemporary Dramatists*. Ed. James Vinson. 2nd ed. London: St. James Press, 1977.

Chapters or Portions of Books

Browne, Terry W. *Playwrights' Theatre: The English Stage Company at the Royal Court Theatre*. London: Pitman Publishing Co., 1975.

Craig, David. "David Storey's Vision of the Working Class." *The Uses of Fiction: Essays on the Modern Novel in Honour of Arnold Kettle*. Ed. Douglas Jefferson et al. Milton Keynes, England: Open University Press, 1982. 125–38.

Dutton, Richard. "*Home* by David Storey." *Modern Tragicomedy and the British Tradition: Beckett, Pinter, Stoppard, Albee, and Storey*. Norman: University of Oklahoma Press, 1986. 151–61.

Ecker, Gisela. "David Storey: *Home*—'schones Wetter heute' oder Strukturen des 'small talk.'" *Englishes Drama von Beckett bis Bond*. Munich: Fink, 1982. 250–71.

Gray, Nigel. "Show Them You Can Take It" [on *This Sporting Life*]. *The Silent Majority: A Study of the Working Class in Post-War British Fiction*. New York: Barnes & Noble-Harper & Row, 1973. 133–59.

Hayman, Ronald. *British Theatre since 1955: A Reassessment*. Oxford: Oxford University Press, 1979. 55–58.

Hidalgo, Pilar. "David Storey." *La ira y la palabra: teatro inglés actual*. Madrid: Cupsa, 1978. 171–80.

Hilton, Julian. "The Court and Its Favours." *Stratford-upon-Avon Studies 19: Contemporary English Drama*. Ed. Malcolm Bradbury and David Palmer. London: Edward Arnold, 1981. 139–155. Rpt. as "The Court and Its Favours: The Careers of Christopher Hampton, David Storey, and John Arden" in *Modern British Dramatists: New Perspectives*. Ed. John Russell Brown. Englewood Cliffs, N.J.: Prentice-Hall, 1984. 50–74.

Hutchings, William. " 'Much Ado about Almost Nothing' Or, The Pleasures of Plotless Plays." *Within the Dramatic Spectrum*. Ed. Karelisa V. Hartigan.

Bibliography

Comparative Drama Conference Papers 6. Lanham, MD: University Press of America, 1986. 107–114.

———. " 'Poetic Naturalism' and Chekhovian Form in the Plays of David Storey." *The Many Forms of Drama*. Ed. Karelisa V. Hartigan. Comparative Drama Conference Papers 5. Lanham, MD: University Press of America, 1985. 79–85.

Kerensky, Oleg. "David Storey." *The New British Drama: Fourteen Playwrights Since Osborne and Pinter*. London: Hamish Hamilton, 1977. 3–17.

Morley, Sheridan. *Review Copies: Plays and Players in London, 1970–1974*. London: Robson Books, 1974.

Olsson, Barbara. "Pitman and Poet: The Divided." *A Yearbook in English Language and Literature*. Ed. Max Gauna. Vienna: Braumuller, n.d. 39–52.

Randall, Phyllis R. "Division and Unity in David Storey." *Essays on Contemporary British Drama*. Ed. Hedwig Bock and Albert Wertheim. Munich: Hueber, 1981. 253–65.

Roberts, Philip. "David Storey's *The Changing Room*." *The Royal Court Theatre, 1965–1972*. London: Routledge & Kegan Paul, 1986. 107–20.

Rosen, Carol. "*Home*." *Plays of Impasse: Contemporary Drama Set in Convining Institutions*. Princeton: Princeton University Press, 1983. 128–46.

Taylor, John Russell. "David Storey." *The Second Wave: British Drama of the Sixties*. London: Eyre Methuen, 1971; rev. 1978. 141–54.

Thomann, Claus. "David Storey, *Cromwell*." *Englische Literatur der Gegenwart, 1971–1975*. Ed. Rainer Lengeler. Dusseldorf: Bagel, 1977. 197–217.

Weaver, Laura H. "Rugby and the Arts: The Divided Self in David Storey's Novels and Plays." *Fearful Symmetry: Doubles and Doubling in Literature and Film*. Ed. Eugene J. Crook. Tallahassee: University Presses of Florida, 1981. 149–62.

Wieselhuber, Franz. "David Storey: *Home* (1970)." *Das zeitgenössische englische Drama*. Frankfurt: Athenaum, 1975. 262–73.

Wimmer, Adlof. "David Storey." *Pessimistisches Theater: eine Studie zur Entfremdung im englischen Drama, 1955–1975*. Salzburg: Institut fur Anglistik and Amerikkanistik, Universitat Salzburg, 1979. 116–30.

Worth, Katharine J. *Revolutions in Modern English Drama*. London: Bell, 1973. 26–30 and 38–40.

Young, B. A. *The Mirror Up to Nature: A Review of the Theatre, 1964–1982*. London: William Kimber, 1982. 71–73.

Pamphlet

Taylor, John Russell. *David Storey*. Writers and their Work 239. Ed. Ian Scott-Kilvert. London: Longman, 1974.

Articles

Anderson, Lindsay. "On David Storey." *Cinebill: The American Film Theatre—The Second Season*. New York: AFT Distributing Corp, 1975.

Bibliography

Bygrave, Mike. "David Storey: Novelist or Playwright?" *Theatre Quarterly* 1.2 (April–June 1971): 31–36.

Churchill, Thomas. "Waterhouse, Storey, and Fowles: *Which Way Out of the Room?*" *Critique: Studies in Modern Fiction* 10.3 (1968): 72–87.

Duffy, Martha. "An Ethic of Work and Play." *Sports Illustrated*, 5 March 1973: 66–69.

Free, William J. "The Ironic Anger of David Storey." *Modern Drama* 16.3–4 (December 1973): 306–17.

Free, William J., and Lynn Page Whittaker. "The Intrusion Plot in David Storey's Plays." *Papers on Language and Literature* 17 (Spring 1982): 151–65.

Gray, Paul. "Class Theatre, Class Film: An Interview with Lindsay Anderson." *Tulane Drama Review* 11 (Fall 1966): 122- 29.

Hashiguchi, Minoru. "England, karera no England—David Storey: *Radcliffe* wo megutte." *Eigo Seinen* (Tokyo) 117 (1972): 730–31.

Hutchings, William. " 'Invisible Events' and the Experience of Sports in David Storey's *The Changing Room.*" *Proteus: A Journal of Ideas* 3.1 (Spring 1986): 1–7.

———. "The Work of Play: Anger and the Expropriated Athletes of Alan Sillitoe and David Storey." *Modern Fiction Studies* 33.1 (Spring 1987): 35–47.

Joyce, Steven. "A Study in Dramatic Dialogue: A Structural Approach to David Storey's *Home.*" *Theatre Annual* 38 (1983): 65–81.

Kalson, Albert E. "Insanity and the Rational Man in the Plays of David Storey." *Modern Drama* 19.2 (June 1976): 111–128.

Kedzeielska, Alicja. "David Storey: świat bez gniewu i trwogi." *Dialog* (Warsaw) 18.1 (1973): 77–83.

Knapp, Bettina L. "David Storey's *In Celebration* and Gabriel Cousin's *Journey to the Mountain Beyond*: From 'Maw' to Mater Gloriosa." *Theatre Annual* 33 (1977): 39–55.

McGuinness, Frank. "The Novels of David Storey." *London Magazine* ns 3.12 (March 1964): 79–82.

Mellors, John. "Yorkshire Relish: The Novels of John Braine and David Storey." *London Magazine* ns 16.4 (October–November 1976): 79–84.

Newton, J. M. "Two Men Who Matter?" *Cambridge Quarterly* 1 (Summer 1966): 284–95.

Nightingale, Benedict. "Everyman on His Uppers." *New Statesman*, 19 April 1974: 558–59.

Papajewski, Helmut. "Unbestimmtheit also struktureller Grundzug von David Storey's *Home.*" *Literatur in Wissenschaft und Unterricht* 4 (1975): 164–76.

Pearce, Howard D. "A Phenomenological Approach to the *Theatrum Mundi* Metaphor." *PMLA* 95.1 (January 1980): 42–57.

Peel, Marie. "David Storey: Demon and Lazarus." *Books and Bookmen* 17 (March 1972), 20–24.

Porter, James E. "*The Contractor*: David Storey's Static Drama." *University of Windsor Review* 15.1–2 (1979–80): 66–75.

Quigley, Austin E. "The Emblematic Structure and Setting of David Storey's Plays." *Modern Drama* 22 (September 1979): 259–76.

Bibliography

Reinelt, Janelle. "The Central Event in David Storey's Plays." *Theatre Journal* 31 (1979): 210–20.

Rosen, Carol. "Symbolic Naturalism in David Storey's *Home*." *Modern Drama* 22.3 (September 1979): 277–89.

Shelton, Lewis E. "David Storey and the Invisible Event." *Midwest Quarterly* 22 (Summer 1981): 392–406.

Shrapnel, Susan. "No Goodness and No Kings." *Cambridge Quarterly* 5 (Autumn 1970): 181–87.

Stinson, John J. "Dualism and Paradox in the 'Puritan' Plays of David Storey." *Modern Drama* 20.2 (June 1977): 131–43.

Taylor, John Russell. "British Dramatists: The New Arrivals, III—David Storey, Novelist into Dramatist." *Plays and Players* June 1970: 22–24.

Weaver, Laura H. "The City as Escape into Freedom: The Failure of a Dream in David Storey's Works." *West Virginia University Philological Papers* 28 (1983): 146–53.

Reviews of Selected Productions

Andrews, Philip. *"Phoenix." Stage and Television Today* 2 May 1985: 11.

Ansorge, Peter. *"The Contractor." Plays and Players* May 1970: 46.

Barber, John. " 'Changing Room' One of Year's Best." *Daily Telegraph* 10 November 1971: 10.

———. "Defeated Anti-hero of 'Life Class.' " *Daily Telegraph* 11 April 1974: 13.

———. "Laboured Bad Taste in Orton-Type Farce." *Daily Telegraph* 23 September 1976: 13.

———. "Rich Contrast of Idealist and Two Wastrels." *Daily Telegraph* 16 August 1973: 13.

———. "Tart Comedy of Men with the Marquee." *Daily Telegraph* 7 April 1970: 16.

———. "Verbal Torments of Marquee Men." *Daily Telegraph* 21 October 1969: 15.

Barnes, Clive. " 'Home' and 'Contractor' Shine in London Season." *New York Times* 17 August 1970: 32.

———. "On the Stage, King Comedy Reigns." *New York Times* 26 September 1976: 54.

———. "Stage: 'Changing Room.' " *New York Times* 19 November 1972: 79.

———. "Stage: 'The Contractor.' " *New York Times* 9 December 1971: 63.

———. "Stage: Two Plays by Storey in London." *New York Times* 11 September 1973: 55.

———. "Storey's 'In Celebration.' " *New York Times* 31 May 1974: 22.

———. "Stage: 'Changing Room' Opens at Morosco." *New York Times* 7 March 1973: 37.

———. "Theatre: David Storey's 'Contractor.' " *New York Times* 18 October 1973: 66.

———. "Theatre: 'Home' Arrives." *New York Times* 18 November 1970: 41.

Bibliography

Billington, Michael. "A Play Worth Having." *Times* (London) 23 April 1969: 16.

————. "Dramatising Work." *Times* (London) 7 April 1970: 8.

————. "First Nights: *The Restoration of Arnold Middleton.*" *Plays and Players* September 1967: 30.

————. "Guys Hold More than Guy-Ropes." *Times* (London) 21 October 1969: 14.

Brooks, Jeremy, and J. A. Lambert. "David Storey Week: Triumph and Disaster." *Sunday Times* 26 September 1976: 35.

Brown, Geoff. "*Mother's Day.*" *Plays and Players* December 1976: 35–36.

Brustein, Robert. ". . . Or Just 'Conscientious Naturalism'?" *New York Times* 18 March 1973, sec. 2: 1.

Bryden, Ronald. "Cromwell." *Plays and Players* October 1973: 47–49.

Cahn, Victor L. "The Joy of Being Part of a Team." *New York Times* 10 June 1973, sec. 2: 11.

Chaillet, Ned. "Pale Shadows of Old Court Days." *Times* (London) 23 April 1980, 13.

————. "Sisters." *Times* (London) 14 September 1978: 12.

Chapman, Robert H. "In the Play Pen: Contemporary Drama Cornered." *Harvard Magazine* 82.1 (September–October 1979): 54–61.

Clurman, Harold. "Films & Plays." *Nation* 30 October 1976: 443- 44.

————. "Theatre." *Nation* 26 March 1973: 410–11.

————. "Theatre." *Nation* 5 November 1973: 478.

Coveney, Michael. "*The Farm.*" *Financial Times* 27 September 1973.

————. "*Sisters.*" *Financial Times* 13 September 1978.

Darlington, W. A. "Hero Talked On Till He Had a Fit." *Daily Telegraph* 6 July 1967.

————. "Is This a Plot or Isn't It?" *Daily Telegraph* 3 November 1969: 11.

————. "Where Do They Go From Here?" *Daily Telegraph,* 20 July 1970: 7.

Dawson, Helen. "*The Farm.*" *Plays and Players* November 1973: 42- 43.

Day-Lewis, Sean. "New Instalment [*sic*] of the Storey Story." *Daily Telegraph* 12 April 1969: 14.

Elsom, John. "Nude with Qualms." *Listener* 18 April 1974: 514.

————. "Old Bottles." *Listener* 1 May 1980.

Frankel, Haskel. "All the World's a Locker Room in Superlative New David Storey Play." *National Observer* 9 December 1972: 24.

————. "Mr. Storey's Cosmic 'Contractor': Nothing Less Than a Masterpiece." *National Observer* 11 December 1971: 24.

Gilbert, W. Stephen. "*Life Class.*" *Plays and Players* May 1974: 26–27.

Gill, Brendan. "Goal to Go." *New Yorker* 19 March 1973: 92.

Gussow, Mel. "David Storey's 'The Farm' Is Family Play about Forces That Hold People Together." *New York Times* 12 October 1976: 45.

————. "New Drama Goes Off Off Broadway." *New York Times* 12 November 1976: C–3.

————. "Stage: 'Life Class' at the Theatre Club." *New York Times* 15 December 1975: 43.

————. "Strength of Yorkshire Unfurls with Truth." *New York Times* 15 October 1974: 44.

Bibliography

Hastings, Ronald. "Song of the Living Tent." *Daily Telegraph* 18 October 1969: 15.

Hayman, Ronald. *"Early Days." Plays and Players* May 1980: 28.

Hewes, Henry. "Knights at a Round Table." *Saturday Review* 12 December 1970: 63.

———. "Storey Theatre." *Saturday Review of the Arts* April 1973: 77.

———. "Theatre in England." *Saturday Review* 25 July 1970: 20.

———. "True Storey." *Saturday Review/World* 18 December 1973: 47.

Higgins, John. "David Storey: Night and Day." *Times* (London) 16 September 1976: 13.

Hobson, Harold. "The Quality of 'Life Class.' " *Sunday Times* 23 June 1974: 28.

———. "Rural Rites." *Sunday Times* 30 September 1973: 29.

Holland, Mary. *"The Changing Room." Plays and Players* January 1972: 44–47.

Holmstrom, John. "Keep It Mum." *Plays and Players* June 1969: 26–29.

Hughes, Catherine. "Broadway Hails Britannia." *America* 16 January 1971: 47.

———. " 'The Farm'; 'Poor Murderer.' " *America* 8 April 1972: 304.

———. "Four Hit Plays—A London Review." *America* 8 April 1972: 379.

———. "Mixed Metaphors." *America* 31 March 1973: 290.

———. "Tenting Tonight." *America* 3 November 1973: 334.

Kalem, T. E. "Duet of Dynasts." *Time* 30 November 1970: 48.

———. "Family Communion." *Time* 10 June 1974: 106.

———. "Laureate of Loss." *Time* 27 December 1971: 55.

———. "On to the Triple Crown." *Time* 5 November 1973: 84.

———. "Rock of Ages." *Time* 25 October 1976: 87.

———. "Sisyphus Agonistes." *Time* 18 December 1973: 84–85.

Kalson, Albert E. Review of *Mother's Day* and *The Farm. Educational Theatre Journal* 29.2 (May 1977): 260–62.

Kauffmann, Stanley. "Notes on Naturalism: Truth Is Stranger as Fiction." *Performance* 1: 33–39.

———. "On Theatre." *New Republic* 14 April 1973: 92.

———. "On Theatre." *New Republic* 12 December 1970: 33.

Kerr, Walter. "British Writers." *New York Times*, 9 September 1973, sec. 2: 1.

———. " 'The Changing Room': Something Like Magic . . ." *New York Times* 18 March 1973, sec. 2: 1.

———. "Like Pinter, Except . . . " *New York Times*, 29 November 1972, sec. 2: 1.

———. "Too Many Questions." *New York Times* 24 October 1976, sec. 2: 1.

———. "Without Accent, without Energy." *New York Times* 28 October 1973, sec. 2: 3.

Kroll, Jack. "The Playing's the Thing." *Newsweek* 16 June 1980: 82–83.

———. "Raising the Roof." *Newsweek* 13 January 1971: 114.

———. "Sporting Life." *Newsweek* 19 March 1973: 86.

———. "Team of Destiny." *Newsweek* 11 December 1972: 71.

Lambert, J. W. "Globetrotting Theatre." *Drama* 133 (Summer 1979): 15.

———. "Lost Horizons." *Times* (London) 14 April 1974: 34.

———. "Plays in Performance." *Drama* 111 (Winter 1973): 16–18.

———. "Plays in Performance." *Drama* 113 (Summer 1974): 39–41.

———. "Romanian Roundabout." *Drama* 133 (Winter 1979): 17–18.

———. "To Be a Pilgrim." *Sunday Times* 19 August 1973: 27.

Lanouette, William J. "Digging Away, Storey Unearths a Biting Drama." *National Observer* 23 November 1970: 20.

Lewsen, Charles. " 'The Changing Room.' " *Times* (London) 16 December 1971: 18.

Marcus, Frank. "Ring of Truth." *Sunday Telegraph* 30 September 1973: 18.

Mayer, David. "*Sisters.*" *Plays and Players* November 1978: 21.

Nightingale, Benedict. "Three Sons." *New Statesman* 2 May 1969: 631–32.

Novick, Julian. "Can 'the Facts' Alone Make a Play?" *New York Times* 3 December 1972, sec. 2: 13.

———. "Two Plays at Washington's Arena Stage About the Work Ethic." *New York Times* 3 December 1972, sec. 2: 3.

O'Conner, J. J. "English Presence." *Wall Street Journal* 8 November 1970: 22.

Oliver, Edith. "Off Broadway: Change and Decay in All Around I See." *New Yorker* 25 October 1976: 61–62.

———. "Off Broadway: David Storey's Tent Show." *New Yorker* 29 October 1973, 107–9.

———. "The Theatre: Off Broadway." *New Yorker* 29 December 1975: 43.

Rich, Alan. "Rocky Life on the Farm." *New York* 1 November 1976: 75.

Ridley, Clifford A. "Oops—The British are Coming." *National Observer* 2 November 1974: 23.

Shorter, Eric. "Family Home Truths Grippingly Studied." *Daily Telegraph* 23 April 1969: 21.

———. "*Phoenix.*" *Daily Telegraph* 13 March 1985. Rpt. in *London Theatre Record* 27 February–12 March 1985: 230.

———. "Regions." *Drama* 133 (Summer 1979): 70–72.

———. "Strained Plot Leads to Anticlimax." *Daily Telegraph* 27 September 1973: 14.

Simon, John. "*Life Class.*" *New York* 23 September 1974: 67.

———. "Theatre Chronicle." *Hudson Review* 27 (1974): 82–83.

Taylor, John Russell. "First Nights: *The Restoration of Arnold Middleton.*" *Plays and Players* September 1967: 42.

———. "*Home.*" *Plays and Players* August 1970: 30–34.

———. "Plays in Performance: London." *Drama* 140 (2nd quarter 1981): 24.

Thorber, Robin. "*Phoenix.*" *Guardian* 13 March 1985. Rpt. in *London Theatre Record* 27 February–12 March 1985: 230.

Wall, Stephen. "Kitchen Agonistes." *Times Literary Supplement* 2 May 1980: 495.

Wardle, Irving. "David Storey's Needless Chronicle on War." *Times* (London) 11 August 1973: 9.

———. "*The Changing Room.*" *Times* (London) 10 November 1971: 12.

———. "Flawless Tone." *Times* (London) 18 June 1970: 8.

———. "*Life Class.*" *Times* (London) 10 April 1974: 13.

———. "Mr. Storey Brilliant When in Focus." *Times* (London) 6 July 1967: 8.

———. "New Play by Storey Stars Two Knights at the Royal Court." *New York Times* 20 June 1970: 23.

———. "Storey Returns Home to Yorkshire." *Times* (London) 29 September 1973: 9.

Bibliography

————. "Unanswered Questions After Coming Home to the Finest Family in the Land." *Times* (London) 23 September 1976: 13.

————. "What about the Workers?" *Times* (London) 8 November 1969: 3.

Waterhouse, Robert. "*The Contractor*." *Plays and Players* November 1969: 26–27.

Weales, Gerald. "A Change for the Best." *Commonweal* 6 April 1973: 114.

Weightman, John. "Art versus Life." *Encounter* September 1974: 57–59.

————. "Life and Death of the Common Man." *Encounter* December 1969: 53.

————. "The Outsider in the Home." *Encounter*, September 1976, 40–44.

Weintraub, Bernard. "The Rugby Field on the Stage." *New York Times* 13 December 1971: 52.

Young, B. A. "*Cromwell*." *Financial Times* 17 August 1973: 3.

————. "*Early Days*." *Financial Times* 23 April 1980: 21.

————. "*Life Class*." *Financial Times* 10 April 1974: 3.

————. "*Mother's Day*." *Financial Times* 24 September 1976: 3.

Index

Index

Index

203

Index

Index

William Hutchings is an associate professor of English at the University of Alabama at Birmingham. He has published articles on a number of contemporary writers, including Samuel Beckett, Alan Sillitoe, Peter Shaffer, Lindsay Anderson, and Joe Orton, as well as studies of such earlier modern writers as James Joyce, H. G. Wells, and Yevgeny Zamyatin. His essays have appeared in *Modern Fiction Studies, Papers on Language and Literature, Twentieth Century Literature,* the *James Joyce Quarterly, College English,* and the *Journal of Modern Literature,* among others.

DATE DUE

GAYLORD			PRINTED IN U.S.A.